GAY GUERRILLA

GAY GUERRILLA

JULIUS EASTMAN AND HIS MUSIC

EDITED BY
RENÉE LEVINE PACKER
MARY JANE LEACH

UNIVERSITY OF ROCHESTER PRESS

The University of Rochester Press gratefully acknowledges the Robert D. Bielecki Foundation, the Robert and Carol Morris Center for 21st Century Music, and the Howard Hanson Institute for American Music for their generous support of this publication.

First published 2015
Reprinted in paperback 2018

University of Rochester Press
668 Mt. Hope Avenue, Rochester, NY 14620, USA
www.urpress.com
and Boydell & Brewer Limited
PO Box 9, Woodbridge, Suffolk IP12 3DF, UK
www.boydellandbrewer.com

Hardcover ISBN-13: 978-1-58046-534-2
Paperback ISBN-13: 978-1-58046-956-2
ISSN: 1071-9989

Library of Congress Cataloging-in-Publication Data

Gay guerrilla : Julius Eastman and his music / edited by Renee Levine Packer and Mary Jane Leach.
pages cm — (Eastman studies in music, ISSN 1071-9989 ; v. 129)
Includes bibliographical references and index.
ISBN 978-1-58046-534-2 (hardcover : alkaline paper) 1. Eastman, Julius. I. Levine Packer, Renee, 1940– editor. II. Leach, Mary Jane, editor. III. Series: Eastman studies in music ; v. 129.
ML410.E21G39 2015
780.92— dc23
[B] 2015028034

This publication is printed on acid-free paper.
Printed in the United States of America.

CONTENTS

FOREWORD

George E. Lewis

This volume constitutes an early and signal contribution to the growing corpus of scholarship and commentary on the music of the composer and singer Julius Eastman. The individual essays confront the several challenges Eastman's life and work pose to canonical narratives of American experimental music. This book is the result of the combined tenacity of its two coeditors. First, there is Renée Levine Packer, a chronicler of late twentieth-century American experimental music who knew Eastman since his early days as a Creative Associate at the University at Buffalo.[1] The other driving force behind this book is the composer Mary Jane Leach, a central figure in Downtown experimentalism, whose relentless musicological sleuthing has been crucial to unearthing new knowledge about Eastman's life and work.

Leach's experiences while researching Eastman included unusual dreams and inexplicably malfunctioning software that did not allow her to read e-mails associated with the project. "I began to wonder," Leach recalls, "if Eastman's spirit was trying to sabotage the dissemination of his music."[2] In a lecture I attended at a Harlem theater in 2009, historian Robin D. G. Kelley recounted a similar story about his extraordinary book, *Thelonious Monk: The Life and Times of an American Original*.[3] Strange things began to happen to Kelley as he pursued knowledge about Monk, culminating in a hit-and-run car accident that left him with severely reduced mobility for months. Kelley told a friend that he was wondering if Monk were somehow involved in what was happening to him. The friend responded, "Did you ask Thelonious's permission to write the book?" Kelley decided to create an atmosphere that would allow him to make that request, and somehow, the strange occurrences came to an end. The possibility that Eastman could be similarly contacted through spiritual methodologies seems less odd when we consider the extent to which, as this book shows, a kind of pan-religious spirituality and ethics often permeated encounters with Eastman and his work.

Most of the contributors to this book, including me, actually met Eastman at some point in his turbulent career. I do not quite remember when I met Julius for the first time, and for reasons that I hope will become clearer later, I will refer to him by first name just this once. As someone who came of musical age in part in several Downtown New York music scenes in the late 1970s, I have my own reminiscences about Julius, some of which go back to my attendance at live performances of his work. Other traces of memory remain from the fall 1980 Kitchen tour of Berlin, Stockholm, Paris, and Eindhoven, in which I participated along with Douglas Ewart, Eric Bogosian, Robert Longo, Molissa Fenley, Rhys Chatham, Joe Hannan, Bill T. Jones, Arnie Zane, and others.[4]

Prior to Eastman's emergence, the African-American presence in the Downtown New York music scene of the 1960s and 1970s was marked by two important figures: the composer and artist Benjamin Patterson, a key figure in the Fluxus movement, and the composer Carman Moore, who in the early 1960s founded the *Village Voice*'s tradition of a regular, composer-written column on new music, providing important early exposure for colleagues such as La Monte Young.[5] As this book shows, Eastman was a prominent member of this scene; his collaborators, colleagues, and associates comprise a Who's Who of American experimentalism.

For me, Eastman represented a singular figure of presence; as a newcomer to New York in 1975, I did not know Moore, and Patterson appeared to me as a legend living in Germany.[6] Certainly, Julius's demeanor and comportment at that time gave me no hint of a working-class origin and upbringing that, as I have come to discover through the work of Leach and my Columbia University colleague Ellie Hisama, was very much like my own. John Patrick Thomas gives us a hint of Eastman's self-fashioning: "If it is true, as is said, that he never had serious vocal training—he at least paid attention to models who were 'classically' trained; Julius seemed to admire that kind of vocal resonance and color. Then again, his speaking voice . . . was also extraordinarily resonant."[7]

A recent article by Hisama calls on scholars to apprehend Eastman's work "as a black, gay man who worked in a primarily white new music scene . . . with respect to both of these social categories, rather than to disregard them within a 'post-race or sexuality-neutral context.'"[8] Eastman himself issued an explicit call, avant la lettre, for this kind of intersectionality, with the notorious title of one of his works: *Nigger Faggot* (1978). Once again, we can point to African-American letters for antecedents, notably in the work of James Baldwin, and afterward, in the work of Marlon Riggs and the gay-sibling artists Thomas Allen Harris and Lyle Ashton Harris.

This presents us with at least two axes of interpretation, but to claim that both were equally mediational would warp the case. Though sexual acts between consenting adults of the same sex were illegal in the United States until late in the twentieth century, homosexuality could nonetheless be acknowledged and even quietly celebrated across large swatches of the art world. The same could not be said of blackness; black artists were far less in evidence in the Downtown New York music scene than queer ones, and one could never be quite sure when the products of backgrounds similar in most details to Eastman's might suddenly be denigrated (in the exact sense of that term), either openly or cryptically.

None of the authors in this volume identify any instances where homophobia posed an issue of collegiality for Eastman in the new music scene; indeed, his alliances with other emerging gay composers of his approximate generation, such as Arthur Russell, indicate that there was a considerably more extensive network of gay artists in this scene than of African-American artists. Eastman's home and public lives, however, were another matter. According to Hisama, Eastman's mother was accepting of his sexual identity, and disturbed by his father's lack of accommodation to it.[9]

The protest against the titles of the pieces on a controversial 1980 Northwestern University concert of Eastman's music resulted in their eventual removal from the printed concert program.[10] Since the titles could not be printed, Eastman explained them in spoken remarks, which were audio-recorded. Although the protests and censorship focused on "racism" rather than references to homosexuality, this did not mean that Eastman's explicit invocation of queer values was somehow passed over. As Hisama heard it, after Eastman's explanation of the motivation for *Gay Guerrilla*, "the applause that usually concludes a composer's pre-concert remarks is palpably absent from the audience—all we hear are his footsteps as he walks to the piano."[11]

As a final invocation of intersectionality, Eastman referred to himself in a 1976 interview as "a kind of talented freak who occasionally injected some vitality into the programming" of the Creative Associates.[12] Talented we can understand, as well as the reference to hybrid vigor—but what made Eastman a "freak"? His extended vocal range? His blackness? His gayness? Or an assemblage of these and other factors, including the context of American experimental classical music? The remark evinces Eastman's understanding of his own presence on the scene as inherently performative, after the fashion of a similar observation attributed to Miles Davis, who was notorious for turning his back on audiences during performances and cursing out patrons at intermission. After one such episode, Davis was said to reflect, "When you have stock in Con Edison and make all the money I make, you have to act the way people expect you to act—they want me to be their evil nigger, and that's what I'm ready to be."[13]

You Don't Know My Place

In many respects, the tenor of reminiscences on and around Eastman do recall American narratives associated with jazz, even more so than with the world of classical music. There is Eastman's early autodidact background, teaching himself as a boy to read music—a standard feature in the backgrounds of jazz musicians from the beginning of the genre to the advent of jazz schools in the 1950s and 1960s.[14] Moreover, parallels abound between the way Eastman is described by contemporaries (and authors in this book) and the epic tropes surrounding Charlie Parker. Both were described as cultured, erudite, handsome, possessing a resonant speaking/playing voice, and unusually magnetic. Both were seen as unpredictable geniuses who succumbed to substance abuse and came to a tragic, premature end.

Part of the legend in both cases involves invocations of the ineffable, as with Harry Partch, another important queer composer, whom one biographer called "an inexplicable, almost unknowable figure."[15] Ryan Dohoney quotes Ned Sublette, a central contributor to the Downtown scene who (as I recall) was as close to Eastman as anyone, to the effect that Eastman "didn't run with anybody."[16] Indeed, did anyone really know Eastman? It is for this reason that I hesitate to invoke his first name in these reflections; Dohoney observes that Eastman "held himself apart" from his collaborators, and the clear import of R. Nemo Hill's memoir in this book is that this distancing extended even to friends and loved ones.

Although Hill feels that "protestations of a hostile environment, either racial or otherwise, while undeniable in their own right, seem to beg the question of the use to which Julius put every aspect of every dilemma," I would add that the binary between institutional and personal agencies is not quite so easily elided; we often despair of finding a bright line that allows secure apportionment between them. If we become obliged to identify whiteness as one staging ground for new music, we are not similarly compelled to advance simplistic notions of individual racism as overdetermining. In a field already marked by whiteness, Eastman's life and works, like those of his colleagues of any ethnicity, would logically be similarly marked, in interaction with individual subjectivities, however socially mediated.

In that light, we can reconsider the infamous incident around John Cage's reaction to Eastman's performative queering of Cage's *Song Books* at the 1975 June in Buffalo new music festival, which Ryan Dohoney interprets in another article as "this story of white paternalism correcting unruly black youth [that] was not so much touching as it was condescending and troubling with regard to how Cage conceived of his role as compositional rule maker."[17] As Dohoney points out, whereas "both Eastman and Cage were part of a network of gay and lesbian experimental musicians going back to the 1930s," the two composers differed between "Cage with a so-called homosexual aesthetic and Eastman with a queer experimentalism."[18]

I read this encounter in part as a meeting of the generations, but I also want to consider it via an intersectional transposition of Houston A. Baker Jr.'s opposition between two African-American expressive strategies: *mastery of form*, a cryptic masking favored by Cage that, in Baker's words, "conceals, disguises, floats like a trickster butterfly in order to sting like a bee,"[19] and Eastman's *deformation of mastery*, a phaneric strategy that "distinguishes rather than conceals. It secures territorial advantage and heightens a group's survival possibilities."[20] Using primate behavior as a metaphor, Baker notes that, "The gorilla's deformation is made possible by his superior knowledge of the landscape and the loud assertion of possession that he makes."[21] It was this raucous, post-Stonewall assertiveness that proved unsettling to Cage.

Eastman's performance that day may also have constituted an intersectional testing of the limits of his membership—or, in American racial parlance, his "place"—in the experimental scene. Extending that discussion of place, Hisama sees the need to more fully explore the reasons for Eastman's absence in scholarship on African-American composers,[22] including volumes edited and compiled by African-American scholars, such as Eileen Southern's canonical survey *The Music of Black Americans*, the *International Dictionary of Black Composers*, and a number of others. A similar erasure marks Benjamin Patterson's presence/absence in histories of the Fluxus movement, despite his obvious centrality to the collective as it saw itself at the time.[23]

However, I despair of finding the smoking gun in either case—or rather, evidence can be best gleaned by tracing a network/assemblage with attention to both individual human actants and factors such as class, genre, and community, expressed with a view toward defining what markers such as "composer" and "composition" signify.[24] On this view, I keep returning to critical theorist Fred Moten's identification of "a vast interdisciplinary text representative not only of a problematically positivist conclusion that the avant-garde has been exclusively Euro-American, but of a deeper, perhaps unconscious, formulation of the avant-garde as necessarily not black."[25]

Fifty-Two Niggers

Whether or not Luciano Chessa's contribution to this book is entirely on point in claiming that Eastman's use of the crazy/evil nigger trope precedes Richard Pryor's 1974 album *That Nigger's Crazy*, the presence of the trope in African-American public discourse precedes both, and would have surely been available to Eastman as he was growing up.[26] In 1964, the prominent African-American comedian Dick Gregory published *Nigger: An Autobiography*, and in the same year, we have a public talk by Malcolm X that could easily serve as an anthem for Eastman:

> You'll get freedom by letting your enemy know that you'll do anything to get your freedom; then you'll get it. It's the only way you'll get it. When you get that kind of attitude, they'll label you as a "crazy Negro," or they'll call you a "crazy nigger"—they don't say Negro. Or they'll call you an extremist or a subversive, or seditious, or a red or a radical. But when you stay radical long enough and get enough people to be like you, you'll get your freedom.[27]

In Eastman-like words: *Stay On It*. In fact, Eastman's discussion of his "nigger" pieces at the 1980 Northwestern University concert invokes one pole of Malcolm's well-known dichotomy between the house, or good nigger, whose obsequious acquiescence to oppression values survival over freedom, and the field nigger, also known as the "bad" or "evil" nigger—the embodiment of up-front resistance, celebrated by Eastman as "fundamental."[28] Malcolm saw the field-nigger trope as the engine of radical change; Eastman's sense of intersectionality draws him to invoke the same image about the gay guerrilla: "That is the reason that I use 'gay guerrilla' in hopes that I might be one, if called upon to be one."[29]

Again, deformation of mastery comes to the fore—in Houston Baker's words, like "Morris Day singing 'Jungle Love,' advertising, with certainty, his unabashed *badness*—which is not always conjoined with violence. *Deformation* is a go(uer)rilla action in the face of acknowledged adversaries."[30]

Eastman and others in his home community might have been familiar with the series of novels by the African-American Robert Beck, writing under the pseudonym "Iceberg Slim," who became famous for depicting the "real world" of the black underclass. Evil, bad, crazy, and dirty niggers, as well as hybrids and variations thereof, overpopulated the pages of books like *Pimp: The Story of My Life* (1969) and *Trick Baby: The Story of a White Negro* (1967).[31]

Another popular book of the period that sought to represent the real life of the streets was Claude Brown's 1965 *Manchild in the Promised Land*:

> The bad nigger thing really had me going. I remember Johnny saying that the only thing in life a bad nigger was scared of was living too long. This just meant that if you were going to be respected in Harlem, you had to be a bad nigger; and if you were going to be a bad nigger, you had to be ready to die. I wasn't ready to do any of that stuff. But I had to. I had to act crazy."[32]

The last sentence tells us that in the end, the evil nigger and the crazy nigger are more similar than different. Whether by choice or necessity, both become desperadoes, outlaws, to whom it is prudent not to get too close—you might get burned. Another danger was that anyone could suddenly "go nigger." Harvard law professor Randall Kennedy, who has published a history of the "troublesome word," recalls that some were adamant: "'Never give up your right to act like a nigger,' by which they meant that Negroes should be unafraid to speak up loudly and act up militantly on behalf of their interests."[33]

Richard Pryor played the nigger-as-griot, bringing uncomfortable perspectives and ambivalence home through performance. Novelist Cecil Brown's memoir of Pryor recalls that the title of that influential album came from an exclamation of an audience member, amazed at hearing these opinions spoken aloud: "That Nigger's crazy!"[34] Brown goes on to maintain that "What Black people meant by the expression 'That Nigger's Crazy' is different from how white Americans understand the phrase. For

Black people, it meant that in most instances, acting crazy was the right thing to do."[35]

Eastman's life spanned an American cultural naming that moved from colored to Negro to black to the first stirrings of "African American." The designation "nigger" persisted throughout all those incarnations and beyond, even as a certain pretense of politesse in current American media culture has euphemized the term as the "N-word." Eastman's dual and very public politicization of race and sexuality disrupted complacencies not only in white avant-garde circles but also in African-American communities such as those at Northwestern University in 1980, who were beset with their own issues of campus racism and thus were not quite ready to fully support Eastman's invocation and exegesis of the word.[36] Only later, with the emergence of gangsta rap, were large numbers of African Americans positioned to understand Eastman's enumeration of "52 niggers"—as it happens, one for every week in the year.[37]

Works such as *Crazy Nigger* and *Evil Nigger* were roughly coterminous with the emergence of the word *nigga* in rap as a *Verfremdungseffekt* that exposed the wan accommodations of traditional society. Eastman's peculiar genius was to introduce these specifically African-American tropes of highly politicized resistance to a classical music world in which such tropes had been in rather short supply. In that regard, we see that as with African-American culture more generally, Eastman felt able to make "nigger" available for uses beyond what Ryan Dohoney rightly, but perhaps too narrowly, observes as "repurposing of hate speech."

Repetition

It is difficult to avoid allowing race to overdetermine perspectives on African-American artists, even as race indelibly marks one's experiences. Even so, one dominant direction in critical commentary, while celebrating Eastman as a protominimalist, cannot help framing him (borrowing the title of a book by critic Greg Tate), as a token "Flyboy in the Buttermilk."[38] One gathers the sense that except for Eastman, minimalism's progenitors would all be white. However, one of the signal influences on early musical minimalism, and one still largely unacknowledged in many music histories, was John Coltrane. Coltrane was a major influence on La Monte Young, Steve Reich, Terry Jennings, and Terry Riley, and a piece such as the 1960 recording of *My Favorite Things* (particularly the McCoy Tyner solo) is essentially a minimalist improvisation using repetition as a primary element.[39] Coltrane's use of repetition precedes Reich and Glass, and is roughly coterminous with that of Young and Riley, both soprano saxophonists who, like many, were taken with Coltrane's sound on that instrument.[40]

As Benjamin Piekut has perceptively observed, "To explain what experimentalism has been, one must attend to its fabrication through a network of discourses, practices, and institutions. This formation is the result of the combined labor of scholars, composers, critics, journalists, patrons, performers, venues, and the durative effects of discourses of race, gender, nation, and class."[41] This perspective makes it easier to understand why, in histories of musical minimalism, Coltrane (if he is mentioned at all) is largely portrayed as an outside source rather than an insider member. This case, as well as the present volume, shows the extent to which genre (i.e., minimalism, classical music, jazz, experimentalism, etc.) functions as a socially improvisative assemblage that operates epistemologically to produce what "counts" as knowledge.

To the assemblage around Eastman we must add sound itself. By 1965, Coltrane's movement toward a relentlessly intense combination of freely fractal nonlinear repetition with sheer noise established a strong sonic distance from early minimalism. In the same vein, even Eastman's more minimalist-oriented work incorporated the kind of ecstatic affect that, like late Coltrane, eschewed musical minimalism's storied sense of cool—itself genetically connected with Miles Davis's *Kind of Blue*. Eastman's widely acknowledged connection with jazz surely went beyond the influence of his jazz-musician brother Gerry, toward a culturally literate, deep-structure engagement with this and other forms of African-American music. Imagine the driving rhythm of the opening of *The Holy Presence of Joan d'Arc* as a work song, full of grunts, and you can see what I mean.

In theorizing Eastman's protominimalism, Hisama draws on the art historian Briony Fer's observation about new artmaking strategies after modernism emerging through repetition, a thesis that inevitably draws on Deleuze, but even more directly, on Rosalind Krauss's theorization of the grid as a defining trope of late modernist visual art.[42] I found it intriguing to juxtapose Fer's understanding of repetition—marked by a Eurological ambivalence exemplified by the terrifying sentence of Sisyphus, whom the gods punish eternally by compelling him to push an enormous boulder up a hill, only to see it roll down, again and again—with the literary critic James Snead's influential discussion in his 1981 article, "On Repetition in Black Culture."[43]

Hisama's article muses on an intriguing question that Fer poses: "Could it be that art is one of the very few places in culture that allows a margin of freedom within repetition rather than a place exempt from its demands?"[44] This question is subsumed within Snead's discussion of the vast gulf separating African and Afrodiasporic framings of repetition from pan-European culture's engagements with it; one can see Snead responding to Fer by asking whose "culture" we are discussing. Both authors deploy Kierkegaard's essay on repetition epigraphically, but Fer's epigraph asks, "What would life be like if there were no repetition?" Snead highlights another passage from the same essay, one that frames Kierkegaard's advocacy of repetition as transgressive in relation to the dominant Western belief of the day that "there is no repetition in culture, but only a difference, defined as progress and growth."[45]

In Snead's formulation, it becomes clear that black culture is not one of the places in which freedom within repetition is marginal; art is only one site for this expression of freedom through repetition. What Coltrane, Eastman, and the early minimalists discovered was how to overcome the Sisyphean horror, by signifying on Nietzsche's eternal recurrence to reveal, through recursion, that the practice of freedom draws its main power from freedom itself. For Snead's Kierkegaard, "Repetition is reality and it is the seriousness of life. He who wills repetition is matured in seriousness. . . . Repetition is the new category which has to be brought to light."[46]

Although in the end, one cannot be sure what drove Julius Eastman to his untimely departure, to the extent that his very presence in the putatively white avant-garde became a site for political and social contestations that went well beyond Eastman himself, it is not difficult to imagine intersectional pressures exercising a strongly and personally destabilizing series of blows, of a sort that few of his colleagues in what became Downtown classical music would have been prepared to fully analyze or appreciate. That level of Sisyphean loneliness, I feel, marks Eastman's life and colors his work, and we see intimations of it in a number of the essays in this book. Even well-meaning whites, queer or not, were trapped along with everyone else in a complex system of discursive, social, and institutional signification and differential access to infrastructure that few knew how to combat effectively, and I can easily imagine Eastman's internal, resigned shrug, intoned in that unforgettably resonant way: "You just don't understand."

Notes

1. See Renée Levine Packer, *This Life of Sounds: Evenings for New Music in Buffalo* (New York: Oxford University Press, 2010).
2. As recounted by Mary Jane Leach in chapter 6.

3. Robin D. G. Kelley and Randy Weston, "Randy Weston and Robin Kelley: Dialogue on Monk, October 13, 2009," *Jazz Studies Online*, accessed June 2, 2015, http://jazzstudiesonline.org/resource/randy-weston-and-robin-kelley-dialogue-monk-part-ii. Interestingly, the audio on the interview drops out and does not return, so readers will not be able to hear Kelley's story.

4. A Dutch-language flyer for the Eindhoven tour stop is available at http://alexandria.tue.nl/vanabbe/public/publiciteit/folders/1980/FolderTheKitchen1980.pdf, accessed June 2, 2015.

5. See George E. Lewis, "Benjamin Patterson's Spiritual Exercises," in *Tomorrow Is the Question: New Directions in Experimental Music Studies*, ed. Benjamin Piekut, 86–108 (Ann Arbor: University of Michigan Press, 2014). See also Lewis, *A Power Stronger Than Itself: The AACM and American Experimental Music* (Chicago: University of Chicago Press, 2008), 588n214.

6. George E. Lewis, "In Search of Benjamin Patterson: An Improvised Journey," *Callaloo* 35, no. 4 (Fall 2012): 979–91.

7. As recounted by John Patrick Thomas in chapter 5.

8. Ellie M. Hisama, "'Diving into the Earth': The Musical Worlds of Julius Eastman," in *Rethinking Difference in Music Scholarship*, ed. Olivia Bloechl, Melanie Lowe, and Jeffrey Kallberg (Cambridge: Cambridge University Press, 2015), 263.

9. Ibid., 279.

10. Ibid., 273. See also Andrew Hanson-Dvoracek, "Julius Eastman's 1980 Residency at Northwestern University" (MA thesis, University of Iowa, 2011), accessed June 2, 2015, http://ir.uiowa.edu/etd/1226.

11. Hisama, "'Diving into the Earth,'" 280.

12. Quoted in ibid., 269.

13. Martha Bayles, "Miles Davis and the Double Audience," in *Miles Davis and American Culture*, ed. Gerald Early (St. Louis: Missouri Historical Society Press, 2001), 154. Bayles interprets this apocryphal anecdote as an example of cynicism and inauthenticity, while Stanley Crouch sees it as an example of "ugliness." See Stanley Crouch, *Considering Genius: Writings on Jazz* (New York: Basic Books, 2007), 247.

14. Hisama, "'Diving into the Earth,'" 266.

15. Bob Gilmore, *Harry Partch: A Biography* (New Haven, CT: Yale University Press, 1998), x.

16. As recounted by Ryan Dohoney in chapter 7.

17. Ryan Dohoney, "John Cage, Julius Eastman, and the Homosexual Ego," in *Tomorrow Is the Question: New Directions in Experimental Music Studies*, ed. Benjamin Piekut (Ann Arbor: University of Michigan Press, 2014), 50.

18. Ibid., 40.

19. Houston A. Baker Jr., *Modernism and the Harlem Renaissance* (Chicago: University of Chicago Press, 1987), 50.

20. Ibid., 51.

21. Ibid.

22. Hisama, "'Diving into the Earth,'" 272.

23. See Lewis, "In Search of Benjamin Patterson."

24. For an important early analysis, see Lloyd Whitesell, "White Noise: Race and Erasure in the Cultural Avant-Garde," *American Music* 19, no. 2 (2001): 168–89.

25. Fred Moten, *In the Break: The Aesthetics of the Black Radical Tradition* (Minneapolis: University of Minnesota, 2003), 32.

26. As recounted by Luciano Chessa in chapter 12.

27. Quoted in Dave Zirin, *A People's History of Sports in the United States: 250 Years of Politics, Protest, People, and Play* (New York: New Press, 2008), 136.

28. Hanson-Dvoracek, "Julius Eastman's 1980 Residency at Northwestern University," 34.

29. Hear "Julius Eastman's Spoken Introduction to the Northwestern University Concert," on Julius Eastman, *Unjust Malaise*, New World Records CD 80638, 2005.

30. Baker, *Modernism and the Harlem Renaissance*, 50.

31. Iceberg Slim, *Pimp: The Story of My Life* (New York: Cash Money Content, 1969 [1987]); *Trick Baby: The Story of a White Negro* (Los Angeles: Holloway House, 1967 [1997]).

32. Claude Brown, *Manchild in the Promised Land* (New York: Touchstone, 1965 [2012]), 111.

33. Randall Kennedy, *Nigger: The Strange Career of a Troublesome Word* (New York: Vintage Books, 2003), xvii.

34. Cecil Brown, *Pryor Lives! Kiss My Rich, Happy Black . . . Ass! A Memoir* (Berkeley, CA: Cecil Brown, 2013), 120.

35. Ibid.

36. For a recent account providing historical corroboration and theoretical context for the experiences of African-American students at Northwestern University, see Sarah Susannah Willie, *Acting Black: College, Identity, and the Performance of Race* (New York: Routledge, 2003). See also Lewis, *A Power Stronger Than Itself*, 289–91.

37. Hanson-Dvoracek, "Julius Eastman's 1980 Residency at Northwestern University," 34.

38. Greg Tate, *Flyboy in the Buttermilk: Essays on Contemporary America* (New York: Simon and Schuster, 1992).

39. Hear John Coltrane, *My Favorite Things*, Atlantic 13420, compact disc, 2009 [1961].

40. For an account of Coltrane's influence on early minimalist composers, see Edward Strickland, *Minimalism: Origins* (Bloomington: Indiana University Press, 1993), 131, 148–50.

41. Benjamin Piekut, *Experimentalism Otherwise: The New York Avant-Garde and Its Limits* (Berkeley: University of California Press, 2011), 7.

42. See Rosalind Krauss, "Grids," *October* 9 (Summer 1979): 50–64.

43. Snead's life bore some parallels with Eastman's. A jazz musician as well as a scholar, Snead was a gay African American. A devout Christian, he died of AIDS in 1989, after holding academic posts at Yale and the University of Pittsburgh. Philosopher Cornel West, who arranged for the posthumous publication of Snead's writings, wrote a poignant remembrance of him that seems to resonate with Eastman as well: "Jamie . . . represents a new breed of black intellectual produced by a culture on the underside of modernity. And by 'new breed,' what I mean is that, given his energy and the quality of his mind, he was willing to no longer confine himself to the Afro-American terrain, but rather to try to redefine the whole in light of his understanding of that terrain." See the Yale AIDS Memorial Project (YAMP) page on Snead at http://yamp.org/Profiles/JamesSnead.

44. Briony Fer, *The Infinite Line: Re-Making Art after Modernism* (New Haven, CT: Yale University Press, 2004), 4.

45. James A. Snead, "On Repetition in Black Culture," *Black American Literature Forum* 15, no. 4 (Winter 1981): 147.

46. Ibid., 152.

ACKNOWLEDGMENTS

The editors wish to thank Gerald Eastman for the Julius Eastman estate, Mrs. Frances Eastman (in memoriam), and the Eastmans' cousin, David Lisbon. We are grateful to George E. Lewis and the contributors to this volume, who each spent untold hours over several years with us on this project.

We are grateful to D. W. Burkhardt for the use of his photographs including the cover, and to John Bewley at the University at Buffalo Music Library, who was always there for us, Thomas Sokol, William Thomson, Karl Singletary, Joseph Kubera, Petr Kotik, Pauline Oliveros, Bobby Previte, Ned Sublette, Daniel Di Landro for the SUNY Buffalo State *Buffalo Courier Express* Collection, the *Buffalo News*, David and Rachel Tuttle for Jim Tuttle's estate, Stuart Bratesman, Chris Rusiniak, the ISRO Publications Unit, Tania León, and R. Nemo Hill. Our appreciation also to supporters Robert D. Bielecki and David Felder.

Renée Levine Packer: I extend heartfelt thanks also to Eberhard Blum (in memoriam) and Ann Holyoke Blum, Frederic Cohen, Rocco Di Pietro, Joseph Ford, Charles Gayle, David Gibson, Jon Gibson, Dennis Kahle (in memoriam), Cristyne Lawson, Beatriz Lima, Marta Garcia Renart, Terri Rubinstein Steve Schmal and the Ithaca High School class of 1958, John Spitzer, and Zeyda Ruga Suzuki. And in gratitude for their unwavering support over the many years this book was in development, I thank my husband Arnold Packer, Irene Kraas, and David Wolfe, as well as Diana Childress, Jan and Diane Williams, and Carol Plantamura.

Mary Jane Leach: There are so many people for me to thank, starting with the initial search to find the music of Julius Eastman, which soon began to cross-fade with stories about his life, beginning with Lois V Vierk and C. Bryan Rulon (in memoriam), and building to this long list of composers, musicians, and other people in the arts, each providing an important piece of the jigsaw puzzle that was Eastman's life, so that eventually a clearer picture began to emerge. I am grateful to Charles Amirkhanian, Tom Bogdan, David Borden, Warren Burt, Steve Cellum, Nicholas Chase, Anthony Coleman, Joseph Dalton, Andy de Groat, Rocco Di Pietro, Ryan Dohoney, John Driscoll, Werner Durand, Maurice Edwards, Frank Ferko, Kyle Gann, David Garland, Peter Gena, Don Gillespie, Sean Griffin, RIP Hayman, Joe Hannon, Bill Hellermann, Ellie Hisama, Ralph Jackson, Philip Johnston, Donald Knaack, Petr Kotik, Stuart Leigh, Garrett List, Lyn Liston, Steve Lockwood, Mary Luft, Evan Lurie, Al Margolis, Francis McKee, Paula Mlyn, Charlie Morrow, Roy Nathanson, Phill Niblock, Frank J. Oteri, Hélène Panhuysen, William Parker, Nora Post, Judith St. Croix, Elliott Sharp, George Steel, Ned Sublette, Paul Tai, Nurrit Tilles, and John Zorn. I hope I haven't forgotten anyone, but if I have, I offer my sincere apologies—it has been seventeen long years. I also thank my mother, Juliet Cooke Barton for her support and tolerance. Dennis Bathory-Kitsz, Amy C. Beal, Paul Epstein, Sabine Feisst, Alan Gasser, Charles, K. Noyes, and David Toub, who all offered help and advice when I really needed it. And to the two people who acted as my prime sounding board during this publishing process: Nicholas Chase and Jody Dalton—many thanks for your advice and for being there.

Finally, to Ralph Locke, Sonia Kane, Julia Cook, Ryan Peterson, Tracey Engel, Rosemary Shojaie, our copy editor Therese Malhame, the anonymous readers, and the staff at the University of Rochester Press, we offer our sincere thanks.

INTRODUCTION

Julius Eastman and His Music

Renée Levine Packer

"The queen's name is Esss-ther," growled the distraught voice from the stage. In royal brocaded gown and furred cap, Julius Eastman played-sang-acted the pitiable monarch King George III as stricken and crazy but endlessly human as he roved the stage or sank, spent and muttering on his centered throne. . . . The underlying agony, the imploring for human understanding, the wrenching effect of the king's straining for reason amid the whirlwinds of his own mind, these were the heights of the Eastman performance.

—John Dwyer, "Eastman's 'Mad King': Mighty Work of Theater," *Buffalo Evening News*, November 1, 1970.

Julius Eastman is regarded as a brilliant composer as well as a magnetic performer. He was a slender man of medium height and graceful mien. If he wasn't being swish, or doing heavy metal with engineer boots and chains, or in his do-rag, you might think he was just another bookish university intellectual in thick-rimmed glasses and a modified Afro. He changed costume and hairstyles periodically in his quest for identity, appearing toward the end of his life in all white toga-like garb, a tacit proclamation of spiritual endeavor.

As with his dress, Eastman's music moved between styles—from traditionally notated scores, to more open graphic renderings. He used improvisation throughout his composing life, sometimes working in minimalist (or what he called "organic music") and jazz idioms. While a good deal of his work has been lost, the music that remains is increasingly performed and discussed in the United States and abroad, abetted by a growing audience for *Unjust Malaise*, the 2005 New World Records three-CD set of his music so ably produced by Mary Jane Leach and Paul Tai.

Julius Eastman should have lived a long life. His mother and his maternal grandmother died in their early nineties, his father, at ninety-seven. Instead, Julius was dead just months short of his fiftieth birthday, an architect of his fate, rather than its victim. What were the forces that shaped him? What happened between the years 1968, when Julius premiered his *Piano Pieces I–IV* in Buffalo, and 1980, when he presented his newest works *Evil Nigger*, *Gay Guerrilla*, and *Crazy Nigger* for performance at Northwestern University?[1] What triggered the downward spiral that led to his premature demise? And what of the work he left behind?

This is a book about searches, primarily Julius Eastman's search for identity as a black, gay musician, and for the form that his art would take. It is about my search for the person underneath the poses and the choices he made. It is about Mary Jane Leach's search for his music; and it is about new material that, through research and analysis, young musicologists, who find themselves riveted by Eastman's music, are continuing to uncover.

One can easily identify the loci of Eastman's life—his childhood in Ithaca, New York, his solid musical training at the Curtis Institute of Music, his productive professional years in Buffalo, and his final years spent largely in New York City. I met Julius in 1968, in Buffalo, New York, where he began to flourish. There he found well-placed sponsors, such as the astute musicologist and administrator Peter Yates, and the composer-conductor Lukas Foss. He found a community of like-minded people—the resident group of young virtuosi at the University at Buffalo known as the Creative Associates, one of the most important and influential collectives of musicians devoted to contemporary music in the country at that time. Eastman fit right in. In Buffalo he had enviable performance opportunities as pianist, singer, and composer; an attentive press; a stable financial situation; and, eventually, an assistant professorship in the university's music department. But, after six years, something didn't feel right; it was not enough.

"What I am trying to achieve," he told Renate Strauss in an interview with the *Buffalo Evening News*, shortly before he left Buffalo, "is to be what I am to the fullest—Black to the fullest, a musician to the fullest, a homosexual to the fullest." Turning away from the classical avant-garde, he told Strauss that his intense involvement with jazz during this period was a revelation. "I really enjoy playing with my group, the Space Perspective," he said.

> What happens now, instead of getting up every morning composing, I get up and practice the piano, improvise—it's jazz, that's the difference. . . . Jazz is so exciting because it allows for instant expression of feelings; it has immediacy and it also has style. . . . I feel it comes closer than classical music to being pure, instantaneous thought. When I am playing this music [jazz], I feel as if I am trying to see myself—it's like diving into the earth, that's what it feels like.[2]

Eastman moved to New York City in 1976 with no job in hand, but convinced that he had sufficiently good contacts and a better than fifty–fifty chance he could pull it off. Ryan Dohoney notes in his essay (chapter 7), that Eastman's refusal to reside in a specific musical camp mirrors not only his "multiply directed aesthetic practice," but also his seemingly effortless lifestyle transitions, from commodious private home and comparatively measured university life, to a gritty downtown existence. His impatience with boundaries plays out in the ballet he composed and choreographed for three dancers in 1970, *The Moon's Silent Modulation*. Here he "looks beyond the planet to the moon and sun and stars to the universe of conflicting forces." He concludes: "Truth is light and darkness."[3]

The issues of race and sexual orientation in late 1960s America, when Julius Eastman was achieving adulthood, were fraught with hostility and humiliation. James Baldwin wrote that to be a Negro in America was to be in a rage almost all the time. The great tennis player Arthur Ashe said in his autobiography that, for him, it was easier to die of AIDS, than to be black in America. "AIDS isn't the heaviest burden I've had to bear," he wrote.[4] Eastman was nearly twenty-nine years old when the Stonewall Inn riots in Greenwich Village protested the perennial police harassment of gays. "To be gay was to risk being continuously called out."[5] As his brother Gerry Eastman remarked, "Julius was black and gay so that was like a double whammy. He had to have double 'fuck you' armor to survive."[6]

Julius and I were the same age. In my capacity as managing director of the Buffalo contemporary music group, the Creative Associates, we traveled together; we broke bread together; we danced together; we talked together—he was my friend—and yet, as I have discovered, what I thought I knew, saw, intuited, was but the merest glimpse, limited access.

Originally, I considered calling this volume *Oh Sweet Boy: Julius Eastman and His Music*. "Are you tone-deaf," one would-be contributor asked? "You can't use the title *Oh Sweet Boy*. You're a white woman for

God's sake! Don't you get it?" As it happens, *Oh Sweet Boy* is a quote from a poem Eastman wrote for one of his most frequently played compositions, *Stay On It*, a love note to someone he cared for deeply (see chapter 10). For me, it captured something of the core of Julius Eastman as I knew him—a funny, irreverent, totally arresting person. And what about the current title of this book, one may ask? Was Julius Eastman an activist, a guerrilla? At some point in time between his benignly titled *Piano Pieces I–IV* dated 1968 and his comment to percussionist Dennis Kahle in 1973 that *Stay On It* was part of his "Nigger" series, the answer has to be "yes, he became one."[7] Art has long been used as a weapon to speak out to power. Pablo Picasso's *Guernica* and, more recently, Andres Serrano's *Piss Christ* are examples. Luciano Chessa places Eastman's piano work *Gay Guerrilla* in the same tradition (see chapter 12). Similarly, Eastman's use of the deliberately provocative title may be seen as preemptive "signifying," another guerrilla tactic.[8]

Very little, if anything, was off limits to Julius Eastman, whether he was appropriating John Cage's work *Song Books* as a platform for a sexually explicit performance, using *nigger* in the titles of his own musical compositions, or disregarding the sanctity of other people's property. His personal indifference toward possessions bled over to disdain for any notion of "mine-yours." He helped himself to his brother's or friends' belongings, and when they became predictably outraged he would protest: "Don't be so angry; they're only THI-INGS!" As far as he was concerned, "what's yours is mine" applied. The reverse was also true. His mother, Frances Eastman, recounted the time when she and her son were walking in the snow together. They passed an older man shivering in the street. Julius promptly took off his overcoat, placed it on the man's shoulders and continued walking with his mother. When Mrs. Eastman complained that he was going to get pneumonia from the cold, he just shrugged.

Karl Singletary, Julius Eastman's former roommate in Buffalo, described Eastman as a spiritual man. His classmates in Curtis and his New York companion, R. Nemo Hill, remarked also on his lack of interest in making money or making profitable connections. Singletary recalled their many conversations about Jesus, whom Eastman revered, not as the Son of God, but as one of the great prophets of the world, along with Moses and Buddha. Hill remembers, "He would never lock the door—even after he was robbed by one of those homeless people he brought around. He used to go to the men's shelter and give pedicures to the guys there. He was so brave. He just would not compromise" (chapter 1).

In 2005–6 while writing a book on the Buffalo Creative Associates, I dreamed that Julius gave me permission for this book, and so I contacted his family. Both Frances Eastman and Gerry Eastman knew me from the Buffalo days and welcomed the idea. The best way to achieve an authentic portrait of such a complex man, it seemed to me, would be through the lens of people who knew him. I believe that the multiplicity of voices in this collection evokes not only the man and his work but also the richness of his world.

Perhaps inevitably in a volume such as this, the reader will find varying versions of particular episodes such as speculation about a job that didn't materialize at Cornell, or Eastman's motives in the controversial *Song Books* incident. From time to time, redundancies will crop up as contributors refer to milestone events. The relatively brief biography lingers with more detail on Eastman's Buffalo years to demonstrate the breadth of his musical exposure and interests, and provides a stage for the ensuing chapters, which zoom in on material that is both instructive and revealing (chapter 1).

David Borden, who met Eastman when they were both in their twenties, recounts Eastman's attitudes, eccentricities, and thinking about music. While discussing his interpretation of *Evil Nigger*, Borden takes on the startling title of the piece, an action he sees as Eastman's attempt to transcend the always present "flashpoint of condescension and irrational hatred" (chapter 8). In his analysis of *Crazy Nigger*, Andrew Hanson-Dvoracek declares that such controversial titles were Eastman's way of insisting on the conversations he wanted his listeners to have (chapter 9). Poet R. Nemo Hill provides insight into what daily life with Eastman involved, suggesting that "from bedroom to bathroom to street corner to concert hall . . . the man and his music were not at war with one another—but in perfect, if discomforting, alignment" (chapter 3). Musicologist Ryan Dohoney guides us through Eastman's chameleonic presence in the downtown New York of the late 1970s and 1980s, caroming from the underground disco scene to the Brooklyn Philharmonia and Lincoln Center (chapter 7). Veteran critic-composer Kyle Gann, long interested in Eastman and his music, relates his various encounters with Eastman over the years, commenting particularly on the "organic" aspect of the music and the "astonishing" revival of interest in his work (chapter 4).

Eastman's impact is strikingly evident in the writings of the younger musicologists who did not know Eastman personally. Coeditor Mary Jane Leach, who had already dedicated so much of her time and effort to bringing about the immensely valuable recording of Eastman's music, worked primarily with this group of scholars. We believe that we are presenting the reader with a broad and deep portrait of the man, the composer-performer, the lover, the provocateur. As an early reader of the collection put it, "by combining biography, musicology, analysis, and reminiscences, we are tuning in to the very heterogeneity that makes Eastman's music so unforgettable."

Mary Jane Leach underscores the fragility of all artistic legacy as she describes her multiyear quest for Eastman's extant scores and tapes that led to the production of a commercial recording of his work (chapter 6). In a subsequent essay, she discusses Eastman's instrumentation, titles, and working methods, with particular attention to the *Joan d'Arc* pieces and their influences (chapter 11). Eastman's colleague in the Music Department at the University at Buffalo, singer-composer John Patrick Thomas, writes about Eastman's development as a singer, and the relationship between performance and composing (chapter 5). Matthew Mendez examines *Stay On It*, placing it within the experimental "downtown" new music and dance music worlds (chapter 10); Andrew Hanson-Dvoracek provides an analysis of the 1978 work *Crazy Nigger*, which, along with *Evil Nigger* and *Gay Guerrilla*, form the core of Eastman's mature style (chapter 9). In closing, Luciano Chessa writes about *Gay Guerrilla*, which he describes as the finest example of what Eastman called his "organic music." It is the piece, Chessa declares, that guarantees Eastman a firm place in the history of twentieth-century music (chapter 12).

Julius Eastman wrote radical works. An item in a *New Yorker* magazine column subtitled "Bad Boys" noted that Eastman was "an extreme composer" who demands "complete commitment."[9] He was also charismatic, arresting, charming, and as I said to critic Kyle Gann when he called me in early January 1991 with the news of Julius Eastman's death, "sometimes he was just damned outrageous."[10]

Notes

1. This point was astutely noted by Mary Jane Leach.
2. Renate Strauss, "Julius Eastman: Will the Real One Stand Up?" *Buffalo Evening News*, Lively Arts Section, July 16, 1976.
3. Thomas Putnam, "Julius Eastman Works Scheduled," *Buffalo Courier Express*, April 19, 1970, 32.
4. Arthur Ashe, *Days of Grace* (New York: Ballantine, 1993), 139–40.
5. Jonathan D. Katz and David C. Ward, *Hide/Seek* (Washington DC: Smithsonian Books, 2010), 31.

6. Gerald Eastman interview with the author, September 14, 2009.

7. The author is tempted to postulate that the 1971 uprising at the nearby Attica Correctional Facility, which was intensely monitored by the University at Buffalo community, may have been a significant factor in Eastman's growing activism.

8. See Henry Louis Gates Jr. on "signifying" in Afro-American culture, *The Signifying Monkey: A Theory of African-American Criticism* (New York: Oxford University Press, 1988); also Ellie M. Hisama, "'Diving into the Earth': The Musical Worlds of Julius Eastman," in *Rethinking Difference in Music Scholarship*, ed. Olivia Bloechl, Melanie Lowe, and Jeffrey Kallberg, 260–86 (New York: Cambridge University Press, 2015).

9. Russell Platt, "Classical Notes: Bad Boys," *New Yorker*, August 26, 2013, 14.

10. Kyle Gann, "That Which Is Fundamental: Julius Eastman, 1940–90," *Village Voice*, January 22, 1991.

CHAPTER ONE

JULIUS EASTMAN, A BIOGRAPHY

Renée Levine Packer

I dreamed about Julius before I was pregnant, you know. Julius was a different kind of baby. The odd thing was that he didn't like to be touched. Most babies want to be bounced, but you had to put Julius down. He didn't want to be held. When he was about two years old, I used to read him stories and, while standing in his crib, he would repeat the story word for word. So I knew right away there was something special going on.

—Frances Eastman interview with RLP, October 11, 2006.

The "lords of in-between," writes Lewis Hyde in his book *Trickster Makes This World*, are the boundary crossers who travel "a spirit road as well as a road in fact." Hyde continues, "Every group has its edge, its sense of in and out. . . . We constantly distinguish—right and wrong, sacred and profane, clean and dirty, male and female, young and old, living and dead—and in every case trickster will cross the line and confuse the distinction. . . . Trickster will appear to suggest an amoral action, something right/wrong that will get life going again."[1]

There was something of the contrarian, of the trickster about Julius Eastman. He never let people think that he worked hard. Everything he did was calculated to seem effortless. He had a commanding presence but employed masks, as we learn, not only in performance.

Julius Eastman appeared in my office unannounced one day—a slim, handsome black man of medium height dressed in a long army-green trench coat and white sneakers, carrying some music scores under his arm. "Lukas Foss said I should come over and talk to you," he said in a low, modulated voice. "I have a string quartet I'd like the Creative Associates to play." My office at that time was a dreary little alcove tucked between the entrance to the men's room and a floor-to-ceiling wall of dark gray windows overlooking a parking lot in Baird Hall, home of the Music Department at the University at Buffalo. This unlikely site was a beehive of activity—the headquarters of the Center of the Creative and Performing Arts (the Center), a virtual "roundhouse" for contemporary music performance during the 1960s and 1970s. At that time, young composers and performers (called Creative Associates or CAs) came to the Center from all over the world on yearlong resident fellowships to study and perform new music. Foss hadn't mentioned a thing about Julius Eastman to me, which meant that I hadn't approached any of the musicians—some of whom could be quite surly—about agreeing to do anything that might encroach on their free time. I gave him a list of the musicians' phone numbers, suggesting that he call them directly. "Good luck," I said with some skepticism.

As it turned out, Julius Eastman stuck around, becoming a guest performer with the Center in that 1968–69 season, and an official member of the Center's roster of musicians in fall 1969. One year later, he was invited to join the faculty of the university music department as an instructor of music theory. His biographical sketch in the Center's concert programs reads: "Pianist-composer. Diploma in composition from the Curtis Institute of Music. Among his works are two ballets, songs, orchestral and piano works." He was twenty-eight years old.

The Buffalo years, which comprised Eastman's most productive period artistically and his most stable financially, merit broad and deep attention. One notes the avalanche of performance activity, the multifaceted ability he brought to the music as composer, pianist, singer, conductor, actor, choreographer, and dancer; the dizzying schedule that also included teaching, touring, and recording; and the confidence of his reach.

Early Years

Men of the Eastman family were builders and engineers. Phillip Walter Eastman was of West Indian descent, a self-educated carpenter/contractor who crafted, among other things, beautiful staircases. Well versed in mathematics and European history, he named his children after important historical and Biblical figures such as Oliver Cromwell, Julius Caesar, Esther, and Rebekah. Julius Dunbar Eastman Sr. was born on March 26, 1913, in Purdy, Virginia, the second boy of ten children. When the Depression hit, Phillip Eastman refused to take on menial work, relying instead on his eldest boys to shoulder much of the family support.

Julius Sr. went to elementary school in Virginia, to high school in New York City, and attended City College at night to obtain his bachelor's degree. He became a civil engineer, and at one time oversaw the flood control stations between Buffalo and New York City. He married Frances Famous (also of West Indian descent) in New York in the 1930s. Twenty-three years old, she too attended City College and had studied piano for many years. At the time of their marriage, Julius Sr. made it clear that he preferred not to have any children because he had already supported a family. In fact, he could do without friends, too. He told her that he was happy being just the two of them alone. But despite her husband's preferences, Frances Eastman gave birth to a son, Julius Dunbar Eastman Jr., at Harlem Hospital in Manhattan on October 27, 1940.

The family moved to Syracuse from Manhattan in the early 1940s. Julius Sr. enlisted in the army, and Frances Eastman went to work at General Electric as an inspector.

> I put Julius in nursery school but, after ten weeks or so, I had to quit my job because every day around 3:00 P.M. they would call me from the school and tell me that he was running a fever. He used to have earaches, so I had to pick him up and take him home. He was very close to me at that time. In Syracuse when he was three, four, and five, and until adulthood, he was too attached to me.[2]

Perhaps to be near Mrs. Eastman's mother when the new baby came, the family returned to Manhattan, where Gerald Eastman was born on May 11, 1945. Two years later, citing the desire for her sons to have a yard to play in and ride their bikes, the family relocated to a comfortable two-story house on a tree-lined street in the Southside neighborhood of Ithaca, New York.

Problems in the marriage were emerging. For one thing, Julius Sr. saw young Julius as the interloper. According to Mrs. Eastman, he was "never nice to his first son." Soon after the move to Ithaca, Frances and Julius Eastman Sr. separated, and Mrs. Eastman got a job as a clerk in the Cayuga Medical Hospital, later becoming the first woman of color to be supervisor of medical records there.[3] "From early childhood," Mrs. Eastman recalled, "Julius had a mind of his own. Even at two years old, I could recognize what his personality was going to be like. He would not compromise. If I told him to behave and sit down, he would stand rigidly erect (like a board) with fists clenched and you would have to kill him and break his bones to make him sit down. He never changed."[4] When Julius was nine or ten, Mrs. Eastman took him along to visit her Trinidad-born mother, Caroline Famous, in New York, where she owned a small apartment house in the South Bronx. While walking past a music store one day, Mrs. Eastman mentioned that when she had been a piano student, she always purchased her music in that store. "Oh," Julius said, "I want to go in and buy something." The Eastmans had a grand piano in their Ithaca house, although Julius had not yet had any training, other than beginning general music lessons in school. Mrs. Eastman purchased a simple book, and they brought it home. In the book was Beethoven's *Für Elise*, which, she reported, Julius played "right off."

According to Mrs. Eastman, when Julius was "just a kid," Julius Sr. asked her if she "noticed something" about Julius. Mrs. Eastman thought that he might have intuited a homosexual proclivity in his son. Mrs. Eastman replied, "No. I think he's just fine," and "that was the end of that." But Mrs. Eastman felt that her husband knew that Julius might be homosexual early on.[5]

Young Julius sang in a production of Engelbert Humperdinck's *Hansel and Gretel* in grade school, and soon thereafter became a paid soprano singer in the boys' choir of St. John's Episcopal Church on Buffalo Street. He continued his singing in the glee club at Boynton Junior High School. A classmate remembers that he performed a solo at their eighth grade graduation. "[Julius] sang 'Stormy Weather,' which seems like an odd song to sing at graduation. . . . I remember being impressed then by the richness of his baritone voice."[6] By age fourteen, Julius's voice had grown deeper, and he became a bass-baritone. During this period, he began studying piano with Roger Hannah, the organist at the Episcopal Church in town. Throughout his high school days, Julius was a member of the Ithaca High School Glee Club, directed by Vito E. Mason, who was also choir director of the First Presbyterian Church. Classmate, Miriam (Heinicke) Monfredo recalls:

> I didn't know Julius well. . . . He was one of not very many Blacks in our class, and he was so quiet and slight of frame that I suspect he often went unnoticed. But one morning in second period choral club, . . . we started rehearsing this piece that called for a male solo and, as far as we knew, had not yet been assigned to anyone. When we reached the solo section everybody's voice straggled off since we expected Vito Mason to stop us there as he had done in the past. But this time, he nodded instead

> to someone in the front row. And suddenly, seemingly out of nowhere, came this big, glorious, bass voice. We gave a collective gasp, and shivers run down my spine even now, when I remember it all these years later. It was Julius's bass, and although in all likelihood he was the physically smallest person in the room, he had indisputably the largest, most magnificent voice there. I talked to him after rehearsal, telling him how stunned I had been, and I think that was the first time I had ever seen him smile. It was, typically, a shy self-effacing smile. Julius was one of the most modest, least self-aggrandizing people I have met in my lifetime, and yet he owned a voice that the gods give to very few.[7]

Once Julius started taking piano lessons, his mother recalled, "He would sit at that piano, and I would have to make him do his homework and go to bed. I had taken piano lessons for years, but Julius, after six months, was better than I ever was. He was a natural. I don't know where it came from."[8] By 1957, Julius was playing piano well enough to have a job accompanying dance classes at the Iris Barbura Studio. His musicality was immediately evident to Thomas Sokol, professor of music at Cornell University, who, after dropping his daughter off for a ballet class, stayed to listen to the young pianist, who he sensed was an unusually gifted musician.[9] Barbura's friend, the Romanian-born choreographer, Vergiu Cornea, was the dance instructor at Ithaca College, and the founding director of the Ithaca Ballet. Julius studied ballet with Cornea, eventually composing a work titled *Vergiu's Dance*.

Ithaca did not have a large black population in the 1950s and 1960s. When asked, neither Professor Sokol, nor Julius's high school classmates, could pinpoint incidents of racism. In fact, one of Julius's classmates wrote, "We were in a science club project, and even then one could see he was extra smart and a very talented young man. There was [*sic*] no race cards to be played in those days. . . . Ithaca was a good place to grow up in."[10]

Frances Eastman saw it somewhat differently, however. Julius had been singing since grade school, and was an admired soloist in the high school glee club, even winning an award from the Hollis Dann Glee Club Fund, which had been established in 1945 to be given to an outstanding glee club member. She thought his grades were good, but near the end of his senior year, the school counselor called her in for discussion of college possibilities, and said "no school will accept Julius." To Mrs. Eastman, it just didn't add up. She knew that the counselor had taken pains with two young girls in Julius's class who wanted to go to Bryn Mawr, making sure they were invited to the proper teas and such. Yet for Julius, the counselor couldn't think of anything to promote his candidacy for admission to a college.[11]

In 1957, the year before his high school graduation, Julius Eastman began to study piano with George Driscoll, who recognized and supported the young man's talent. Following graduation, Julius entered Ithaca College, where he studied in what Mrs. Eastman called "the concerto program" with Driscoll. After a few months, Driscoll recommended that Julius move on to a music conservatory, and suggested that he audition for the Juilliard School. He auditioned for Rosina Lhevinne, the acclaimed teacher of Van Cliburn, John Browning, and others. Lhevinne concurred that Eastman had talent, but felt that he was not yet sufficiently prepared to study with her. If he would agree to devote the entire next year exclusively to practicing the piano, she said that she would hear him again, and would probably accept him as her student. According to his cousin, David Lisbon, who accompanied Julius to the audition, Julius was sorely disappointed because he felt that the audition had gone well. Both wondered if race had been an issue in the decision. In those days, Lisbon recalled, "one never really knew."[12]

Driscoll was not satisfied with the Juilliard results either, and urged Julius to audition for the Curtis Institute of Music in Philadelphia. On January 28, 1959, he wrote a note to Curtis stating that Julius Eastman was applying to the school "with the consent of his current backer."[13] In early May, Julius auditioned for the faculty, playing Chopin, and was accepted for admission as a piano major with Mieczyslaw Horszowski. In addition to his piano studies, he would study solfège, music dictation, and Elements of Music I. All Curtis students were accepted on full tuition scholarship.[14] Upon learning of his acceptance, on May 14 Julius wrote to the admissions director: "Dear Sir: I have received your letter of acceptance and am overjoyed. I will do my best to deserve this gift. Sincerely yours, Julius Eastman."[15]

Curtis

In 1959, Zeyda Ruga (Suzuki), a Cuban pianist and classmate of Eastman's, entered Curtis at age sixteen. There were two other girls from Latin America in the class: Marta Garcia Renart from Mexico and Beatriz Lima, a Brazilian. All three became good friends with Eastman. In their class of just over one hundred students, the only other black student was Homer Lee, a clarinetist.[16] Ruga lived in a residence for young girls run by the Dominican nuns, the only condition upon which her father would give his permission for her to study in the States. Eastman lived at the YMCA.

According to Ruga, Eastman was not "chummy" with many students other than the Latin Americans. She noted that some people in the school may have "steered clear," because Julius was homosexual, and that he did not seem "at ease" with the others. Although she was not aware of any overt bias about race or Eastman's sexuality, she speculated that "it was probably hard for him." They studied harmony, solfège, and counterpoint together, and had many conversations about music.

Ruga and Eastman were very poor, but student tickets were often available, enabling them to attend concerts together fairly regularly, including one by Arthur Rubinstein.[17] Marta Garcia Renart and Eastman shared an interest in modern dance, in addition to their musical focus. They had German class together, and she remembers that he made a small cantata called "Wo ist mein Bleistift?" (Where Is My Pencil?), hinting at Eastman's endearing sense of humor.

To both Ruga and Marta Garcia Renart, it was evident that their friend lacked the high quality of training that many of their classmates had before coming to Curtis. Ruga's impression was that he needed more technique, and that he did not have a particularly beautiful sound on the piano. She thought that insecurity, because of this comparative lack of musical training, may have accounted for his shyness and reticence.[18] Possibly because of these technical limitations, Garcia Renart speculates, he may not have been taken as seriously as he should have been by the other students. On the other hand, Ruga recalled, "Julius was intelligent, handsome and graceful. He had a beautiful voice and was a graceful dancer. And he had a spiritual side. He could see through people. Music wasn't a business for him. He wasn't interested in making connections or making money. Things had to mean something spiritually to him." Ruga Suzuki added, "We gave friendship freely to one another."[19] Beatriz Lima remembers when she and Eastman gave a joint recital for a group of women at a home in a suburb of Philadelphia. They journeyed by train, pretending to be concert artists on tour. Since they were usually short of money, they were looking forward to the tea portion of the event, hoping for a free meal. They both played; Eastman also sang to Lima's accompaniment. But the refreshments were slight, in no way replacing a meal. To make matters worse, Lima recalls, they were paid by check, which could not be cashed until the next day. Back in Philadelphia, Eastman offered to pay for Lima's supper as she had completely run out of money. When she thanked him, he answered: "It's good to be poor because you learn to be generous."[20]

Eastman's academic record at Curtis was uneven. He entered as a piano student and received a B grade from Horszowski in both years as a piano major. During those first two years he received mostly A's in his Elements of Music class, but got a D in Music Dictation. During the summer of 1960, following his first full year at Curtis, Julius wrote to the Curtis registrar to request Zeyda Ruga's Cuban address. In the note, he includes a description of his daily routine:

> The days spent here this summer have been a continuous sameness, producing an infinite amount of progress and change. At present I practice from 8 o'clock to 12 in the early afternoon. I read in the library. Late afternoon I practice or compose. Speaking of composing, I have taken a composition course at Ithaca College from a Mr. Benson, who knows Giannini and has worked together with him. To continue my schedule I used to cook dinner in late afternoon but my mother is now on vacation so at present I let her do it. At night back to practice [*sic*] and a combination of composing and reading.[21]

In Eastman's second year at Curtis he encountered Dr. A. Constant Vauclain, with whom he studied Counterpoint, Harmony I, and Aural Harmony I. Evidently a rapport existed between student and teacher because Eastman received good grades in Vauclain's classes, and as Zeyda Ruga Suzuki remarked, "It was from Dr. Vauclain that Julius learned to hear."[22]

In February 1961, during his second year at Curtis, Eastman petitioned the school for permission to switch his major from piano to composition, necessitating a formal application review and recommendations. Warren Benson, associate professor of music at Ithaca College, with whom Julius had studied during the summer of 1960, wrote to the Curtis admissions officer on April 2, 1961: "My knowledge of his work is somewhat limited to his efforts of one six-week summer course in 1960 at Ithaca College. He has talent, industry and a flair for dramatic writing. He needs discipline and much training. I would endorse his candidacy, based on this limited acquaintance with his work."[23]

All students who apply to the Curtis Institute of Music are asked on the application form the question, "What is your ultimate goal in studying music?" In 1959, Eastman's response was "I would like to become an excellent musician and pianist." A year and a half later on his application form to gain acceptance as a music composition major, he wrote in response to the same question, "To obtain wisdom."[24] This provocative response prompts one to wonder whether he was speaking of obtaining wisdom to understand the world? Wisdom to bring to his music? Or wisdom to deal with a difficult daily circumstance? When he arrived in Philadelphia at age nineteen in 1959 to attend Curtis, it is probable that he had not spent any sustained period of time in a big city, other than a two-month summer stay in New York following his high school graduation while taking lessons with the pianist Seymour Lipkin. The nature of his experiences in those first two years at Curtis (1959–60, 1960–61) is open to speculation. As those who knew him have attested, he was shy and did not have many friends beyond the three girls from Latin America. We know there were very few blacks in the school; many of the students were far more musically sophisticated than he; his grades were mediocre (especially in the first year); he was not particularly outgoing; he was poor; he weighed 140 pounds and lived in a small room at the YMCA. In another exchange of letters with Miss Hill, the Curtis registrar wrote to Eastman, presumably to remind him of the date of his first lesson that fall, and may have referred to his previous living arrangements as "barracks." Eastman seems to be feeling down:

> I doubt that you will realize what pleasure just your little note has given. The fact is that fruitfull [*sic*] dialogue between me and members of this earth have been at a near standstill. Recent letters that I have written have not been answered except for one which I have not answered. The reason being that I wrote once to this person and after a long wait I received nothing. I imagined losage [*sic*] in the mail. I wrote again. Shortly after I received the reason for the delay. "Too busy." So I have not answered. Between stubbornness and laziness I know not which the greater sin be.
>
> Barracks indeed! If I have to live there one more year I shall die a morbid death of claustrophobia. But even worse than inevitably living in my cell is the fear and dread of having to call and knock at the door of strange people looking for a room. This is why I stayed at the Y all last year without effort on my part to move. But since I have written my father only once this summer (laziness on my part this time) my chance of escaping the terrible fate is very slim.
>
> Thanks again for the card.
> Sincerely yours,
> Julius
>
> P.S. I play two of my own pieces Sunday at a tea. First I shall delve into their form and style (the Bernstein way) then I shall proceed to play them.[25]

In his first and second years at Curtis, Eastman never received better than a B grade from his major teacher Mieczyslaw Horszowski. His academic record is plagued with absences, explanations running from "mental lapse," "forgot," to "just didn't go." In one instance, he does note that he had been playing at a fundraising dinner for the school, the only concrete excuse offered. In his final two years at Curtis, after being accepted by Dr. Vauclain as a composition major, he consistently received A grades. By the middle of his second year, a health history form in his file indicates that he was underweight at 125 pounds, and that he needed glasses to correct his vision. The form mentions a family history of tuberculosis on his father's side, and that Eastman had a heart murmur.[26]

During his third year at the Curtis Institute, there are further indications that Eastman may not have been in good health. A doctor's communiqué to school officials notes that he is suffering from exhaustion and recommends that he take at least a week's rest.[27] In late September of his final year at Curtis, Eastman sent a note to Mrs. Anne Smith, the staff receptionist, stating, "Something has come up and I will not be able to be in on the 27th. I shall be there on Monday, the 1st." In response, a telegram sent to Eastman and signed by Efrem Zimbalist, Director, reads "Report for classes Friday, 9/28 or dismissal."[28]

Eastman's graduation recital, consisting entirely of his own compositions, took place on February 27, 1963. The first piece, *The Blood*, enlisted a mixed chorus of nine singers. Richard Goode was the piano soloist. Beatriz Lima, who sang in the chorus, describes *The Blood* as "so beautiful." In her opinion, it was "a tribute to man's suffering," reflecting her classmate's profound respect for each human being, rather than a tribute to any godly figure. As she recalled:

> Julius could have invited any of the wonderful voice students at Curtis to sing his composition, but, instead, he asked some of his friends who were not singers. This is how I, who really couldn't sing at all (although Julius had the strange notion that I sounded like a boy soprano), got to sing in Curtis Hall along with pianist Marta Garcia Renart and, if I remember correctly, pianist Richard Goode and clarinetist Frank Ell.[29]

His work *Song Trilogy* followed with text by the composer. The sections are titled "O, Go Not"; "Birds Fly Away" (for voice, cello, and piano); and "I Love the River." Closing the first half was *Piano Compositions* comprising *Chorale on a Theme of Vauclain, Plié, Vergiu's Dance*, and the first movement of the Sonata for piano—"allegro," performed by the composer.[30] On May 11, 1963, Julius Eastman was awarded a diploma in music composition from the Curtis Institute of Music.

Information about the five years following Eastman's graduation from Curtis is sketchy. He returned to Ithaca, where he continued his studies in piano and composition at Ithaca College and, possibly, for a time, in New York at Mannes College of Music with Frances Dillon. It may have been at this point, as Frances Eastman reported, when Eastman auditioned, and was accepted, for a position in the Metropolitan Opera Chorus. He declined the offer. While living in Ithaca, he gave music therapy classes at Willard State Hospital on nearby Lake Seneca, continuing to perform when occasions arose. He was vocal soloist in regional productions, including a 1964 production of Leoncavallo's *Pagliacci*, and participated in the Cornell University Summer Series concerts with Thomas Sokol, director of the Cornell University Glee Club, who early on had taken an interest in his development. In July 1966, Eastman presented a recital at the Alice Statler Auditorium at Cornell University, on which he performed as bass soloist (with Virginia Marks as accompanist) on the first half of the program, and as pianist on the second half. His own composition *Song Trilogy* for pianist, soprano, cellist, and dancer closed the first half of the program. In it, Eastman performed as the dancer. The event was reviewed by critic Nina Sobelman for the *Ithaca Journal*:

> The second concert of the Cornell Summer Series brought the talents of Julius Eastman back to the Ithaca community. Mr. Eastman is an Ithacan whose many-faceted artistry as composer, bass, pianist and even dancer was most evident in his masterful display Thursday evening. His well-disciplined and balanced vocal selections were superbly accompanied by Virginia Marks. . . . Mr. Eastman's brilliant use of diction as a technique of interpretation was evident in all his English songs, notably Morley's *Now Is the Month of Maying*. This quality was also present in the Schubert lieder. . . . Mr. Eastman's song trilogy further displayed the vast scope of his creative talents. Many of his modern dance forms were perhaps a bit too punctuated for his intensely descriptive music. Nevertheless, this section of the program was most rewarding. The second portion of the evening featured Mr. Eastman at the piano. The rendition of the Rameau suite . . . showed an independent and intensely experimental style. . . . The Ravel *Sonatine*, although somewhat disappointing in its lack of precision, was nevertheless the epitome of impressionist piano playing. Once again the pianist's control of dynamic effects was evident, enabling the audience to be enticed into the colorful and subtle world of impressionism. Well received by the audience was Mr. Eastman's improvisation. His facility was demonstrated especially in the third movement, in which the motives were masterfully woven together. Incredibly, nothing was left hanging at the end, as is so frequently the case. This imaginative array of musical diversity, most artfully chosen, attests to Mr. Eastman's sensitivity, making him one of the (most) intense—and rewarding—musicians we have seen.[31]

Professor Sokol received a phone call that summer from the conductor Eugene Ormandy, saying that he needed three male singers for minor roles in a performance of *Der Rosenkavalier* at the Saratoga Performing Arts Center. Sokol told Ormandy he thought he had three good people, and selected Arthur Neal, Jack Burns, and Julius Eastman. He arranged for the music department voice coach, Barbara Troxell, to work on the singers' German pronunciation. According to Sokol, Eastman "did wonderfully well."

On December 8, 1966, Eastman selected a program, similar to his Cornell recital from the previous summer, to present on his New York City debut concert at Town Hall. This review is by Alvin K. Fossner, an assistant professor of music at Jersey City State College:

> Julius Eastman, pianist . . . showed himself to be a young man to watch. He obviously is one of those rare persons who has enough insight into the contemporary compositional technique to specialize in that area of performance. Most pianists include something new in their recitals because it's the thing to do. The results are usually quite bland. In Eastman's case, it is difficult to assess whether the music he chose is really that good or it is what he did with it. In the *Three Epigrams* by Robert Palmer, a group of well-constructed, dissonant pieces, he skillfully brought out all of the thematic material. *The Prelude* by Constant Vauclain was interpreted in the Baroque spirit and made much musical sense. His own compositions, *Chorale and Fugue on a Theme of Constant Vauclain* which has some of the flavor of Hindemith and *Vergius's Dance*, were given brilliant, colorful readings. . . . The most intriguing part of the recital was the selection in which he actually improvised a theme and variations. In our own time the late Alec Templeton did it regularly but before this we must go back to Mozart and Beethoven to find a precedent.[32]

It is in 1967 that Buffalo turns up for the first time in any accounting of Eastman's working life. Karl Singletary, a dancer with Kathleen Crofton's Buffalo-based Ballet Center company, met Eastman that year through Billie Kirpich, director of dance at the University at Buffalo. Eastman was composing music for Kirpich's dances and, presumably, accompanying Kirpich's dance classes as well.[33] In conversation with Singletary, Eastman mentioned that he needed a place to stay. Singletary offered to rent Eastman a room in his apartment for the summer. A few months later in fall 1967, Singletary left Buffalo to study in Berlin and relinquished the apartment. He asked his father to let Eastman stay as a tenant in his family's spacious house. The arrangement lasted for a month or so. Eastman, it seems, was bringing "strange" people to the house, and the elder Mr. Singletary asked him to leave.[34]

In November 1967, Thomas Sokol invited Eastman to perform in Stravinsky's *Oedipus Rex* with the Cornell Symphony Orchestra and the Glee Club. The stellar cast included Lili Chookasian, contralto; David Lloyd, tenor; David Pelton, tenor; Robert Farrell, baritone; Julius Eastman, bass; and G. Wallace Woodworth, speaker. In act 1, Eastman sang the role of Tiresias (a learned priest in Thebes). In act 2, he sang the Messenger who proclaims "divine Jocasta is dead!" announcing Queen Jocasta's suicide, when she realizes that Oedipus (her son) had murdered the old King (her husband) and subsequently married her: "The lights had been darkened in the auditorium for part of act 2. At the moment for the Messenger to shout the news of the Queen's death, Julius turned on a music stand spotlight directed at his face, which (unknown to anyone but himself) he had painted silver. This powerful theatrical moment underscores Eastman's brilliant theatrical imagination."[35] A month later, Eastman was engaged to perform the role of King Balthazar in Menotti's *Amahl and the Night Visitors* with the Buffalo Philharmonic Orchestra.

The year 1968 was a breakthrough year for Julius Eastman. He toured with the Gregg Smith Singers in Europe and the United States, and traveled often between Buffalo and Ithaca for performances as vocal soloist. In late April, Eastman participated in a Cornell Music Department production of Stravinsky's *L'Histoire du Soldat*, produced by Kenneth Fung, in which he performed and choreographed the part of the Devil. In late May, he was bass soloist in the role of Adam in the Buffalo Choral Arts Society's performance of Haydn's *The Creation*, conducted by Robert Schulz.[36] In October he returned to Ithaca to perform as vocal soloist in the American premiere of *The Prophecy of Isaiah* by Bohuslav Martinů, and during that fall, he was hired on a four-month temporary appointment as teaching assistant in the SEEK program at the State University College (formerly Buffalo State Teachers College) Music Department. The job description is "musical accompanist for dance."[37]

For a period during the 1968–69 academic year, Eastman lived in an apartment in Allentown, a section of small stores and restaurants in downtown Buffalo that had "a scruffy casualness to it that appealed to local artists" and had the whiff of a miniscule prefashionable Greenwich Village.[38] By December 1968, he had made notable contacts in the music and dance world of Buffalo. He had impressed Peter Yates at the State University College, and had a part-time appointment there as a dance accompanist; he was composing and playing piano with Billie Kirpich in the modern dance department across town at University at Buffalo; and he was performing as vocal soloist with the Buffalo Philharmonic. At some point, Julius showed his music to Lukas Foss, the conductor of the Buffalo Philharmonic Orchestra and founder of the highly regarded new music group, the Center of the Creative and Performing Arts, in residence at the University at Buffalo.

Buffalo, New York, in the 1960s and 1970s was—unlikely as it may seem—a world-renowned hotbed of the musical avant-garde. Based on a plan devised by Foss, the Rockefeller Foundation provided support for annual fellowships for young composers and virtuoso instrumentalists (called Creative Associates) to live in Buffalo for up to two years, thus creating a community of musicians who would spend their time studying, creating, and performing difficult, often controversial, new works. The Center of the Creative and Performing Arts, the initiative's formal name, was housed in the Music Department of the University at Buffalo, and presented its Evenings for New Music concert series regularly, at the Albright-Knox Art Gallery in Buffalo and in Carnegie Recital Hall in New York. Essentially an artists' colony embedded in a university, the now legendary lineup of Center musicians over the years included Maryanne Amacher, John Bergamo, Buell Neidlinger, Cornelius Cardew, George Crumb, Don Ellis, Terry Riley, Frederic Rzewski, David Tudor, Andrew White, and Jan Williams.[39]

Foss was sufficiently impressed to invite Eastman to present his four new pieces for piano as a guest artist on the Center's Evenings for New Music concert at the Albright-Knox Art Gallery. Thus, on December 15, 1968, Julius performed *Piano Pieces I–IV* (1968) on a program, with works by Roger Reynolds, Morton Subotnick, Bruno Bartolozzi, and Stanley Lunetta. The pieces were repeated in New York several months later, on February 4, 1969, at Carnegie Recital Hall.[40] In late December 1968, Eastman performed for a second time as soloist in the Buffalo Philharmonic's Christmas presentation of Menotti's *Amahl and the Night Visitors*.

During this holiday period, the young medical intern Donald Burkhardt and Julius Eastman meet.

> It was Christmastime when I met Julius. One of the fellows at the hospital where I was doing my residency knew some people in my neighborhood on the West Side not too far from Kleinhans Music Hall. After that, we often got together for dinners, played cards and just had a nice evening together. On one of those evenings Karl Singletary came over with Julius and so that's how I met Julius. It was as simple as that. All those people were black.[41]

According to Burkhardt and to Singletary, Eastman was gregarious, flirtatious, and surrounded himself with a lot of friends. At the conclusion of his year at the American Ballet Theatre School, Karl Singletary returned to Buffalo, discouraged and depressed, because he could not afford to continue studying in New York. By then, Eastman was living with Burkhardt in his apartment on Plymouth Avenue.

> Julius heard that I came back [from New York]. He felt that I was very talented and that I should stick with the dance. I remember I was wearing ballet slippers with holes in them and had to use duct tape to hold them together. Julius bought me a new pair because I just couldn't afford to. I always remembered how thoughtful he was. He was the one who encouraged me to stay with the dance and not to just give it up totally. He sort of stuck with me and helped me out.[42]

In the Center

On September 1, 1969, Eastman officially joined the Creative Associates as pianist-composer. CA fellowship appointments ran through the academic year, from September through June. The Center's well-known concert series, Evenings for New Music, was presented approximately six times a season in Buffalo and New York City. In 1969, most of the concerts were performed at Rutgers University just preceding, or following, the New York concerts. Donald Burkhardt remembers that Eastman was very excited about being invited to be a Creative Associate.[43] The coveted appointment appears to have been a boon for him. He was now a member of a prestigious contemporary music ensemble, along with a dozen or so talented colleagues from Europe and the United States; he had the resources of a fine university at his disposal; he had a wide range of performance opportunities including regular appearances in New York City, an attentive local press, and a regular paycheck—an ideal environment for a young composer.[44]

Eastman's first assignment as a member of the new music group was as pianist in two ensemble pieces on the 1969–70 season's Evenings for New Music opening concert—*For Norma* (1968) by his fellow Creative Associate, trombonist-composer James Fulkerson, and *Jack's New Bag* (1967) by California-based Barney Childs. Later that season, Eastman played the organ in the US premiere of Norwegian composer Arnie Nordheim's work for organ, percussion, and electronics, *Colorazioni* (1968), and played the piano in a work for large ensemble by the Budapest-born Canadian composer Istvan Anhalt, *Foci* (1969). Both visiting composers, Nordheim and Anhalt, were on hand to mount or conduct their works, providing valuable experience for any young composer.

Another musician new to the Creative Associates that fall was the Czech flutist-composer Petr Kotik, who had arrived in Buffalo in November 1969 directly from Europe. Kotik was not altogether happy with the programming of Center music directors Lukas Foss and Lejaren Hiller and, four months after his arrival, he started his own group, the S.E.M. Ensemble, enlisting colleagues percussionist Jan Williams, graduate student clarinetist Roberto Laneri, and others. As composer George Crumb, a CA in the mid-sixties said, "You found the folks in the group who were on your wavelength and got to know those people pretty well.[45] In that spirit, Eastman joined in the ensemble's second public performance in September 1970, and continued as a member of S.E.M. for the next four years, during which time Kotik and Eastman saw each other almost daily.[46] S.E.M.'s focus on collaboration, improvisation, and the use of controlled chance systems corresponded to Eastman's interests, affording him an even broader musical life.

In the Center's earliest days, the musicians inaugurated an independent concert series that was held primarily on the university campus, as opposed to the Center's more prominent Evenings for New Music series at the Albright-Knox Art Gallery. The campus-based concerts (known as the Creative Associate Recitals) quickly developed their own profile, and were highly valued by the Center members, who programmed Schubert, Mozart, William Walton, jazz, or anything else they wanted to do. Creative Associate cellist Robert Martin remembered, "We all came to each other's concerts. I played Elliott Carter's *Sonata* with Carlos Alsina. In a way, I have more vivid, happier memories of the Baird Hall recitals. It was a 'homey' kind of thing."[47] In his early years as a Creative Associate, Eastman frequently participated in his colleagues' recitals. In December 1969 he played works for flute and piano by Herbert Brün and Stefan Wolpe with the flutist Thomas Howell. In January 1970, he participated as vocalist and pianist in five pieces on Creative Associate soprano Gwendolin Sims's recital, including playing in two ensemble works by Morton Feldman, *Vertical Thoughts* (1963) and *For Franz Kline* (1962). In late March he was both pianist and speaker on a joint Creative Associate recital performing works by Ann Loomis Silsbee and Petr Kotik.[48]

A few weeks later on April 19, 1970, Eastman premiered his large, ambitious multimedia opus, *The Moon's Silent Modulation*, a ballet for three dancers, with choreography, music, and libretto by the composer.

Eastman's score calls for flute, percussion, two pianos, speaker, mixed chorus, and string quintet. The performance took place in Domus, a large, loft-like space in Buffalo that was once the Pierce-Arrow plant.

Ralph Ellison has written that although the ideal of achieving a true political equality eludes us in reality, there is a fictional vision available to us.[49] So too, the composer arranges a musical version of the world as he would have it. In an interview about his piece with Thomas Putnam, music critic for the *Buffalo Courier Express*, Eastman calls the ballet an "allegory" having "blocks of sound that enter and exit." The work describes "the ego mechanism" that is the conflict between the sun and the earth. "Each considers itself superior," Eastman remarks. "It is a simple work—clear, almost religious," he explained. The message is: "There are no superior persons or beings that can be identified."[50] Composer-choreographer Eastman also served as narrator, reading his own poem. In the interview, he states that it is the first work in which he used graphic notation and "dealt with things other than notes."[51] A review of the performance in the *Buffalo Evening News* the next day gives a sense of the event, "This is a big work, full of gesture, its core based on an oft-repeated three-note motif. Slicing block-chords, tone clusters and a long crescendo-diminuendo of two stolidly opposed repeated chords were played by Mr. [Ronald] Peters with an excellent sense of timing, heightening the drama."[52] Thomas Putnam described the score as "heavy with dense string and choral sound, percussion clamor, and electronic flashes of flute."[53]

Less than two weeks after the premiere of *The Moon's Silent Modulation*, Eastman's work *Thruway*, also written in 1969–70, was presented by the Center at Rutgers University, Carnegie Recital Hall, and in the Sculpture Court of the Albright-Knox Art Gallery. Burkhardt remembers:

> He was composing everywhere we went. He always had something [his materials] and he was writing things down—even when we went camping across the country. That's how the name *Thruway* came about. I had a van with a table in it—an old Volkswagen camper. So he could easily sit in the back while we were driving along and he'd write his music. But always it was his music that he was concerned with.[54]

Thruway is scored for soprano, chorus, jazz combo, instrumental ensemble (violin, clarinet, cello, and flute), film projections, and tape. Eastman conducted all the performances. As in *The Moon's Silent Modulation*, *Thruway* employs blocks of improvised sections, prompting Putnam to write that the movement in *Thruway* seemed "more carefully plotted than the sound, whose random character was emphasized by the separation in space of the instrumentalists. There was some fine dissonant singing by the East High Choir, who skillfully added notes to notes until a cluster was rich."[55] And Herman Trotter, who reviewed the piece for the *Buffalo Evening News* wrote:

> Eastman conducted *Thruway*. . . . A prologue of jazz in an adjacent room and amoebic projections on the back wall ushered in a scene of recumbent bodies, running figures, religious chanting, abstract busy vocal noises, the chorus walking through the audience as though blind . . . followed by instruments, a barrage of film images . . . choir singing and collapsing one by one, more jazz, out. It all had a riveting dramatic effect, but don't ask me what it meant.[56]

Raymond Ericson of the *New York Times* wrote, "an ominous mélange of jazz, tape and live vocal sounds, brilliantly performed by some black high-school singers.[57]

Donald Burkhardt and Julius Eastman lived together for a year and a half. Burkhardt recalls that they led a fairly quiet life during their time together and did not do much socially.

> He was too bold with his language (at least during the last years that I knew him). He upset people. My parents came to visit when Julius and I were living together and we all went to see Niagara Falls. Julius kept using bad four-letter words and I had to tell him "Julius, we don't talk like that in our family." My mother was sitting right there. Later, she thanked me. And at Christmas 1970, Julius and I took a Christmas tree with all the decorations to Syracuse to my grandparents' house because they were too old to be able to manage it. We opened our gifts there. The gift he gave me was two very pornographic magazines wrapped up in tissue paper that you could see through. Now, we were all there together in the same room, and I could see as I was getting ready to open it, what was coming so I said, "Julius, do you think I should open this here?" And he said, "Oh yeah, go ahead." But I didn't open it because I knew what it was. My grandparents would have been shocked.[58]

In June 1970, Don Burkhardt finished his medical internship, entered the navy, and was sent to New London, Connecticut. As he recalls, Eastman was very upset about the impending change in their lives. For one thing, Eastman depended on Don. "Julius just didn't know how to do things. He was always composing, and really didn't manage very well on his own. He needed stability. I remember that his mother even said to me once, 'Make sure when he's onstage at concerts that he wears black socks.'"[59]

The Creative Associate fellowship ran through June, after which Eastman joined Burkhardt in New London, where he stayed over the summer months and well into the fall. During one of Burkhardt's free periods, they drove to the Berkshires, where they attended a performance of the Dance Theatre of Harlem at Jacob's Pillow. Burkhardt remembers that Eastman was keen to meet Arthur Mitchell, the brilliant ballet dancer and soon-to-be company director. After the performance, Eastman introduced himself to Mitchell and stayed to chat. Mitchell called Eastman a "triple threat" (referring to his talents as musician, dancer, and choreographer), provoking a hearty laugh all around.[60]

During that same summer, Eastman returned to Ithaca to mount performances of his latest works, *The Moon's Silent Modulation* and *Thruway* in the Statler Auditorium on the Cornell University Summer Concert Series. As Thomas Sokol describes it, Eastman introduced his audience to his new works in a special way. After obtaining tickets in the lobby, audience members proceeded into a large, resonant, marble-floored foyer leading to the auditorium doors. There, they were met, unannounced, by three instrumentalists seated in three corners (a violist, a cellist, and a trombonist—each playing his own favorite solo sonata—simultaneously) while Eastman sat alone in the mezzanine, sounding at intervals, a C on one suspended orchestral chime. Following this unusual introduction, the concert began.[61]

Eastman's appointment as instructor in the University at Buffalo (UB) Music Department, in the fall of 1970, included the requirement that he would teach only one course in order to accommodate his performance responsibilities with the Creative Associates. With Burkhardt away in the navy, Eastman rented his own apartment on Elmwood Avenue, directly across from Kathleen Crofton's school, the Ballet Center of Buffalo.[62] He invited Karl Singletary, who had returned to Buffalo and was a dancer in Crofton's ballet company, to move in with him.

> I lived there with Julius for about a year and a half. We were like brothers. In a way, I liked staying with him because he was always out of town so it was like having the apartment all to myself. Julius paid the rent. I bought the food and helped cook because I knew how, even as a teenager. I knew I was good for Julius because I maintained the house and did the laundry. I was neat. Julius was not. He was slack about housekeeping. I had my own room in another part of the house because, again, Julius would bring people to the house all the time. So I would just go to my room and close the door. To me, it seemed that Burkhardt was the best thing for Julius. Julius was so spaced out and never really took any one person seriously. He was just too

> gregarious—too surrounded by so many people. Burkhardt and I weren't that way. But Julius would just laugh it off. He did that a lot. Eventually, it got too much and I couldn't stay with him anymore.[63]

Eastman also referred to his busy social life in Suzanne Metzger's interview in UB's campus paper, the *Reporter*, stating that he had "almost too many friends—mostly downtown people who have nothing to do with music. I had to get rid of some of my friends recently. You know, for a clean living fellow, I like to get to bed by eleven o'clock and they were coming to my door at three in the morning. That's too much."[64]

As Singletary observed,

> This was the Martin Luther King era, and I remember one time especially when Julius made me very proud. Kathleen Crofton, I learned some years later, didn't take me in her company originally because of my color. Eventually she did, though I was the only black person in the company. Crofton employed an Asian pianist for classes and rehearsals who used to play from scores. At the time, we were rehearsing *Les Biches* with a famous British guest ballerina who had been brought in to choreograph the piece. The staff accompanist got sick at the last minute and couldn't be there to play the Poulenc score, so I suggested that Crofton engage Julius as a substitute. Julius came to the studio having never seen the big ballet score before. He looked it over a couple of times and began playing. He was even able to conduct the rehearsal with the dancers. Everybody was just amazed that this guy (and the only other black person there beside me) was able to look at this huge score and tune in right away. People were just wowed, and I was so proud.[65]

In an interview with Renate Strauss for the *Buffalo Evening News* in July 1976, Eastman comments, "I did a lot of things between 1970–75. Zubin Mehta invited me to sing *Essay* by Hans Werner Henze with his orchestras in Los Angeles and Tel Aviv. I premiered Henze's *El Cimarrón* in Pittsburgh. Lukas Foss had me conduct one of my pieces, *Seven Trumpets*, on his Marathon Series with the Los Angeles Philharmonic."[66]

The reporter goes on to note, "[Eastman's] portrayal of the mad King George III in Peter Maxwell Davies's music-theater piece *Eight Songs for a Mad King* created waves of excitement both here and in New York. He repeated the role with the New York Philharmonic under Pierre Boulez on the Prospective Encounters series, and made a recording of the piece in London with the composer and the Fires of London."[67]

The Maxwell Davies piece was a tour de force for Eastman and the headlines after each performance were close to ecstatic. "[*Eight Songs for a Mad King*] hits the listener like a collective shriek from Bedlam. . . . [Eastman] is not a trained singer, but he had the style and the vocal command . . . he lurched around like a mad Lear. Toward the end, he snatched the violin from the player, tore off its strings and smashed it. . . . This was theater."[68]

On November 1, 1970, Eastman performed the piece at the Albright-Knox Art Gallery. The Buffalo performance evinced the headline, "Eastman's 'Mad King': Mighty Work of Theater." The *Buffalo Evening News* reviewer, John Dwyer, called it "The dramatic sensation of this town over many seasons."[69]

"I Always Thought I Was Great but Why Does Making It Big Take So Long?" is the title of an interview with Eastman published in the UB Campus newspaper the *Reporter* in late September 1971. Eastman's question was not just a glib remark. Teaching music theory in the university while performing with the CAs was OK, he announced to the reporter, but his aim was to attain the level of a Menotti or Barber or Copland—professionals who made their living by composing alone.

> I would just like to compose, but that's only a dream. I always thought I was just great and it shouldn't be so hard, but I was shocked that the processes were so slow. . . . I'm not a world figure, but certain people know me. I've never pushed my music at all. Maybe that's not a good quality particularly, but I've always figured that once one is known, the publishers will come to you.[70]

Publishers or not, Eastman was living a rich musical life and earning a steady income, amplified by his reappointment that fall as instructor in the UB Music Department.

Curiously, Eastman does not refer in his interview to a stunning event that had occurred in the region just weeks before—the uprising at the Attica Correctional Facility, when more than twelve hundred mainly black and Hispanic inmates took control of all five cell blocks and seized forty-three white guards as hostages. The four-day revolt, precipitated by unaddressed inmate complaints, resulted in the deaths of twenty-nine inmates and ten hostages. According to his colleague Andrew Stiller, Eastman suffered acute distress over the Attica events, prompting Stiller to write, "I don't think any of us at the time fully understood how deeply divided he [Eastman] was inside between being an African American on the one hand, and an openly gay classical musician of the most esoteric sort."[71]

Later that fall, in addition to teaching and working with the S.E.M. Ensemble, Eastman conducted the Creative Associates in four performances of Makoto Shinohara's *Consonance* (1964–67) on concerts in Buffalo, Albany, and New York. He wrote *Comp 1*, a work for solo flute, for his colleague Petr Kotik and *Macle*, for four amplified voices with electronics, which was performed in February 1972 by the composer along with Petr Kotik, Roberto Laneri, and Jan Williams in Buffalo, in Carnegie Recital Hall, and on a short tour of State University of New York campuses.

Jan Williams no longer has the score of *Macle*, but he remembers that it consisted of a grid of twelve or sixteen squares, each square indicating an action for the performer to execute. No instruments were used, only vocal sounds were permitted. One action, for instance, might be "sing a popular song." Williams believes that all the performers received the same score.[72] John Dwyer voiced his opinion of the piece in the *Buffalo Evening News*:

> *Macle* for four grunters, moaners and howlers and a similar tape was by Julius Eastman, the very gifted and versatile composer, singer, dancer, actor and poet, who has done so many things here so well and at least one, the Maxwell-Davies "Mad King" to national attention. *Macle* is a work that seems to me so embarrassingly bad and unrelievedly ugly as to raise the question whether the composer had not wrought some kind of revenge on either art or audience, or both.[73]

Weeks later, at the end of February, Eastman appeared as "guest artist" in a modern ballet based on Jean Genet's *The Blacks*, which was produced by UB dance professor Cristyne Lawson and her Company of Man. Choreographed and directed by Lawson, *Black Ivory* was "a ballet for masked spectators and players." The title alludes to a trade name of the nineteenth century describing the human cargoes dispatched as merchandise from Africa to the markets of the "civilized" world. The score was by Roberto Laneri. Upon arrival at the Albright-Knox Art Gallery Sculpture Court where the event took place, audience members were asked to choose between two entrances to the performance area. At each entrance, audience members were issued a standard mask, which they were requested to don. Only once they are inside the court do the audience members realize they have been segregated into an area for white-masked people and, on the other side of the court, people with black masks. The space between them is the stage for the action of *Black Ivory*.

There follow episodes of black-masked players marching, strutting, cakewalking, and, finally, tap dancing. Then white-masked players dance minuets, including a *Grand Pas de Deux* by the dancers Karl Singletary and Graham Smith. At one point, the queen—an eighteen-foot high, pearly masked totem of white laces and ribbons—enters. Critic John Dwyer in the *Buffalo Evening News* described the effect:

> As with Genet, the Lawson fantasy not only challenges color identity but sexual identity, and fearfully enough, the idea of identity itself. Julius Eastman is weirdly wonderful as this 20-foot-high, campy duenna in a pale-silver mask and halo of feathers. His art of the mime makes his monstrous grotesque come alive to our horrified delight in its preposterous court manners and royally maternal if slight concerns for life or death.[74]

Cristyne Lawson remembers, "We did *The Blacks* by Jean Genet, and Julius was the Black Queen. He stood on a high scaffold in a long [white] dress that covered the base, and was in a white mask. At the very end of the piece, he takes off the mask and laughs—and the audience sees that it's a black man underneath. That was Julius's idea. He was a genius."[75]

Several weeks later, on March 8, 1972, Eastman played piano and woodblocks in Stockhausen's *Refrain*, for three instrumentalists, on his colleague Garry Kvistad's Creative Associate recital. Kvistad recalls the collaboration with pleasure, adding "There are some vocal requirements for *Refrain* (velar clicks with different pitch inflections) which Julius had no problem executing flawlessly. And I do remember how funny he was."[76] Additional performances with clarinetist-composer Roberto Laneri and group improvisations with the S.E.M. Ensemble followed throughout the winter.

Eastman's formidable performance skills were evident once again in spring 1972. *Requiems for the Party Girl* by Canadian composer R. Murray Schafer was written for voice and ensemble. The composer had always thought "the heroine should be a woman" and was skeptical when he learned that Julius Eastman was scheduled to perform his piece on an Evenings for New Music concert. Schafer's fears that the piece might be perceived as campy were allayed when he attended the performance and, upon subsequent reflection, came to agree that the part could be performed by a musician of either sex, particularly since it is a requiem.[77]

During the summer of 1972, Eastman visited Don Burkhardt in Winter Park, Florida, where he was serving at the Naval Training Center. One might speculate about the reasons, but on July 27, 1972, Eastman wrote to the Curtis Institute, asking that a copy of his transcript be mailed to the Main Office of Rollins College.[78]

By fall 1972, Eastman was back in his Elmwood Avenue apartment commencing his third year on the faculty of the UB Music Department.

Newly promoted to assistant professor, his three-year reappointment again specified a curtailed teaching load to reflect his continuing performance duties with the Creative Associates. Thus, his life was consumed with teaching, performing, and composing. By then he had made new friendships, both inside and outside of the university, and his musical life in Buffalo extended well beyond the university and the occasional appearance with the Buffalo Philharmonic.

Sometime in the early 1970s Eastman called on his university colleague, saxophonist Charles Gayle, at his house in Buffalo, and began going over to visit and to hang out with other musicians with whom Gayle played, including drummer Ameer Alhark and bassist Ray Combs. Gayle, a native of Buffalo, was on the UB faculty from 1970 to 1973, where he taught jazz history, theory, and ensemble. In the mid-sixties, he had met and played with bassist Buell Neidlinger, percussionist John Bergamo, and saxophonist Andrew White III, when they were Creative Associates. Eastman impressed Gayle as an educated guy. He spoke well, had high energy (in fact, may have been a little "hyper"), and had a lot of ideas. They talked in depth about music. "Julius was ambitious to the hilt; he wanted to be heard, to be on the map. He was interested in the accessibility of his work." Eastman, Gayle recalled, treated everyone nicely and the musicians took to him, although they didn't have comparable musical backgrounds. Gayle and his colleagues were the only ones doing free jazz in Buffalo at that time. According to Gayle, Eastman was open to experimental jazz, but he was not tied to "bop" and "post-bop" chord structures, although he was aware of both streams. In those years, the transition from conventional (or straight) jazz to free jazz didn't transfer so easily, and people fell out with each other over playing "regular" jazz and free jazz. Gayle left Buffalo in 1973 because he felt that there were no outlets for his kind of music, "unless you wanted to play in attics somewhere." Even then, Gayle sensed that Buffalo was not the right place for Eastman, saying that he needed access to musicians who played in different kinds of ensembles including, but not exclusively, orchestras.[79]

Saxophonist-composer Joseph Ford met Julius Eastman through his friends Leroy Jones and Jack Thomas, who were students at UB. He played in several of Eastman's pieces, including *Stay On It*, in Buffalo and at Carnegie Hall, and with the S.E.M. Ensemble as well. Ford grew up in Buffalo and began playing piano as a child. After high school, he went to Central State University, a historically black college in Wilberforce, Ohio, where he studied with Ken McIntyre in his senior year, and was conversant with twentieth-century classical music, such as Hindemith, Webern, Berg, and Bartok. To Ford, it seemed that Eastman "knew what he wanted and seemed reasonably disciplined." He commented, "The more we rehearsed, the further away I got from traditional roles and tones. . . . Julius said interesting things such as 'reverb tunes things up,' meaning that if you put reverb on things, it kind of hides intonation problems." To Ford, "Julius was the closest I've ever been associated with a genius as far as music is concerned. You could just hear it."[80]

Whether they were aware of it or not, Eastman and his colleagues were part of a growing sociological sea change—the blurring between popular and high culture, and an increasing disregard for established borders within traditionally accepted disciplines.[81] Although Duke Ellington, Ornette Coleman, Leroy Jenkins, and other African-American composers had been working in both the jazz and classical idioms for years, the genres were perceived as separate continents.[82] In the seventies, neatly tagged categories seemed increasingly porous, prompting the *New York Times* music critic John Rockwell to remark on the collapsing border between "experimental jazz" and contemporary music. "The same faces," he noted, "have been turning up among the performers at avant-garde jazz concerts and avant-garde 'serious' new-music concerts."[83] Performance venues were expanding into art galleries, clubs, and lofts—often the composers' and the players' preferred environments.

Jazz assumed an even larger presence in Julius Eastman's life when his brother Gerry moved to Buffalo in 1973. An accomplished jazz bassist and guitarist, who played with Count Basie's band for a time, Gerry Eastman studied at Ithaca College after his release from the service. He moved to Buffalo for two reasons: he and Julius wanted to work together, and Julius needed help dealing with his newly purchased house. The Tralfamadore Café had recently opened on Main Street, and soon Gerry convinced the owners to let him play there on weekends. Using the "Tralf" as a lab, he booked Julius and other bands into the club, substantially enlivening jazz life in his new town.

Julius began giving his brother piano lessons when Gerry was still in grade school.

> I grew up hearing all that piano literature all the time and I became a great "notey" person. I began playing the guitar. When I got out of the service, a professor from Ithaca College heard me playing in a club and asked if I would like to go to Ithaca College. I said, "Sure; why not?" The guy spoke to the dean and I just got in—no auditions, no nothing. After all that was done, I went up to Buffalo with Julius. Julius was blending African rhythms and twentieth-century music techniques. Sometimes

> his music sounds Caribbean to me. His early stuff has the characteristics of Caribbean steel band music. What we did in Buffalo was more of a new form of small traditional jazz ensemble; black new music that was rooted in African America.[84]

The 1972–73 Evenings for New Music season in Buffalo had a festive sheen: even the Albright-Knox's key benefactor, Seymour Knox, and director Robert Buck attended. The featured works, both written in 1972, were by two new Buffalo residents: the thirty-five-year-old David Del Tredici, a recently appointed Creative Associate, and new UB Music Department faculty member Morton Feldman. The program opened with Del Tredici's *Vintage Alice*, the first of a long series of compositions by the composer based on Lewis Carroll's *Alice in Wonderland*. After intermission, the audience was guided to the Gallery Sculpture Court, where five majestic Steinway B pianos, lids fully open, awaited. The American premiere of Morton Feldman's new forty-three-minute work, *Pianos and Voices* (later retitled *Five Pianos*) was performed by an impressive group of composer-pianists: Feldman himself, his student William Appleby, David Del Tredici, Julius Eastman, and Lukas Foss. As Thomas Putnam described it in the *Buffalo Courier Express*, "The music is floating clouds, spaced out voices [the softly humming pianists] which are intended not to cohere, but drift in separate slow times. The music is triadic, with a minor tonality implied. . . . The voices seemed to be all around, as if members of the audience had caught on to Feldman's idea of filling out his harmonic piano tapestry with human sounds."[85] It was a magical evening.

A few months later, Eastman sang the countertenor part in David Del Tredici's *Night Conjure-Verse* (1965) on Evenings for New Music concerts in Buffalo and in Carnegie Recital Hall that December. According to a colleague, Del Tredici was not happy with Eastman's performance, and felt that he had not prepared his part sufficiently.

The pace accelerates. In addition to his teaching duties, Eastman performed in another Feldman work, *Voices and Instruments II*, on the February Evenings for New Music in Buffalo and in Carnegie Recital Hall. The following night, Eastman, Petr Kotik, Stuart Dempster, and John R. Adams performed works of Cage, Eastman, Donald Erb, and Kotik at a concert at the WBAI Free Music Store. Later that spring, Eastman performed as actor and pianist in Jani Christou's *Anaparastasis III* (1969), and as speaker in Gardner Read's *Haiku Seasons* (1970).[86]

During this period Eastman composed *Wood in Time* for Karl Singletary to use on a program featuring the Buffalo Inner City Ballet Company.[87] In a performance later that summer, music critic Herman Trotter described *Wood in Time* as "a counterpoint of amplified, cross-timed metronomes interpreted by mechanical body movement with graceful edges, gradually becoming more abandoned and freely expressive."[88]

From time to time some of the Center fellows would agree to visit the public schools in town to talk about new music and what it means to be a musician. Alyssa Rabach, a student intern with the Center in the early 1970s, accompanied Julius Eastman and Benjamin Hudson on one of those dates. She remembers:

> The kids were totally intrigued. Julius started just banging on the floor and the kids banged on the floor, tapping their pencils, tapping on their arms; they were yelling. I suggested they pass out the music so the kids could see the graphic nature of the scores. A lot of these children were taking instrument lessons at school and were used to the standard stuff. Ben and Julius brought the students to the stage so they could see the unorthodox notation and choose which page would come next in the performance, showing them that the music was not necessarily in a fixed order. That way those kids became collaborators.[89]

Eastman's involvement with Buffalo's varied musical community, both inside and outside the university during this period, provided a rich and demanding artistic life. Henry James has written that "every man works better when he has companions working in the same line, and yielding to the stimulus of suggestion, comparison, emulation."[90] Eastman was surrounded with superb colleagues who encompassed a multiplicity of musical styles and approaches. Although Eastman and Morton Feldman may have regarded one another as being from different planets musically, Eastman and Petr Kotik became friends (musically and personally) instantly. Eastman absorbed it all. Figures in the Buffalo universe, such as Foss, Frederic Rzewski, Terry Riley, and Charles Gayle, were to have significant influence on his work (see chapter 10).

Eastman's astonishing productivity during this stimulating but demanding period continues. With the Buffalo/Ithaca connection still strong, in July 1973, he presented a new work for fourteen voices and tape, *Colors*, in Barnes Hall at Cornell University. According to Thomas Sokol, who conducted the performance, Eastman grouped the singers into subunits by assigning them different colors (i.e., three blues, three reds, one black, one yellow, etc.). With this scoring device, each color represented an instrumental line to which Eastman assigned various specific tasks such as "mumbling," "arguing," "sustain a long note," "sing any small notes."[91]

Colors was paired with the first performance of *Prometheus* (1971–72), a dramatic cantata, written by his friend Ann Silsbee.[92] Silsbee dedicated *Promethus* to him.

Not only was Eastman teaching and performing large works such as Maxwell Davies's *Eight Songs for a Mad King*, Del Tredici's *Night-Conjure Verse*, and Feldman's *Voices and Instruments II*, but he was composing all the while. *Macle* (1972) for four voices and tape may be seen as a precursor to the larger vocal work *Colors* (1972–73), which precedes by a matter of months *Stay On It* (1973). These works were followed by *440*, a piece for voice, violin, viola, and double bass, which was performed on a CA recital in 1974 by Benjamin Hudson and colleagues.[93]

Eastman performed *Eight Songs for a Mad King* again in October 1973, this time with Foss and the Brooklyn Philharmonia. Further contributing to Eastman's escalating reputation that year was the release by Nonesuch Records of a remastered recording of the Maxwell Davies, with Eastman and the Fires of London. The recording, conducted by the composer, was nominated for a Grammy Award.

Just weeks later, in mid-November, Julius Eastman and three instrumentalists (playing flute, guitar, and percussion) performed Hans Werner Henze's ninety-minute *El Cimarrón* (1969–70) in the Sculpture Court of the Albright-Knox Art Gallery. A left-wing political piece, it is subtitled "a recital for four players," and uses a text based on the memoirs of a 104-year-old former Cuban slave, Esteban Montejo. Eastman, percussionist Dennis Kahle, and guitarist Stuart Fox had already presented the American premiere of the piece in Pittsburgh in 1971. Fellow Creative Associate, Eberhard Blum, flutist in the Buffalo performance, has written about the episode:

> Besides their musical parts, all of the musicians have to perform visual actions, especially the singer, who has to act almost all of the time. We had the very best conditions. Julius was ideal for the singer/actor part, and our group had enough time for rehearsals. . . . But during the rehearsals it became ever clearer to all of us that Julius had personal difficulties with playing the role of a runaway black slave. He was unable to identify himself with the role he had to fill as an actor. He refused to memorize certain passages of the libretto, as well as the actions he was to perform. He needed to refer to the score for his theatrical cues or simply did not perform them at all. The impact of certain statements in the piece was thus lost, and Henze's musical and political message became weak and unclear. . . . We all would have understood if he had decided not to perform such a part.[94]

Eastman's ambivalence about the work, and lack of focus, made rehearsals unpleasant and frustrating. Thomas Putnam reviewing the concert for the *Buffalo Courier Express* stated that "the didacticism of *El Cimarrón* is a deterrent to dramatic interest."[95]

The Center's tenth anniversary (1973–74) was celebrated with a five-week European tour, the program designed as a platform for American composers. Feldman wrote a piece for the occasion; Lejaren Hiller revised his work *Algorithms I* (1968–74); Foss was represented with *Paradigm* (1968).

In preparation for the tour, Eastman's *Stay On It* (1973) and Feldman's *For Frank O'Hara* (1973) were performed on the December Evenings for New Music concert at Carnegie Recital Hall and repeated in Buffalo eleven days later, giving the musicians ample opportunity to develop definitive interpretations of those works. Years later critic Kyle Gann would call *Stay On It* "one of the first minimalist-based pieces to show pop music influence, and an early use of improvisation in a notated context."[96]

Eastman's reputation as a mesmerizing musician was growing, due to the wide acclaim for his Grammy nomination, and to his continuing exposure as composer and performer in New York. In 1973 Eastman also won a $3,000 Creative Artists Public Service grant for music composition from the New York State Council on the Arts.[97] He used the prize money as the down payment for a spacious house on Bird Avenue on Buffalo's West Side.

Buffalo's West Side, in the early 1970s, was almost exclusively white. During and after World War I, African Americans migrated to Buffalo in ever increasing numbers, most settling on the East Side of Main Street, the city's major north–south artery. According to historian Mark Goldman, one of the earliest known descriptions of the emerging African-American community appeared in 1921, in a story published in a weekly called *Buffalo Saturday Night*. The story, titled "Local Color: A Visit to Buffalo's Black Belt," noted the tremendous influx of blacks at that time.[98] By 1950, the black community, which continued to grow throughout World War II, was nearly 7 percent of the city's total population, more than 36,645 people. By 1960, the number had nearly doubled, African Americans being second only to Poles as an ethnic group.[99] Slums, neighborhood blight, overcrowding, and high rents resulted, fed in no small part by discriminatory housing policies.

Bird Avenue is a pedestrian-friendly, tree-lined street. The three-story wooden houses are spaced fairly close to one another, most with commodious front porches and generous windows. When Eastman bought his house on Bird Avenue, between Richmond and Grant, in 1973, he was one of the first, if not the first, black person to purchase property on that street on that side of town. Gerry Eastman, who lived there with Julius for two years or so (1973–75), remembers that occasional incidents did occur, such as when someone hurled a beer can at them from about twenty feet away, yelling "niggers go home; go back to Africa." Saxophonist Joe Ford, who was raised in Buffalo, and lived on East Ferry Street at the time, terms Buffalo "a very racist town," and remembers feeling uncomfortable whenever he visited Eastman at his West Side Bird Avenue home. Some have speculated that Eastman bought the Bird Avenue house in the hope of reuniting with Donald Burkhardt. Upon his release from the navy, however, Burkhardt settled as a general practitioner in Arcade, New York, a rural town forty-six miles outside of Buffalo.

On his occasional visits to Arcade, Eastman persisted in irritating his friend. Burkhardt recalled a time when he took Eastman to visit a neighbor who had children. They stayed for dinner. "The problem came afterwards," Burkhardt notes, "when Eastman began using his large vocabulary of foul language, including the F-word, in their living room in front of Steve, his wife, and their several young children. Julius was playing chess, a game he loved, with one of the kids [who was] probably ten or eleven years old, using those words whenever a move was made that surprised him." The next day, Burkhardt's neighbor asked him never to bring Eastman to his house again. Burkhardt concurred, saying "I could not have that sort of thing in my life . . . it was becoming intolerable."[100]

Perhaps this scenario provides us with a clue to Eastman's emotional state. Was his aggressive behavior calculated to embarrass Burkhardt and give vent to his anger that Burkhardt had relocated to the countryside rather than back to Buffalo with him, or was Eastman testing, "showing off," as Burkhardt suspects? Eastman's life demanded that he navigate with ease in various worlds. On the one hand, he was a highly regarded Grammy-nominated singer-actor in the United States and abroad; a faculty member at a major university; a respected composer-pianist in a prestigious musical ensemble and had, as his brother said, "grown up in a white world," with predominantly white friends; and, on the other hand, he was constantly at risk for being demeaned as a black man or (as his brother termed it—the "double whammy") as a gay black man. He is outside the fold in significant ways, while operating within traditional formulas.

We do know that in 1973, when Eastman composed *Stay On It*, he envisioned it as part of a larger work titled, "the nigger series." His colleague Dennis Kahle wrote, "[*Stay On It*] was part of a larger work, maybe a suite or some such thing, called the nigger songs or something very close to that."[101] The program note supplied by Eastman for *Stay On It*, consists of a poem (see chapter 10). There is nothing more to indicate that it was the first in a planned suite of works. Whatever the case, "the nigger series" is an inflammatory and angry expression.

January 1974 began in a frantic whirl as the Creative Associates prepared for their first European tour. The thirteen-member group planned to visit seven countries over five weeks, highlighting the music of American composers. The new Eastman and Feldman pieces were ready. Foss and Hiller dusted off recent works. Music by George Crumb, Christian Wolff, and Charles Ives would be performed from time to time, just to vary the lineup. In several countries, the state radio stations recorded the music either in concert (such as the BBC at the University of Aberdeen) or in special recording sessions. These broadcasts were a boon to little-known composers, and meant that a new work such as *Stay On It* or Feldman's *For Frank O'Hara* would be heard in multiple airings by listeners all over the United Kingdom, Germany, France, and Italy.

The concerts on tour were robustly attended. For the most part, the group felt elated to be bringing new American music to audiences throughout the continent. In Aberdeen's Mitchell Hall, the largest granite building in the world, there was hearty pounding on the floor by the audience afterward; the concert in Barcelona was sold out; in the taping for the South German Radio in Karlsruhe, Eastman included a Supremes song in the improvisatory section of his piece. Another "Julius moment" took place in Lisbon, at one of two Evenings for New Music concerts for the Gulbenkian Foundation. The musicians were performing Christian Wolff's *Burdocks* (1970–71). The score states that the musicians may use any instrument or sound source. Eastman, who had been playing inside an amplified piano, slid down, snakelike, toward the base of the piano to do something with the pedals. All of a sudden, he released a cascade of beads onto the wooden floor, producing a delicate waterfall of sound, as the beads fell, skittered, and rolled. When I complimented him on his imaginative realization of the score, he answered that it had been a total accident. His necklace of love beads had broken. According to the Center archives, the Creative Associates performed *Stay On It* eighteen times, counting the pretour, tour, and posttour events.[102]

On a late March evening, a few weeks after the Creative Associates' return from Europe, Julius Eastman delivered a riveting performance once again. The piece was Frederic Rzewski's *Coming Together* (1972), a work for reciter and eight players. Saxophone player Jon Gibson and trombonist Garrett List came up from New York City to join Rzewski and the ensemble for the concert; Julius Eastman was the reciter.

The text of *Coming Together* is a letter written by Sam Melville, an inmate of Attica prison, who died during the 1971 uprising there. As mentioned earlier, on the morning of September 9, 1971, more than twelve hundred black and Hispanic inmates took control of all five cell blocks at the maximum-security state prison and seized forty-three white guards as hostages. The uprising ended with the deaths of thirty-nine men, both prisoners and hostages, when, four days later, Governor Nelson Rockefeller ordered the State Police to retake the prison by force. An official report issued a year later by the New York State Special Commission on Attica concluded, "With the exception of the Indian massacres in the late 19th century, the State Police assault which ended the four-day prison uprising was the bloodiest one-day encounter between Americans since the Civil War."

"I think," Sam Melville's letter begins, "the combination of age and a greater coming together is responsible for the speed of the passing time." As John Dwyer recounts in his review for the *Buffalo Evening News*, "Melville speaks of the curious nature of time, his new-found grasp of mental equilibrium and physical wellbeing, and the nourishment he has found in books and meditation." Adding to the drama is the fact that Melville wrote the letter during spring, and the audience knows from the program note that he will die a few months later. Eastman's dignified, restrained reading of the spoken phrases, repeated cumulatively over and over, juxtaposed with "a hammering momentum" of the recurring musical phrases, produced an emotional political statement of great impact. The piece was repeated days later in Carnegie Recital Hall.[103] Back in Buffalo a month later, Eastman performed his own eighteen-minute work *440* (1973) on colleague Benjamin Hudson's CA recital.

The Center commissioned a new work by Pauline Oliveros for the opening of the 1974–75 Evenings for New Music concert season. Her piece, *Crow*, part of a series of "sonic meditations," is a slow-motion ceremonial dance by two combatants who approach each other from opposite directions, each seeming to mirror the other's movements. The slow, dreamy movement is accompanied by drone-type music. According to Oliveros, the meditative content of *Crow* is meant to be a dwelling with, or upon, certain prescribed conditions (a perfectly black spot, for example). Each performer is intended to maintain and connect through these conditions. Ideally, the accompanying musicians surround the audience, the dancers traveling through the space, and the audience—should they choose to participate in the meditation—merge and create community.

The intensity of Oliveros's and Eastman's mime-like duet created powerful theater. Oliveros writes appreciatively about the experience:

"Julius—so naturally charismatic—took on the role I designed for him and seemed to have an in-depth understanding of how the piece was to go from the first moment of working together. He was fearless and beautifully coordinated physically and vocally."[104]

Crow was produced a second time, when the Creative Associates were in residence at Artpark, near Niagara Falls, during the summer of 1975. The composer describes this version in which Eastman was indeed the trickster, a sacred clown, charged with fracturing the communal energy.

> I sat in deep meditation in the blazing sun. I knew that a master artist of unusual powers was stalking me and if I opened my eyes I would be doomed—to uncontrollable laughter. Eastman's role during this performance was to distract me from my meditation in any way possible as long as he did not touch me physically. At that particular moment a body flew over me with a ghastly shriek. I was not fazed or startled out of my meditation. I maintained yet knew that more was to come unpredictably. Some moments later my eyes opened involuntarily and I was very nearly undone as Julius knowingly bent over and peeped into my peripheral vision on the right. I quickly closed my eyes, took a deep breath and managed somehow not to explode in uncontrollable hilarity.[105]

Based on these experiences, Oliveros invited Eastman to participate in a later version of the piece *Crow Two: A Ceremonial Opera*, which she prepared for the inauguration of the Mandeville Art Center at the University of California at San Diego. "Julius," Oliveros wrote, "had a large impact on the development of *Crow Two*. His depth of character and energy had the effect of strengthening all of the other performers. . . . This is because Julius reached beyond any artificiality to authenticity and integrity so that performance was the only reality for the other players and the audience."[106]

Concurrent with his university teaching duties, performances with the Creative Associates, and composing, Eastman was also a member of Petr Kotik's S.E.M. Ensemble. According to Kotik, they had similar ideas about music that veered away from the post-Webern style of avant-garde music-making that was prevalent at the time. Kotik recalls, "We shared ideas and we respected our differences."

Sometime in early December 1974, the group was rehearsing for a European tour that included the premiere of *Instruments*, written for S.E.M. by Morton Feldman, and *John Mary*, a new work that Kotik had written for instruments and voices, with Eastman in mind. "Julius was never disciplined," Kotik recalls, but adds that he was reliable in terms of showing up for rehearsals. In this case, "Julius was somehow unable to learn the piece and he was making mistakes and mistakes and mistakes. His house was very close to mine so I would go over there and we would rehearse together." Nonetheless, at one point in the middle of a group rehearsal in the home of a patron, Julius jumped up announcing, "I can't stand this music anymore," and walked out, leaving his colleagues dumbfounded.[107]

Eastman's abrupt departure from S.E.M., while not a final break, would be the first of several ruptures during this period, signaling a growing discomfort with his professional life. Clearly, he was not fully satisfied with his work in S.E.M. and, as he expressed to Renate Strauss in an interview with the *Buffalo Evening News*, he felt a growing disenchantment with the Creative Associates, who he suspected were losing their spark.[108] As Kotik remembers, he was neither stimulated nor happy with his UB students; and, most probably, he was conflicted between his allegiance to, and identity with, the worlds of classical music and jazz.

A brief recounting of Eastman's career in the Music Department of the University at Buffalo, must begin with his appointment by Lukas Foss as a member of the Center of the Creative and Performing Arts for the academic year 1969–70. At the conclusion of his first year, he was invited to join the official Music Department faculty as an instructor and given a lighter teaching load to reflect his performance duties with the new music group.[109] After two years as an instructor teaching music theory for non-majors and private independent study pupils, Eastman was promoted to assistant professor and given a three-year contract.[110]

In mid-February of the 1974–75 academic year, Eastman received a letter from the Office of the Provost, informing him that he was not being recommended for a renewal of his appointment. "I am obliged to inform you officially that the [following] 1975–76 academic year will be your terminal year."[111] Several factors are mentioned in his file, among them a 1974 memo from the acting chairman of the Music Department regarding unannounced absences from classes, lack of notification from him stating that he would be on tour, or what arrangements he had made to cover his classes while he was away. There were comments from student evaluations noting that he was disorganized and had trouble staying on subject. In one letter, a student expressed displeasure with Eastman's unconventional teaching methods, which, he said, consisted predominantly of sight singing; noting, further, that he had been absent at least six or seven times; and reporting that his apparent lack of enthusiasm was the source of many complaints. Still, in a summary of students' opinions, others considered him "a fine musician who should be doing something besides teaching theory."[112] According to his friend and lawyer Frederick Cohen, Eastman was surprised and upset to learn that his contract would not be renewed. Nonrenewal precluded his ever being eligible for tenure at UB. Eastman told Cohen that the faculty commented that since much of his music was not written out, they were unable to truly evaluate it. This lukewarm view of his work, in addition to his irregular attendance record, was enough to tip the scale. Apparently, he was unable to imagine that his creative gifts would not outweigh institutional strictures and regulations. Eastman was offended and angry, hinting to Cohen that he thought there might have been ulterior motives.[113]

Although he had the option of remaining at the university for one additional year, Eastman wrote to James Blackhurst, the acting Music Department chairman, on April 7: "Dear Mr. Blackhurst: In order to further my professional career, I will resign from SUNY as of September 1, 1975."[114] On April 14, Blackhurst replied: "I have received your resignation letter. . . . There are many here who will miss you."[115]

Files on the music faculty committee meetings, if they still exist, are not available, hence it is impossible to know any details of the discussion or the vote count. We do know that Eastman was less than meticulous about his class attendance, and that he sometimes left on concert tours without addressing the customary notification procedures. Presumably, he was confident that his teaching assistant was capable of taking charge. One wonders, however, if he was aware of the long-term consequences of such breaches of departmental etiquette. Quite possibly his behavior was perceived as arrogant by those faculty members who adhered closely to such protocols. On the other hand, any serious perusal of Eastman's professional productivity during the period 1969–74, would have to impress even diehard skeptics. His suspicion of "ulterior motives" is reminiscent of the uneasiness he experienced after the 1959 Juilliard audition when he and his cousin speculated about racism as a factor in his rejection.[116] Nevertheless, by the mid-seventies, most public universities were intent on improving racial diversity and, although bias may have existed regarding issues of sexual orientation in some quarters, the UB Music Department environment was distinctly tolerant in this regard. Still, from his brother Gerry's perspective, "this is just one more example of Julius's lifelong battle with white people in power."[117]

After deserting S.E.M. just before the European tour, Eastman rejoined the group for a series of previously scheduled concerts that included a performance of Cage's *Song Books* at the Albright-Knox Art Gallery on March 1, 1975, and again in mid-March for a series of concerts at The Kitchen, an alternative artists' space in New York City. The opening concert of

The Kitchen series on Thursday, March 13, was an all-Eastman program that included three works written for the group—*That Boy* (1973), *Joy Boy* (1974), and *Femenine* (1974). *Joy Boy* was commissioned by the Composers Forum in Albany, New York, and premiered there by S.E.M. on November 6, 1974. The score, written for four soprano voices, may either be sung or performed on instruments. John Rockwell, who reviewed the concert for the *New York Times*, was taken with the hour-long performance of *Femenine*, which he described as a predominantly instrumental work (four winds, marimba, piano, electric bass, and mechanically shaken sleigh bells). "The structure," as he described it, "was built around a steadily reiterated marimba-phone [*sic*] figure: three long E flats followed by four short, alternating E flats and F's. This central figure served both as a rhythmic point of reference . . . and as a melodic germ out of which the remaining instruments evolved other notes and motifs."[118]

Eastman's UB class attendance was sketchy following the Music Department's notice of nonrenewal, but he continued performing with the Creative Associates through the end of the season. In all probability, he was already contemplating a more permanent move at this time.

The *Song Books* Incident

Sometime during the winter of 1974–75, Morton Feldman decided to create a new music festival that would be structured as a summer composition seminar for music students from everywhere, similar to the famous Darmstadt Festival in Germany. Concerts would be mainly one-man shows, complemented by the composers' lectures on their work. He called his summer festival "June in Buffalo."[119]

The first three-week June in Buffalo festival in 1975 focused on Feldman's colleagues: John Cage, Earle Brown, and Christian Wolff. The opening week was devoted to the music of Cage. As part of the lineup, Feldman asked Petr Kotik and his group, S.E.M., to prepare a performance of Cage's *Song Books* (1970). S.E.M. had presented several full-evening performances of *Song Books* the year before, notably one attended by Cage and David Tudor at SUNY/Albany. According to Kotik, Cage and Tudor were highly favorable in their comments about the Albany performance, remarking specifically on how much they enjoyed Julius Eastman's contribution to the piece. When Feldman asked Kotik to do *Song Books* at June in Buffalo, Eastman had already left S.E.M., but remembering Cage and Tudor's favorable comments, Kotik invited him to perform it once again. Eastman agreed immediately.[120]

The score for *Song Books* is a sizable tome, consisting of "Instructions," "Solos for Voice 3–58," and "Solos for Voice 59–92." The "Instructions" permit four categories for performance: "1) song; 2) song using electronics; 3) theatre; and 4) theatre using electronics." The singers' parts may be combined, each singer may make a program that will fill an agreed-on program length, and the entire score need not be performed. Some of the songs Cage composed use fairly conventional notation, some use graphic gestures. Texts were drawn from Henry David Thoreau's *Journal* and other thinkers whom Cage admired, such as Buckminster Fuller and Marshall McLuhan. "To prepare for a performance," Cage instructs, "the actor will make a numbered list of verbs (actions) and/or nouns (things) not to exceed sixty-four with which he or she is willing to be involved and which are theatrically feasible (those may include stage properties, clothes, etc.; actions may be 'real' or mimed, etc.)." In addition, Cage explained to Kotik, all parts must be prepared individually without reference to what the other performers might be preparing. In this way, the independently prepared "solos" come together for the first time in the performance.

The performers in the Baird Hall performance were: Petr Kotik, flutist/director; Julius Eastman, voice; Judith Martin, synthesizer; and Jan Williams, percussion. As Thomas Putnam reported in the *Buffalo Courier Express*, "Judith Martin vocalized with the aid of distorted amplification, Jan Williams played an amplified typewriter, and Petr Kotik did a sleepwalking dance with his coat pulled over his head."[121] Putnam does not mention Eastman, but news reviewer Jeff Simon of the *Buffalo Evening News* supplied a brief summary of the incident some weeks later in a longer article about Cage's residency,

> A New System of Love
>
> Wednesday evening, at a public concert, the S.E.M. Ensemble performed [Cage's] 1970–72 *Song Books* in which each performer is supposed to devise his own program of activity independently of the others. One male performer brought out a young, blond man and a young black woman and proceeded to spiel out a broadly funny lecture on "a new system of love" with virulent homosexual overtones. At the end of it, the young man was undressed and the subject of the performer's mocking advances.[122]

Cage was furious. In his seminar the next morning, he was visibly agitated, stamping around the room, breathlessly raising his voice in an uncharacteristic way, even pounding the piano with his fist. He expressed disappointment and immense frustration that his work could have been so misunderstood, especially by such experienced performers, and in a place where he thought surely he could rely on a knowledgeable and sensitive reading.[123]

The incident raises several issues. First, there is the question of the composer's explicit directions that no one is to assume responsibility for shaping the performance. According to Kotik, this is a fatal mistake. Cage approached Kotik after the *Song Books* performance saying, "What was the meaning of this?" Kotik responded "I had no idea what was going to happen." Cage replied, "But you are the director." For Kotik, the event shaped his understanding and attitude toward performance for the rest of his life—namely,

> when one goes onstage to perform, especially in a responsible function as director or conductor, one cannot make excuses based on a composer's misguided performance suggestions. A composer creates the composition, that's one thing. But once the work leaves the composer's desk and is given to the performer, it is the musician who has to decide how to go about preparing the best performance. No excuses. At that point, the issue becomes the composition, not the composer.[124]

A second point relating to the *Song Books* incident, is the question of what prompted Eastman to radically alter his approach to a piece that he had performed several times before, and that had been so positively received by Cage? Kotik reports that Eastman did not repeat himself in the various *Song Books* performances, adding that, as the singer in the group, Eastman was always the star performer. Kotik does not believe that Eastman set out to offend Cage, and characterizes his performance as a misunderstanding. As he sees it, Eastman was enacting a suggested instruction, "Do a disciplined act" by creating a funny, racy divertissement.[125] One may remember that Eastman's friend Donald Burkhardt referred to Eastman's lack of sensitivity in his use of inappropriate language or questionable behavior on various occasions in the presence of Burkhardt's family, and while playing chess with the young son of one of Burkhardt's neighbors. Kotik sees the *Song Books* breach as a similar circumstance, confirming the fact that Eastman never paid much attention to such matters.

Eastman's friend, music historian Ned Sublette, has a theory that Eastman was pointing out the conspicuous absence of sexuality in Cage's work, and unwittingly challenged the whole paradigm of "that little ivory tower white scene." Speaking about the incident a year or so later, Eastman said to Sublette, "Well, it says 'perform a disciplined act,' so I gave this lecture on how to make love. What could be more disciplined? And with a pointer, I noted the various parts involved."[126] What is incontrovertible, however, is that Cage, along with many others, read Eastman's homoerotic performance as a personal provocation and was offended.

Another theory suggests that Eastman wanted to "out" Cage. As musicologist Ryan Dohoney has noted, "Eastman's gay aesthetic, once inserted within *Song Books'* multiplicity, revealed the limits of Cagean acceptance and the degree to which Cagean freedom was contingent on performers having internalized Cage's own tastes and preferences."[127] Here, one may conclude, is a trickster at work.

Three weeks later, Eastman was in New York performing *Eight Songs for a Mad King* with Pierre Boulez and the New York Philharmonic. He returned to Buffalo the next day to appear with the Creative Associates in their residency at Artpark, performing the Maxwell Davies once again and Pauline Oliveros's *Crow*.

Most likely, Eastman spent time in Ithaca that summer, as he generally did, returning to his Buffalo house in the fall, where his principal focus was playing with his brother in a jazz trio at the Tralfamadore Café on Main Street. According to Gerry Eastman, who arranged the bookings for the Café, he would suggest "doing a trio," and Julius would oblige. "His music was close enough to jazz for them."[128]

Ten months later, Julius depicted his postuniversity working life to Renate Strauss at the *Buffalo Evening News*: "I really enjoy playing with my group. What happens now, instead of getting up every morning composing, I get up and practice the piano, improvise—it's jazz, that's the difference." In the interview Eastman explains that he was unwilling to stay at the University, because it was no longer stimulating; he felt his time was up. "If you go on just for the money . . . you know that can't work."

In some sense, Eastman realized that his life with the Creative Associates in the university was a bubble, an unsatisfying artificial world and, as Strauss reports, he was obviously going through a drastic revision of his inner life. "What I am trying to achieve," he declares in the interview, "is to be what I am to the fullest—Black to the fullest, a musician to the fullest, a homosexual to the fullest. . . . It is through art that I can search for the self and keep in touch with my resource and the real me."[129]

Not long after this July 1976 interview, Eastman announced to his brother that he was moving to New York. Gerry Eastman recalls, "He just left. He didn't take anything with him. So, about a year and a half later [winter 1978] when I decided to leave Buffalo too, I packed everything up, repaired the house, painted it, sanded the floors, and sold it."[130]

Downtown

He desired to see the Truth, the time of essential desire
And satisfaction.
Whether this would be an aberration of piety or no,
He desired it. And he possessed extensive human power.

—"Tale," Arthur Rimbaud, from *Arthur Rimbaud, Complete Works*, 157; Translated by Paul Schmidt.

The New York years (1976–90) were the ultimate challenge for Eastman, his stab at "making it big." He was thirty-six years old, not unknown in New York music circles, and had a solid list of accomplishments. During his nearly eight years in Buffalo (1968–76), he composed at least fifteen pieces, in addition to his numerous improvisations with S.E.M., his work with his various jazz groups (Space Connection and Birthright), and his dance/theater collaborations. He had won a Creative Artists Public Service Program award for his musical composition; he had performed the music of nearly one hundred composers of all stripes, as pianist, singer, or conductor; achieved a measure of fame for his recording of Maxwell Davies's *Eight Songs for a Mad King*; he had traveled the world, working under the baton of luminaries such as Zubin Mehta, Pierre Boulez, and Lukas Foss. His lack of success in an academic post would hardly be considered a major gaffe in the professional musical world. In fact, to many, an academic career might have been seen as a retreat from the front lines. Certainly he would not be the only composer denied tenure in a university.

For the initial year or so, Eastman stayed with his grandmother, who owned a small building with six apartments in the South Bronx. Julius and his grandmother were close, and she looked after him. We may assume that one of his first tasks was to alert people that he was in town and ready to work.

Lukas Foss, by this time music director of the Brooklyn Philharmonia, arranged a part-time job for Eastman as cocurator/conductor, along with Tania León and Talib Hakim, of the Brooklyn Philharmonia's community outreach series, a handy base from which he could program and conduct other composers' work in metropolitan area concerts. León remembers that the three composers took a "think-tank" approach to gathering material for the project. Beginning with a roster of black composers exclusively, the program expanded to include women composers and, finally, all composers.[131] Foss also provided Eastman with an occasional platform, as soloist and composer, on the orchestra's "Meet the Moderns" programs. He was already known to the music staff at The Kitchen and other alternative artists' venues around the city.

His friend Ned Sublette had also arrived in New York from Buffalo that summer, after a disastrous semester spent studying composition with Morton Feldman. Eastman would visit Sublette's Upper West Side apartment regularly, and they spent a lot of time hanging out together. Sublette attended Eastman's first concert as a new resident of the city, an improvisation he titled, *Praise God from Whom All Devils Grow*, at the SoHo loft Environ. On Saturday, October 12, 1976, the *New York Times* published a review of the Environ concert, in which critic Joseph Horowitz notes that Eastman characterized his music in terms of "black forces" and describes Eastman's keyboard improvisations as "intense, astringent, often demonic." He paints one section as "an extended crescendo fortified by long trills in both hands. . . . There were also elements of progressive jazz, and a blues color here and there, but overall the idiom seemed genuinely personal." Horowitz's review concludes by saying that "Mr. Eastman's approach was fervent, and the result was surprisingly riveting."[132]

In 1977 S.E.M. performed works by composer Jon Gibson at the Albright-Knox Art Gallery in Buffalo, with Petr Kotik conducting. Julius Eastman heard a recording of that concert, and was particularly taken with two pieces, part 1 of *Melody IV* (1975) and *Song II* (1974). He contacted Gibson soon thereafter, explaining that he wanted to conduct the two pieces together in a continuous fifteen-minute work on the Brooklyn Philharmonia's outreach series. One concert would be in Bushwick, Brooklyn; the other would take place in Harlem. Gibson remembers:

> Julius conducted very well and it sounded great. I was very happy. Years later someone told me that these concerts were supposed to feature black composers and performers exclusively which they did, I think, except for me. I was taken aback when I learned that Julius had to fight long and hard on my behalf to get my music on this program. He never mentioned any of this to me at any time.
>
> He also conducted it along with a new piece of mine, *Equal Distribution 1* (1977) at a concert at The Kitchen a month or so later. *ED1* is a highly structured piece for solo wind instrument, initially for myself to perform on flutes or saxophones. It has a 10-note melody that is permutated, sliced and diced in various overlapping systems which result in a score of stemless notes (fly specks, as it were). I decided to try *ED1* as an ensemble piece with Julius playing the piano. I'm not sure this experiment was successful. In retrospect I deeply wish that I had asked Julius to perform it solo on piano. I dream of that.

> We rehearsed for these concerts in my loft on Thompson Street and sometimes Julius would hang out after rehearsals. One time, several years later, he showed up unannounced in a very strange white costume looking quite North African. I was taking my 2-year old son Jeremy to the local playground so Julius came along. This was a conservative Italian-American neighborhood in those days. Julius ended up over by the backboards with Jeremy and was teaching him some basics of handball. I was doing something else across the way when one of the neighborhood guys came up to warn me about the weird black guy playing with my kid. I told them it was fine, he was a friend. Even so, it got quite tense and we left soon after. . . . I realized that a black person hanging out in that neighborhood had to be very careful.
>
> Julius was very, very direct. Once we were drinking together at a bar after someone's concert and he told me that I should leave my wife, rent a small room in the East Village, and just compose music. I guess it was actually a compliment but still shocking to hear something most people would not even come close to telling you to your face.[133]

Several months before the exchange with Gibson, Eastman presented an evening of vocal improvisations, along with his homemade films, at Phill Niblock's Experimental Intermedia Foundation loft. The films had a fair amount of nudity in them and included shots of dog feces on the street, bringing to mind Rimbaud's rebellious courting of degradation—finding beauty in dross.[134] Another reading of the work may be as a manifestation of racial anger—Eastman's comment on the status of blacks or gays in society. Similarly, seizure of the words "nigger" and "faggot" in the titles for his compositions, is an extension of this device—detoxification through insistent confrontation. The late comedian-writer-actor Richard Pryor (almost exactly the same age as Eastman) tackled similar territory in his sketches and stand-up comedy routines.[135] Ned Sublette remembered that he and Eastman heard a record of Patti Smith singing a song at a Village club in which she repeats the word "nigger" almost all the way through, and that Eastman was much taken with it. (This probably was "Rock N Roll Nigger," which was recorded on her 1978 album *Easter*.) Sublette's perspective on this post-Buffalo period is insightful: "Julius was only on loan to the white music world. Going to New York freed Julius to be who he was. That's what he was trying to define through his music. He told me once that he hated Louis Armstrong but that he loved Coltrane. Coltrane, he felt, was the one who stopped saying 'I'm here to entertain you. I'm playing this for myself.'"[136]

Downtown New York in the late seventies—dilapidated, graffiti-strewn, and still low-rent—was a gay party, and Eastman seemed, more than ever, to be celebrating his membership in the club. Eastman loved to dance and reveled in that disco moment. When Ned Sublette introduced Eastman to Arthur Russell, a fellow musical boundary-crosser, whose work has been termed "structured improvisation," there was immediate rapport. Both men were classically trained—Russell on the cello—and both embraced popular idioms in their music. Over the next few years, Eastman conducted *Instrumentals*, an orchestral work of Russell's, and sang on several of Russell's recordings.[137] During the late seventies/early eighties, he also collaborated with Meredith Monk, a composer, singer, choreographer and dancer, who was working on a new piece for voices. She had been steered to Eastman through the new-music grapevine. As with Russell, there was mutual attraction. They worked together on Monk's 1979 *Dolmen Music* for six voices, cello, and percussion. Eastman is listed as "percussion, voice" on the 1980 recording see (chapter 7).

On a sunny Buffalo weekend morning in the fall of 1977, a few months before I moved to California, my doorbell rang. Julius was at the door. "Hi-i-i-I," he said. "I'm in town so I thought I'd see how you're doing." I was delighted with my surprise visitor and invited him in. In those days, I lived on the second and third floors of an old Buffalo mansion. Three floor-to-ceiling banks of Tiffany-style colored windows lined the staircase, giving the house a beautiful airy glow. Julius was in jeans, with his black engineer boots, and a long metal chain with keys hanging from his pocket. We climbed the stairs and hugged. He didn't want any coffee. His jeans, I saw, were so dirty that they had a caked, stiff quality. "Julius," I said, "please take off those jeans right now so I can put them in the washing machine." I gave him an old kimono to put on and he laughingly complied.

So there we were, sitting around and catching up with all our news about the Creative Associates, about life in New York, when the doorbell rang again. This time it was a gentleman caller—an aging Buffalo socialite, a friend who also "happened to be in the neighborhood." Now we had operetta! I invited Mr. D. in. There, at the top of the stairs, to my visitor's well-concealed surprise, stood the kimono-clad Julius, all smiles and welcoming. Introductions were made, no explanations were given and, with the washing machine gently humming in the background, Julius and I played host and hostess to our guest, showing him around the house and offering him refreshment. Julius seemed to enjoy the swirly effects of the kimono, and we all fell into our roles, as though this was just another everyday occurrence. Eventually, the bewildered Mr. D. departed and Julius's jeans dried. We had relished our little charade and, a short time later, with affection and good cheer, said our goodbyes. Our visits would be few and far between after that.

Gerry Eastman sold his brother's Buffalo house and moved to New York in the spring of 1978. Julius was no longer living with his grandmother, who was by now close to ninety years old, and growing frail. The building she owned was crumbling. Gerry Eastman had already rented an inexpensive loft in Brooklyn, when an acquaintance offered him a first floor rent-controlled apartment on East Sixth Street. Figuring he would use it when he was working late in the city, he took the apartment. The rent was $250 per month. Over the next two years, between gigs, he rehabilitated his grandmother's property, painting and putting in new windows, new stoves, and new refrigerators. Gerry Eastman recalled, "We're talking about the South Bronx where you don't usually have a landlord who aesthetically fixes up the building. Well, I did it for her, so later [when she died] she left me everything. She told me to give Julius money every month because she felt he would just do stupid stuff with it anyway."[138]

In December 1978, Julius produced a concert at the Third Street Music School Settlement in New York, using the money from the sale of his Buffalo house. On the program were *Dirty Nigger*, for two flutes, bassoon, two saxophones, three violins, and two double basses; and *Nigger Faggot* for strings, percussion, and bell. He also programmed a work by his friend Rocco Di Pietro, *Donizetti in Buffalo*, for voice and chamber orchestra.

During this same period the award-winning music critic, now professor of music and journalism at the University of Southern California, Tim Page, was hosting a contemporary music program on the Columbia University radio station WKCR. He knew the Maxwell Davies recording, and had met Eastman at Tanglewood and at parties in the Village. Page was intrigued. His radio program aired from 9:00 P.M. until 2:00 A.M., giving him ample opportunity to explore a composer's music through recordings and discussion. He invited Eastman to be a featured guest, Eastman accepted, and they decided on a date. The event was heavily promoted, but Eastman never showed up. Sometime after midnight, many months later, Eastman appeared at WKCR's Ferris Booth Hall studio. Page thought it looked like something was wrong but he was in the middle of a broadcast and was unable to have more than a brief conversation with him.[139]

Reconstructing Julius's living arrangements, indeed, any sequential accounting of daily life, once he left his grandmother's house, is an iffy proposition. Accounts vary, and timelines do not mesh. Clearly, Mrs. Famous was less than convinced about the merits of her grandson Julius's lifestyle. Eastman lived with a variety of lovers, mostly in lower Manhattan, although he had a continuing relationship for a period with a psychiatrist on the Upper East Side as well. In late 1977, he composed *If You're So Smart,*

Why Aren't You Rich? for Lukas Foss and the Brooklyn Philharmonia. (The title, Eastman remarked, was what his mother always asked him.) In a newspaper interview with Thomas Putnam of the *Buffalo Courier Express*, preceding a performance of the piece on an Evenings for New Music concert in Buffalo in February 1979, Eastman mentions that he wrote the piece "last year" at the kitchen table in his grandmother's house.[140] "It's really a brass piece, with violin and chimes," he explained. "There's no experimentation in it. It doesn't strive to be modern in any way. . . . I would like to know if it has an American flavor."

Foss called the piece "merciless" in his remarks preceding the Brooklyn performance. Critic Putnam describes the piece, which was performed in Buffalo along with works by Schoenberg and Boulez, as follows, "[It] began with a rising chromatic scale and it used this thematic material later in unison scoring for an ensemble of brass instruments and amplified double basses (whose groaning were [*sic*] those of heavy animals). . . . But toughness prevails, a kind of thug simplicity that tells the mind to take a walk."[141] *Buffalo Evening News* music critic John Dwyer, who also reviewed the concert, characterized the piece as "a brass-knuckled chromatic assault on an indifferent or contemptuous society." He closed his review saying that for him the piece "had the feeling of deadly reprisal by a composer who had suffered a deep, deep wound."[142] Eastman supplied a program note for the Buffalo performance. Its bleak Melvillean rant of "sailing with sealed orders" bespeaks not only wound, but depression.

> I feel that we the people, have been given little or no basic information concerning the purpose and direction of this present existence. We do not know what we were before we took on a physical being or if in fact we were. And we have no choice whether to end or not to end our physical being (except in the case of suicide), nor do we know the state of our existence after the demise of our physical body. What we do know is that cold and hunger cause pain. Having been brought into existence on a planet where humans hardly communicate with one another and where there is such a gross lack of meaningful information, I feel that I need not in any way imitate human or universal models in my music. The one thing that I feel that I must do is to respect those with whom I am dealing, and that is all."[143]

At some point during 1979–80, Julius told his brother that he needed a place to stay. Gerry Eastman gave him the keys to the Sixth Street apartment, along with some of the art and furniture he had brought down from the Buffalo house, telling Julius that all he had to do was pay the rent.

Interventions and "an inconsistent period"

Peter Gena, Eastman's friend and colleague from Buffalo, was an assistant professor in the Music Department of Northwestern University when he invited Eastman to present a concert of his music there in mid-January 1980. Eastman decided to program several works for multiple pianos, the titles of which were *Crazy Nigger*, *Gay Guerrilla*, and *Evil Nigger*. Gena recalled the notoriety of the event, which solidified Eastman's reputation as provocateur:

> We did his Nigger series and a couple of the black faculty and the black fraternity thought it was racist. . . . Julius went and spoke to them. But when these neat Ivy League types saw Julius with his engineer boots and leather jacket and Rastafarian hair, there was no way they were going to have common ground. He spoke so eloquently, but they just didn't get it. . . . "You know," he said, "when I was your age, I was either a nigger or a Negro. There was none of this black or African-American stuff." He told them what a badge of honor it was, but they did not get it so we didn't print the titles, which caused a bigger ruckus because then it hit the school newspapers.[144]

That same year, 1980, Eastman went on tour to Europe with a group of artists from The Kitchen. Trombonist, composer, and scholar George Lewis was the music director, and remembers the trip, which included dancers Molissa Fenley, Bill T. Jones, and Arnie Zane, composer Rhys Chatham, visual artist Robert Longo, actor Eric Bogosian, and others. "Julius was doing these improvisations with voice and piano. They weren't about race to the extent that Julius was placing himself out there as a persona. They were more about gay desire, which was very cool, I thought. They were improvised love songs as far as I could tell. If there was a score, I never saw one."[145] For Lewis, who was twelve years younger, Eastman was always the only black guy in the downtown new-music circles at that time—a singular figure, and as a gay, African-American composer, more isolated still. "Here was a guy who was turning race into a situation where it was routinely denied or thought of as being uninteresting but doing it in a very provocative way that was designed to make people a little uncomfortable—kind of an intervention to shake people up."[146]

R. Nemo Hill, a self-described "little white kid from the suburbs," was in his twenties in 1980, when he met the nearly forty-year-old Julius Eastman in The Bar, a thriving neighborhood gay bar on the corner of East Fourth Street and Second Avenue. An aspiring poet, Hill was staying with an old friend on First Avenue, while looking for a place to live. He found Eastman fascinating. The chemistry was immediate and, not long after their meeting, Hill moved in to Eastman's Sixth Street apartment. Eastman claimed that he was going to 'toughen Hill up" so he would know the score. He announced that he was through with sex and that Hill would be the last one. According to Hill, the sexual relationship was extremely satisfying. Eastman, Hill claims, was "into S and M and taught me a lot about the darker side of sexuality."[147]

Hill recalls that, although everybody liked Julius Eastman, trying to get along with him day after day was hard. Eastman had voluntarily left his job with the Brooklyn Philharmonia's community concert series and, although seemingly in good shape, was having trouble getting work.[148] "He wasn't getting work because he was a son of a bitch," says Hill. "He would lay down obstacles, make things difficult for people. Somehow, he felt that it was his mission. You could say that he martyred himself. It didn't seem like a racial issue, since he did it so deliberately. To this day, I have never met anyone who was more an architect of his own fate."

According to Hill, Eastman was not much of a scholar, not a systematic thinker but, as has been mentioned by others who knew him as far back as his student days at Curtis, he was a spiritual man and, referencing Eastman's 1981 composition for ten cellos, *The Holy Presence of Joan d'Arc*, seemed to be on a religious quest. "It wasn't about something that would make you famous or make you feel good or get you rich." Hill continues:

> For the first two months we lived together Julius insisted on calling me Ananda. He'd use tidbits from Buddhist discipline or little proverbs about Allah—and the "thank you Jesus" thing—a little too loud, like an attention-getting ploy. What he was saying was "I'm not just an artist; I'm beyond that."
>
> And he lived the titles of his music. He was the crazy nigger and the gay guerrilla. He was fearsome. He played out those roles. He was an uncompromising man. He liked the idea that he was "a nigger." He loved that because it put him in the position of transgressing some sort of bourgeois status. He liked the idea that he was gay and he pushed it to the extreme. He was filthy dirty. He was a slob. That was the role he wanted to play. He took aspects of his identity and foisted them on people in this provocative way.
>
> But he really did it. He put his money where his mouth was. He didn't care for his possessions. He would never lock the door—even after he was robbed by one of the homeless people he brought around. He used to go to the men's shelter and give pedicures to the guys there. He was so brave. He just would not compromise. He inspired me.[149]

After living with Eastman for approximately six months, Hill found his own apartment, just a few buildings west on Sixth Street. One of Eastman's stray cats followed, crossing rooftops, before appearing at his window a few days later. Not long after Hill moved into his own apartment, Eastman was evicted from Gerry's apartment for failure to pay the rent. Gerry Eastman recalls:

> So he's living in the apartment I gave him. The next thing I know is that he's gotten evicted. He's not making any money. He didn't pay his rent. They [the city marshal] took all his music, his art, and everything else out of the apartment. Julius is saying that he needs a place to stay. I say "Julius, what do you mean, you need a place to stay? Where is all your shit?" "Oh," he says, "the sheriff came and took it." "Where is it?" I say. "Oh, I don't want that shit anymore," he says. So I knew he was going crazy and that his mental state was deteriorating.[150]

Ned Sublette also recalls:

> He was letting it go. My wife felt uneasy when he came by because he was acting crazy. He lost his address book in The Toilet. He couldn't be bothered to pay his rent. He made no effort to reclaim his belongings, which I found out later had been confiscated to a warehouse in Brooklyn. "Julius," I said, "How could you let this happen?" He answered, "It was an inconsistent period."

Now it was R. Nemo Hill who was in a position to accommodate Eastman, reciprocating in a way for Eastman's earlier generosity to him. This time Eastman moved into Hill's apartment. Things between them became increasingly difficult, however. During their time together, Julius brought more stray cats into the small apartment. When one became sick, Eastman wrapped it in a cherished textile wall hanging of Hill's, so that he could carry the cat to the vet. Furious when he discovered that Eastman had used a favorite possession in that way, Eastman admonished him, "You're so attached to things; it belongs to Allah; everything belongs to Allah." That's when Hill told him to take his holy books and leave.

The pianist Joseph Kubera was a member of the new music group in Buffalo in the mid-seventies, but became closer friends with Eastman after Kubera moved to New York in 1979. In those days, he said, composers Beth Anderson, Jeffrey Lohn, and Jon Gibson were all part of the downtown scene and saw each other regularly at performances. Kubera participated in a major performance at The Kitchen in 1980 when he and Eastman performed a two-piano version of *Crazy Nigger*, with Jeffrey Lohn and a group of other musicians joining in at the closing section, adding extra voices to the massive texture. Kubera describes Eastman's multiple piano pieces as:

> built structures, at least in part, using regular blocks of time controlled by a stopwatch, with each new block adding voices to the sonority, or sometimes abruptly changing the texture entirely. Commonly, each voice consisted of repeated notes, with each new voice adding to the harmonic density. But melodic groupings also appeared, as well as specified long tones struck without coordination. Usually, a steady, driving pulse kept the momentum. . . .
>
> A great deal of the performance practice (of the multiple piano pieces) depended on having Julius present to deliver instructions in order to clarify the sometimes vague performance indications. For example, notes were written in a particular octave, but were really meant to be played in various octaves of the pianists' choice. A pianist could also play more than one line of music simultaneously within a section.[151]

Sometime in the mid-eighties, Eastman visited Kubera's Staten Island home. Once again, as was so often the case, he showed up at the door unannounced:

> He just showed up . . . at 9:00 or 10:00 A.M. with boyfriend in tow. He greeted me with his usual growl—"KUBERRAHHH!" Once inside, his first question was, "Got any scotch?" Then he sat down at the old Weber grand I used at the time, played his recent *Piano 2* (1986). As usual, his playing was powerful and poetic. *Piano 2* was quite different from the large-scale "multiples" pieces such as *Crazy Nigger* or *Evil Nigger*. Completely through-composed and exactly notated, though still showing a strong driving pulse in the outer movements.
>
> Julius had a very erratic manuscript, at least at the time he notated *Piano 2*. The notes took up too much space on the page for comfortable reading and were inscribed with a shaky hand. Quarter notes lack stems. There are no dynamics, phrasings, articulations, time signatures, and only one or two bar lines. In the absence of markings, I rely substantially on what I recall of the way Julius played it for me that day at my home. There are a couple of quirks in the notation of the piece. Julius ended each movement with a Japanese character and the word "zen," and he scrawled the word "Chopin" over an accompaniment figure that resembles a Chopin melody. The music itself is assured, firm, and tightly worked. The continuous, driving pulses of the multiple-piano pieces are

> expressed here as long strings of sixteenth notes in the outer movements, coursing up and down the keyboard. Often these are in the left hand, over which long treble melodies soar in quarters and halves. Some of his familiar additive process appears in the opening of the third movement, where rows of repeated notes become repeated chords by addition of a new note with each group of four. The second movement is a lovely slow movement that has an air of desolation about it, yet exhibits poignant chord progressions. Even here a languid, continuous eighth-note motion makes an appearance.[152]

The Late Period

Turmoil, eviction, all his musical scores and tapes discarded, Eastman was still composing, still performing. In 1980 and 1981, he took part in the New Music America festivals in Minneapolis and San Francisco. These were annual gatherings designed to promote the visibility of vanguard artists and the directions their works were taking. Eastman performed *Evil Nigger* and *Gay Guerrilla* in the Minneapolis concerts, and the following year presented his newly composed work, *The Holy Presence of Joan d'Arc*, in San Francisco.

Mary Jane Leach met Eastman in 1981, when they were both hired to be vocalists in a theater piece by Jim Neu for which Hugh Levick was writing the music. At the first 10:00 A.M. rehearsal, Leach reports, Eastman showed up in black leather and chains, drinking scotch (see chapter 6). During the early eighties, he was giving concerts at The Kitchen, conducting for Arthur Russell, and working once again with Meredith Monk, this time playing keyboard in *Turtle Dreams*. There was very little money coming in, and as George Lewis notes, "By the time I left the country in 1982, people at The Kitchen were complaining that Julius was too mercurial. He was developing the reputation of someone who was very difficult to be around."[153] Drugs and alcohol were taking a toll on Eastman's well-being, making it difficult to pinpoint just when his usage began to irreparably invade his working life. Rumors circulated that Eastman was a crack addict, but his friend R. Nemo Hill remains doubtful, because addiction would not have corresponded to Eastman's professed religious views.

Eastman's eccentricities were increasingly disruptive. Another good friend from the Buffalo Creative Associate days, violinist Benjamin Hudson, met Eastman in New York and realized that he needed work. He knew of a church in New Jersey that had a music series, and recommended that Eastman be invited to give a concert, with the possibility of obtaining a larger role in the future. According to Hudson, the concert was fine and actually got a good review, but the church administrators were outraged when they discovered that Eastman had smeared dirt all over the ivory keys of their valuable grand piano. They were convinced he had ruined their prized instrument. The dirt gave him better traction, he said.[154]

Gerry Eastman invited his brother to stay in his Brooklyn loft while he was away on tour. Upon his return he discovered that Julius had sold his tools and his precious coin collection for drug money. Gerry Eastman threw him out. "It got to the point that he couldn't live with me anymore because he was bringing these street urchins into my house and they were robbing me. You know, he was hanging with the lowest of the low."[155]

It was probably fall of 1983 when Thomas Sokol set up a coaching program to help scholarship students who were registered in one of Cornell University's vocal groups, which included a choir, chorale, and the glee club. Sokol engaged Eastman, who had returned to Ithaca at that point, as a vocal coach, but it soon became apparent that he was not happy in the program. As had occurred in a previous assignment with piano students several years earlier, he was unreliable and the students began falling away. According to Sokol, Eastman approached the job as a chore, showing substantially less interest in some students, while demonstrating greater interest in those with whom he could find common ground. From Sokol's point of view, "he seemed unwilling to do the legwork that could have provided a means to help him accomplish his vision."[156]

The Pulitzer Prize-winning Czech-born classical composer-conductor Karel Husa, was a member of the Cornell University faculty from 1954 to 1992, and director of the official orchestra of the City of Ithaca, the Cayuga Chamber Orchestra. For the orchestra's December 1983 program, Husa decided to break with tradition and perform Bach's *Christmas Oratorio* instead of the usual *Messiah* performances. The Bach calls for four vocal soloists, in addition to chamber orchestra and chorus. On Sokol's recommendation, Husa invited Julius Eastman to sing the bass part. Eastman replied that he was happy to do it. Thomas Sokol's recounting of the *Christmas Oratorio* performance indicates that Eastman was, at least on this occasion, "off in another world."[157]

Almost from the outset it became apparent that Eastman lacked the dedicated concentration that is required for performing in such a masterwork. For one thing, he came late to rehearsals, an egregious breach of protocol in these circumstances. During the actual performance, Eastman began to add bits of improvisation not called for in the score, interrupting the flow and causing heart-stopping consternation on Husa's part. Patrick

Will of the *Ithaca Journal* wrote in the review, "Bass Julius Eastman sang his lines with enthusiasm, although his often labored and eccentric dramatic style was sometimes quite distracting and once, during the duet, nearly disruptive."[158] Sokol, who described Eastman as "moving along at his own sense of the Bach line," was convinced that Eastman was "under the influence." Husa was in disbelief.[159]

For all his restless aspirations downward, Eastman coveted a faculty appointment at Cornell. For many years the soprano Barbara Troxell held a position in the Cornell Music Department, and when she became ill with cancer, Eastman thought that he would be in line for the job. Professor Sokol states that he had never discussed any formal openings of that nature with Eastman, although Sokol had hoped a faculty appointment might be arranged with some especially designated "diversity" funds that ultimately never came through. "I was trying to be helpful to Julius. I was leaning over backwards. At times in the late period [however], he was not a reliable addition."[160] As Gerry Eastman remarked, "Julius could not accept that people wouldn't overlook his prima donna crap. Nobody would put up with it."[161] But Frances Eastman remembers how bitterly disappointed her son was when, after Barbara Troxell died in September 1984, he did not get her job. Mrs. Eastman described it as "a nail in the coffin."[162]

A second blow at this time was the death of Caroline Famous. Eastman spoke often and with great affection about his grandmother, and expected that she would leave him money when she died. Mrs. Famous did not have a will, but the deed to the Bronx apartment house was in the names of both Mrs. Famous and Mrs. Eastman. By the time Mrs. Famous died, Frances Eastman was convinced that her son Julius was incapable of using the money wisely. Since Gerry Eastman had worked long and hard for nearly two years to rehabilitate the Bronx property, she advised Mrs. Famous to leave her assets to Gerry. "I said to Gerry, 'Give Julius an apartment' because by that time he was hanging out with bad people—rotten people and drinking people."[163] Julius, feeling cheated out of his inheritance by his mother and brother, was furious, and lashed out at his mother, both verbally and physically. They never repaired their relationship. Julius told his friend R. Nemo Hill, "If they want it, let them have it. I'm above all that." In Hill's opinion, too, this dispiriting situation was a significant factor in Eastman's decline.

As his outward behavior was growing even more erratic, so Eastman's physical deterioration was becoming increasingly visible. Gerry Eastman suspects that his brother had syphilis from an early age, and that he neglected to maintain the simple medical regimen required to contain it.

His friend, Donald Burkhardt, a medical doctor, disagrees stating that "if Julius had syphilis, I would have syphilis. To be assigned to naval submarine duty, which I was, one undergoes the most rigorous medical examinations. I do not have syphilis."[164]

When George Lewis returned to the United States for a brief period in 1984, after having been out of the country for several years, and ran into Eastman on a midtown street, Julius told him that he was living in a homeless shelter. "It's a story associated more with the jazz world than with the new-music world," Lewis comments. "You know, someone who becomes a substance abuser, who deteriorates, and somehow is unreliable. You can't find them when it's time to do the gig. At the end of the day, I felt that Julius was pretty much alone. Who was investing in him?"[165]

In the 1970s and 1980s, a section of Tompkins Square Park, a 10.5-acre public park in New York's East Village, became a kind of squatters' encampment for homeless people, drifters, and drug dealers. Julius visited the park from time to time to play chess with a group of "regulars" there. Facts on the duration of the Tompkins Square Park period are murky, but it is probable that Eastman began staying in the park sporadically throughout the mid- to late 1980s. His friends there always made room for him. Obviously, composing music and learning scores to perform would be difficult, if not impossible, under such circumstances.

Dancer-choreographer Molissa Fenley knew Julius Eastman from their days on The Kitchen tour of Europe in 1980. In 1985–86 she choreographed *Geologic Moments* for the Brooklyn Academy of Music's Next Wave Festival. The evening-length work enlists the music of two composers. Music for the first section is by Philip Glass; the second section is a version of Julius Eastman's *Thruway* for two pianos, performed by the composer and Joyce Solomon; the third segment is a piece for voice and piano performed by the composer, titled *One God*, alluding to the fact that all religions have the idea of a creator.

Fenley remembers that she and Eastman would listen to and discuss the music. He was very good about coming to rehearsals. In one section of the piece, the dancers almost touched, but not quite, at which point Eastman said, "Why don't you just touch each other?" She recalls that he was "shaky" at the Brooklyn Academy of Music performances, and had to sit on a couch in the greenroom backstage to collect himself before going onstage. It occurred to her that he might have had HIV.[166]

During this mid-eighties period David and Kathryn Gibson were having a party in their Albany home, when Julius Eastman showed up unannounced at their door. He was on his way to Buffalo, he said, and decided to drop by the Gibsons' for a visit. Cellist-composer David Gibson had been a Creative Associate in Buffalo in the early 1970s; he and Eastman had worked and toured together over several years. Eastman joined in the party, talking about a piece he was writing. It would be, he explained, a graphic score with notes like flies on the walls. Startled by how gaunt and thin he looked, it was clear to Gibson that Eastman was in terrible health and "in a bad way. . . . At the very best," Gibson notes, "even with his closest relationships, Julius was very elusive." Julius insisted he was OK, stayed for several nights, and departed, leaving the Gibsons with a sinking feeling about their friend's well-being.[167]

Another colleague, saxophonist-composer Joe Ford played in several of Eastman's pieces in the early seventies. On tour in Albany, he and Julius went out to dinner to an Italian place where they were the only blacks. Julius began to talk rather loudly, "Well, Joooooe, what are we going to do tonight?" Joe said he would probably go back to the room, and asked Julius what he was going to do. Julius answered, "Well Jooooe, I think I'll look around for a gay bar or I could go back to the hotel and give you some head!" To Ford it seemed that everyone just turned and looked. Julius, he said, liked to be outrageous. He liked to "hit on straight people—just in case." Ford speculates that Eastman actually liked rejection. He told Joe he should leave his wife. When he called the house, if Joe's wife answered, he would never say hello—just "Joe there?"

Ford left Buffalo after the 1977 blizzard, eventually settling in New Jersey. He would run into Julius at Gerry's Brooklyn studio from time to time. There were rumors that Julius was using drugs but he didn't see it. To him, Julius seemed to be the same as usual. In retrospect, Ford suspects that Julius wanted to be living the role of a tragic figure, and perhaps was "running from the pressure of trying to make it." In the late eighties, one of the last times he saw Julius, Ford was playing at the Public Theater on Lafayette Street in the East Village. He was looking for a parking spot when he saw Julius between Second and Third Avenues. Eastman looked unkempt and had grown facial hair. His appearance was changed, and he had "a little stink going on." Eastman said he was living in a homeless shelter and asked Ford for a cigarette. Ford said, "But you don't smoke. Why should I give you a cigarette?" "Well, gimme fifty cents," Eastman replied. Ford said, "This is crazy. Why aren't you at Gerry's? Don't play this on me. I know you better." "I was pissed," Ford continues. "Why was he doing that?"[168]

There was, in the late eighties, a period of relative stability, when Eastman was living on the Upper East Side of Manhattan with a psychiatrist friend. It seems that he was trying to turn his life around. He applied for a job at Tower Records on Fourth Street and Broadway. Paul Tai, today the vice president and director of Artists and Repertory of New World Records, was manager of Tower's classical music department at the time, and hired Julius. When they discussed schedules, Eastman mentioned that he was in therapy and had to work around his appointments. Tai had no idea at the outset that Eastman was anyone particularly special, but remembers that he was calm and measured and had a compelling presence. Over the few months that he worked in the store, Tai began taking note of the outpouring of affection from people who stopped by to see Julius, or who happened to run into him. Then one day, he just didn't return.[169]

May 1989

What do we know about Julius Eastman? We know he was gifted, ambitious, magnetic, theatrical, with an elegant bearing, a beautiful smile, and a beautiful voice; we know he was impatient and stubborn, arrogant (sometimes), also modest; he was intelligent, undisciplined, highly sexual, dismissive about money and "things." He was also a spiritual man; a searcher who could be a fearsome boundary-crosser, a trickster. We know he was a man of two worlds, probably at home in neither. Ultimately, Julius Eastman could not resolve his contradictions. As he veered more and more into turmoil, he lost his footing in the real world and could no longer do the work to honor his gift. Perhaps Julius Eastman felt that he had come closest to finding his "true self" in Buffalo, the place where he had bloomed, achieved professional recognition, and made his dearest friends.

In May 1989, Julius Eastman returned to Buffalo. Donald Burkhardt, living in that city once again, tells the story:

> He came to my house and my friend Haj went to the door but wouldn't let him in. Haj didn't know Julius but, from my description, he must have realized who it was. Haj telephoned me at the hospital where I was working and his description of Julius was awful. It seems that Julius had slept on the grass in front of my house or in front of the neighbor's across the street. I told Haj not to let him in.
>
> A couple of days later he telephoned, wanting to come over. An experience a few years earlier had left me very upset and I didn't want any more of that. The incident I am referring to took place after I had traveled to India twice. One of my friends there wanted to come to the States for a visit but it seemed almost impossible to get him a tourist visa, so I was thinking of applying to the immigration people for a work visa which

> would allow him to cook or be a housekeeper for me. I was extremely fond of Indian food at that time and thought that the idea might be feasible. Julius' comment about it was that I wanted a slave boy. He was insistent about it—that what I really wanted was a slave boy! From that point on, I couldn't get him out of the house fast enough. So this time when he called to come over, I said, "O.K. you can come over but not in the house. We'll talk on the porch." And he wouldn't come. He said, "I either come in your house, or I don't come." So I said "O.K." And he didn't come.[170]

In what seems like a surreal unwinding of the film, one senses destiny stepping in now. It was late afternoon on a late spring day. Whether it was the day of the Don Burkhardt debacle or the next, we cannot know. We do know that Karl Singletary, the person who introduced Julius Eastman to Don Burkhardt, hadn't heard from Eastman in fourteen years. What unfolds bears uncanny echoes of Eastman's handwritten inscription "Parable" on the title page of his abandoned *Symphony II* written years before (see chapter 3). Singletary describes their encounter:

> Even before Julius left Buffalo back in the summer of 1976, I was beginning to withdraw from him because I was a little nervous and scared of him. I wouldn't let him come up to my apartment anymore. I got that type of fear about him. He was so strange, you know. He had this "open life" and everybody should just put up with it.
>
> Then one late Saturday afternoon fourteen years later, there he was on Main and High Street in Buffalo. He was puny and not very healthy looking. I realized he must have been having financial problems. I didn't have a lot of money either, but I know I gave him some—how much I can't recall. He said he was staying in a shelter around Main near Riley Street. I think it was operated by some Catholic nuns. It was about 6:00 P.M., so we talked and we said goodbye there on Main Street.
>
> Within a week I got a call from the hospital saying that he was dead. He had given my telephone number to the staff there. From what I understand, he had been in the hospital for a couple of days. I felt real bad that I sort of forced him aside, but I just knew that I couldn't take Julius to my home and deal with him and his way of life anymore. So I separated from him right on that corner.[171]

Frances Eastman dreamed about Julius before she was pregnant. She also dreamed about Julius the weekend just before he died.

> I knew that Julius would die before me. I always knew that. And I knew something horrible had happened to him when he died. I love plants and I used to go to Rochester when they had their bonsai exhibit. The

weekend of that exhibit is always the happiest weekend of my year. I went up with a friend and the whole weekend I was so sad and I couldn't really talk to her. We used to chitchat all the way and all the way back. I didn't know what it was and I called up Gerry when I got home and I said, "You know, something terrible has happened to Julius. I don't know what it is." It was Monday when I called Gerry and on Tuesday, I got the call that Julius was dead. And when they brought his ashes here, I fell down crying. I put my hand on the box and had to take my hand off. It was a weird experience. I couldn't touch him. He was very angry. I used to tell him, "Julius take care of your health because, if you live a long life, you will come in to your own."[172]

"That Which Is Fundamental: Julius Eastman, 1940–1990"

In the *Village Voice* on January 22, 1991, Kyle Gann wrote:

> Julius Eastman died May 28, 1990, alone, at Millard Fillmore Hospital in Buffalo. He was forty-nine. According to the death certificate, he died of cardiac arrest. Depending on whom you talked to, it was brought on by insomnia and possible tuberculosis, dehydration, starvation, exhaustion, or depression (supposedly not AIDS). According to his brother, his body was cremated, and there was a family memorial service in Annapolis, Maryland.

Notes

1. Lewis Hyde, *Trickster Makes This World: Mischief, Myth, and Art* (New York: Farrar, Straus and Giroux, 1998). Composer Pauline Oliveros incorporates the "heyoka" or sacred clown concept in her writings about Eastman and in her work *Crow*. Scholar Henry Louis Gates Jr. traces the folk origins of "signifying," which is closely related to the trickster figure in Afro-American culture, see *The Signifying Monkey: A Theory of African-American Literary Criticism* (New York: Oxford University Press, 1988).

2. Frances Eastman, interviews with the author October 11, 2006, and October 1, 2009.

3. In February 2007, on the occasion of her ninetieth birthday and in honor of African American History Month, Frances Eastman was named Senior Citizen of the Year by the City of Ithaca Common Council. The proclamation cites her long-time advocacy and work with the "Southside Community Center and other key community organizations," her championing for social and economic justice, her

"tireless" work on behalf of civil rights, and her "unwavering support for the vulnerable" (Official Notice of Meeting: City of Ithaca Common Council, February 7, 2007). According to David Lisbon, Julius and Gerald Eastman's first cousin, after his discharge from the army where he had served in Greenland as an armed combat engineer, Julius Eastman Sr. attended New York University and was the first African American graduate of the Engineering School in 1954.

4. Frances Eastman interview.

5. Ibid.

6. Peg Cunningham, classmate of Julius Eastman, e-mail to the author, December 10, 2009.

7. Steve Schmal, secretary to the Ithaca High School class of 1958, e-mail to the author, November 30, 2009. The recollection is by Miriam (Heinicke) Monfredo. According to Steve Schmal, there were fewer than fifteen black students in a class of three hundred.

8. Frances Eastman interview. David Lisbon, Julius Eastman's first cousin, states that Eastman's aunt on his father's side, Ann Eastman, was a professor of piano at Howard University. His uncle, Ann's father, was a voice instructor.

9. Thomas Sokol, interview with the author, October 1, 2009. Professor Sokol was the director of the Cornell Glee Club for thirty-nine years and became a champion of Eastman over the years.

10. Jim McCarthy e-mail to the author, December 10, 2009.

11. Frances Eastman interview.

12. David Lisbon telephone conversation with the author, November 15, 2010.

13. George Driscoll, letter to the Curtis Institute of Music, January 28, 1959 (Curtis Institute of Music Archives).

14. All Curtis students were on full scholarship at the time. No living expenses were awarded, however. During this period, although Eastman received a Federation of Music Clubs Award and a National Association of Negro Musicians Award, money for living was always problematic.

15. Julius Eastman to Curtis Institute of Music, May 14, 1959 (Curtis Institute of Music Archives).

16. Ruga Suzuki recalled that Homer Lee developed bone cancer and, tragically, had to have his arm amputated. He could no longer play and, sometime later, committed suicide.

17. According to Ruga Suzuki, a typical daily food expenditure might be 45¢ for a coffee break, 55¢ for lunch, and $1.19 for a special dinner selection.

18. Ruga Suzuki's recollection seems to bear out Rosina Lhevinne's reservations about Eastman's audition for the Juilliard School. Another classmate, his friend Marta Garcia Renart, also recalls that Eastman "was not as good technically as other students" (e-mail to the author, March 4, 2012).

19. Zeyda Ruga Suzuki telephone conversation with the author, February 21, 2010. I want to thank Mrs. Suzuki for "opening her heart" to me. Eastman notes in his curriculum vitae on file at Buffalo State College that he studied dance while in

Philadelphia at the John Hines School of Dance and at the Philadelphia Academy of Dance.

20. Beatriz Lima, e-mail to the author, March 12, 2012. Eastman's statement is reminiscent of writer Jack London's remark, "The very poor can always be depended upon. They never turn away the hungry" (Crain, "Four Legs Good," *New Yorker* 73, October 28, 2013).

21. Julius Eastman undated letter to Anne Hill. Curtis Institute of Music Archives. Eastman refers to the composer Vittorio Giannini.

22. Ruga Suzuki, telephone conversation. Dr. A. Constant Vauclain held teaching positions at the University of Pennsylvania, the Curtis Institute of Music, and Princeton University. He founded the music theory program at the New School of Music, now part of Temple University's Esther Boyer College of Music. He developed a harmonic system called "syntonality" that he felt would open up new expressive paths to musicians (University of Pennsylvania Almanac 50, no. 13, cited in Dana Richardson's blog entry on Constand Vauclain, http://dana-richardson.org/vauclain.htm, accessed November 29, 2010).

23. Warren Benson letter to Admissions Officer, April 2, 1961. Curtis Institute of Music Archives.

24. Curtis Institute of Music Archives.

25. Undated letter to Anne Hill. Curtis Institute of Music Archives. This letter was probably written late in the summer of 1960.

26. Curtis Institute of Music Archives.

27. Dr. Raphael H. Greenstein, March 20, 1962. Curtis Institute of Music Archives.

28. Efrem Zimbalist telegram to Julius Eastman, September 26, 1962. Curtis Institute of Music Archives.

29. Lima, e-mail to the author, March 12, 2012.

30. Curtis Institute of Music Archives. Pianist Richard Goode went on to become a world-renowned concert artist.

31. Nina Sobelman, "Julius Eastman, Cornell Concert," *Ithaca Journal*, July 22, 1966.

32. Alvin K. Fossner, "Eastman in Debut As Pianist," December 1966 (unidentified periodical).

33. In a program note for a performance at Colgate College Summer Theater "Words and Music by Ferruccio Busoni" in July 1968, Eastman writes that he is "composer and pianist for Buffalo University's Dance Department." In an interview in *The Reporter*, a University at Buffalo campus community newspaper, Eastman states that in Buffalo he resumed a friendship with Kirpich, whom he had met years before when he played for her dance classes at Indian Hill Camp in Massachusetts where he was on a music scholarship.

34. Karl Singletary, interview with the author, April 21, 2009.

35. Thomas Sokol telephone conversation with the author, July 23, 2009.

36. Undated curriculum vitae, University at Buffalo, Music Department.

37. The SEEK—Search for Education, Elevation and Knowledge—program was created in 1966 by the New York State Legislature to advance the cause of equality and educational opportunity. (State University College appointment form, October 17, 1968.) This appointment was extended by Peter B. Yates, chairman of the State University of New York at Buffalo Music Department. According to Eastman's friend, Donald Burkhardt, Eastman became good friends with Peter and his wife, Frances. Burkhardt recalls going to the Yates's home with Eastman for Sunday brunch. It should be noted that Peter Yates was the founder of the famous "Monday Evening Concerts" in Los Angeles; his wife Frances Mullen Yates was a noted pianist and Ives specialist.

38. Mark Goldman, *City on the Edge: Buffalo, New York* (Amherst, NY: Prometheus, 2007), 210.

39. Renée Levine Packer, *This Life of Sounds: Evenings for New Music in Buffalo* (New York: Oxford, 2010).

40. University at Buffalo, Department of Music, *Evenings for New Music: A Catalogue, 1964–80* (Buffalo, 1981). In an interview with Suzanne Metzger of the University at Buffalo campus publication the *Reporter*, Eastman says that he "badgered" Foss until Foss invited him to perform with the CAs. "Eastman: 'I Always Thought I Was Great, but Why Does Making It Big Take So Long?'" September 30, 1971.

41. Donald Burkhardt, interview with the author, November 13, 2009. During the academic year 1968–69, Karl Singletary was living in New York on a scholarship with American Ballet Theatre. He was in Buffalo in December 1968 to spend the holidays with his family.

42. Singletary interview.

43. Burkhardt interview.

44. Concurrent with his fellowship with the Center of the Creative and Performing Arts appointment in the 1969–70 academic year, Eastman was still on a part-time (SEEK) appointment at the State University College. In February 1970, the State University College offered Eastman an additional one-year appointment as full-time instructor to replace his SEEK half-time appointment. Eastman declined the offer. On the termination form, State University College at Buffalo Music Department Chairman Peter Yates wrote, "We shall miss him and his unusual gifts as a performer" (State University College, February 4, 1970).

45. George Crumb, interview with the author, November 21, 2000.

46. Ryan Dohoney, interview with Petr Kotik, November 14, 2008.

47. Robert Martin, interview with the author, November 17, 2000.

48. SUNY/Buffalo Music Department, *Creative Associate Recitals: A Catalogue 1964–1980.*

49. Ralph Ellison, "Introduction," in *Invisible Man* (New York: Vintage International, 1995), xx.

50. Thomas Putnam, "Julius Eastman Works Scheduled," *Buffalo Courier Express*, April 19, 1970.

51. Ibid.

52. Herman Trotter, "Eastman's Planetary Work Is Stellar Entertainment," *Buffalo Evening News*, April 20, 1970.

53. Thomas Putnam, "'Moon's Modulation,'" *Buffalo Courier Express*, April 20–21, 1970.

54. Burkhardt interview.

55. Thomas Putnam, "Eastman's 'Thruway,'" *Buffalo Courier Express*, May 4, 1970.

56. Herman Trotter, "Clear Voice, Unclear Work in New Music's Wide Range," *Buffalo Evening News*, May 4, 1970.

57. Raymond Ericson, "5 Works in Finale of Music Evenings," *New York Times*, May 1, 1970.

58. Burkhardt interview.

59. Ibid.

60. Ibid.

61. Sokol interview.

62. The Ballet Center of Buffalo, an ambitious attempt to create an academy for advanced ballet students, was founded in the late 1960s by the noted British ballet mistress and protégé of Anna Pavlova, Kathleen Crofton, with the backing of local arts patron Franz Stone. Graduates became principal dancers in major companies around the world.

63. Singletary interview.

64. Suzanne Metzger, "Eastman: 'I Always Thought I Was Great, But Why Does Making It Big Take So Long?'" *Reporter*, September 30, 1971.

65. Singletary interview.

66. Renate Strauss, "Julius Eastman: Will the Real One Stand Up?" *Buffalo Evening News*, July 16, 1976. Eastman performed the American premiere of Henze's *Essay on Pigs* on the Los Angeles Philharmonic's Contempo 71 series, May 2 and 4, 1971 (Steve LaCoste, Los Angeles Philharmonic archivist, e-mail to the author, April 25, 2011).

67. Ibid. Eastman recorded *Eight Songs for a Mad King* in London in fall 1970. The recording was reissued by Nonesuch Records and nominated for a Grammy Award in 1973.

68. Harold C. Schonberg, "'Eight Songs for a Mad King' a Delight," *New York Times*, December 11, 1970.

69. John Dwyer, "Eastman's 'Mad King': Mighty Work of Theater," *Buffalo Evening News*, November 2, 1970.

70. Metzger, "Eastman: 'I Always Thought I Was Great.'"

71. Andrew Stiller e-mail to the author, May 25, 2011.

72. Jan Williams telephone conversation with the author, May 11, 2011.

73. John Dwyer, "Brave Throng a Tribute to Composers Foss, Smit," *Buffalo Evening News*, February 14, 1972.

74. John Dwyer, "'Black Ivory' Casts Society as a Statue," *Buffalo Evening News*, February 28, 1972.

75. Cristyne Lawson, interview with the author, March 17, 2000.

76. Garry Kvistad, e-mail to the author, June 7, 2011.

77. As he recalls the incident, Schafer thinks that, more than anything, he was startled by the idea of a man in the role. He wrote the piece for a mezzo-soprano and had always thought that "the heroine should be a woman." Upon subsequent reflection and since it is a requiem, he now feels that the part could be performed by either sex (R. Murray Schafer telephone conversation with the author, May 24, 2011).

78. Julius Eastman to Registrar, Curtis Institute of Music Archives, July 27, 1972.

79. Charles Gayle, telephone conversations with the author, January 11, and January 16, 2009; December 20, 2014.

80. Joseph Ford telephone conversation with the author, January 4, 2010.

81. The Beatles' use of a string quartet on their album *Help* in 1965, and their mention of the influence of composer Karlheinz Stockhausen; Andy Warhol's 1964 appropriation of Brillo boxes as visual art works.

82. Leroy Jenkins's pithy comment to Kyle Gann in a 1996 interview says it all. While discussing his 1993 cantata *The Negros Burial Ground*, he tells Gann, "Call it Billie Holiday meets Bartók." Kyle Gann, *Music Downtown* (Berkeley: University of California Press, 2006), 61.

83. George E. Lewis, *A Power Stronger Than Itself* (Chicago: University of Chicago Press, 2008), 331. See Lewis's chapter 9 for a fuller discussion of this topic.

84. Gerry Eastman, interviews with the author, November 2, 2006, and September 14, 2009.

85. Thomas Putnam, "Wall-to-Wall Piano Music Is Hum-Dinger," *Buffalo Courier Express*, October 29, 1972. Portions of this section are quoted from Levine Packer's *This Life of Sounds*, 116–17.

86. University at Buffalo, *Evenings for New Music: A Catalogue*.

87. Singletary had no budget to pay for a musician so Eastman wrote the piece for him using eight amplified metronomes. (Singletary telephone conversation with the author); according to a short program note for a 1975 concert that dates the piece from winter 1973, *Wood in Time* may be performed "with or without dance." *Wood in Time* was actually written in 1972.

88. Herman Trotter, "Inner City Ballet Shows Rare Talent in Varied Styles," *Buffalo Evening News*, August 2, 1973.

89. Alyssa Rabach, interview with the author, April 28, 2000.

90. Henry James, *Hawthorne* (Ithaca, NY: Cornell University Press, 1909), 25.

91. Thomas Sokol telephone conversation with the author, November 12, 2014.

92. Ann Silsbee (1930–2003), composer and poet, took her DMA at Cornell University where she studied with Karel Husa. She was "an accomplished pianist whose music, although carefully notated, gives the impression of improvisation." See liner notes to *Women's Voices: Five Centuries of Song* (Leonarda CD LE338), accessed May 19, 2011, http://www.leonarda.com/composers/comp338b.html. Silsbee dedicated *Prometheus* to Julius Eastman.

93. Violinist Benjamin Hudson became a Creative Associate in fall 1973.

94. Eberhard Blum, "Remarks on 'El Cimarrón,'" June 23, 2010 (unpublished manuscript).

95. Thomas Putnam, "Henze's 'El Cimarrón' Falls Short," *Buffalo Courier Express*, November 18, 1973.

96. Kyle Gann, "'Damned Outrageous': The Music of Julius Eastman." Liner notes written by Kyle Gann for Julius Eastman, *Unjust Malaise*, New World Records CD 80638, 2005.

97. It has not been possible to determine which piece Eastman submitted to the New York State Council on the Arts.

98. Goldman, *City on the Edge*, 81.

99. Richard Brown and Bob Watson, *Buffalo: Lake City in Niagara Land* (Buffalo: Buffalo and Erie County Historical Society, 1981), 189.

100. Donald Burkhardt e-mail to the author, May 15, 2011.

101. Dennis Kahle e-mail to the author, March 11, 2004. CA percussionist Dennis Kahle performed *Stay On It* in all the Center's 1973–74 performances in the United States and Europe.

102. University at Buffalo, *Evenings for New Music: A Catalogue*; see also Levine Packer *This Life of Sounds*, 125–29.

103. Levine Packer, *This Life of Sounds*, 133. According to an entry in the *Evenings for New Music* catalogue, the piece was videotaped in Buffalo on March 1, 1975.

104. Pauline Oliveros, "Special Encounters with Julius: A Man of Power," November 11, 2011 (unpublished manuscript).

105. Ibid.

106. Ibid.

107. Petr Kotik, interview with Ryan Dohoney, November 11, 2008; Petr Kotik, interviews with the author, February 21, 2000, and December 11, 2008.

108. Strauss, "Julius Eastman: Will the Real One Stand Up?"

109. Eastman's year as a Creative Associate was officially considered a half-time appointment since he still held a half-time appointment at the State University College in Peter Yates's music department across town.

110. September 1, 1972, to August 31, 1975. During this period, Eastman took a one-semester leave of absence.

111. John P. Sullivan letter to Julius Eastman, February 14, 1975. University Archives, University at Buffalo, October 23, 2010, and June 3, 2011.

112. University Archives, University at Buffalo, October 23, 2010, and June 3, 2011.

113. Frederick Cohen, interview with the author, September 30, 2010.

114. Music Library, University at Buffalo, June 3, 2011.

115. Ibid.

116. The reader is reminded of comments by Zeyda Ruga that Eastman's technique and sound were not on a level equivalent to that of other Curtis piano students when he arrived there.

117. Gerry Eastman, telephone conversation with the author, July 8, 2011.

118. John Rockwell, "S.E.M. Ensemble Offers Vocal Spark in Kitchen Concert," *New York Times*, March 15, 1975.

119. "You know how they talk about April in Paris? Well, I think we should call it June in Buffalo." Morton Feldman in conversation with the author, winter 1975.

120. Dohoney interview with Kotik.

121. Thomas Putnam, "John Cage Work Not Very Moving," *Buffalo Courier Express*, June 5, 1975.

122. Jeff Simon, "Cage Stung by Careless Followers," *Buffalo Evening News*, Lively Arts Section, June 21, 1975.

123. Portions of this discussion may be found in Levine Packer's *This Life of Sounds*, 144–46. Cage's work, largely misunderstood in his lifetime, is still a mystery to many. Likewise, his sexuality was rarely discussed in public and, although many probably guessed that he was gay, was an obscure aspect of his aesthetic. See Richard Kostelanetz, *John Cage (Ex)plain(ed)* (New York: Schirmer Books, 1996), 167–69; and Ryan Dohoney, "John Cage, Julius Eastman, and the Homosexual Ego," in *Tomorrow Is the Question: New Directions in Experimental Music Studies*, ed. Benjamin Piekut, 39–62 (Ann Arbor: University of Michigan Press, 2014).

124. Kotik interview.

125. Nudity in performance was no longer a rarity in 1975. The musicals *Hair* (1968) and *Oh! Calcutta!* (1969) had been widely discussed and seen by thousands. On a technical note, however, Eastman's interpretation enlisted a "trio" and was not a "solo" as specified in the instructions.

126. Ned Sublette, interview with the author, December 28, 2008.

127. Ryan Dohoney, "John Cage, Julius Eastman, and the Homosexual Ego," in Piekut, *Tomorrow Is the Question*, 47.

128. Gerald Eastman interview.

129. Strauss, "Julius Eastman: Will the Real One Stand Up?"

130. According to Gerry Eastman, he sold the house for the original purchase price of $19,000. Julius Eastman had made a down payment of $3,000, which he recouped. He used the money to produce a concert at the Third Street School Music Settlement.

131. Tania León, telephone interview with the author, September 8, 2011. In the 1978–79 season, the series was expanded from four to six programs, each presented at several venues in Brooklyn.

132. Joseph Horowitz, "Julius Eastman Sings, Plays Piano at Environ," *New York Times*, October 12, 1976.

133. Jon Gibson, "Reflections on Julius Eastman," December 2010 (unpublished manuscript).

134. Arthur Rimbaud, *Arthur Rimbaud: Complete Works*, trans. Paul Schmidt (New York: Harper and Row, 1967), 78. According to Ned Sublette, Eastman sometimes visited a gay bar called "The Toilet" which has been described as "A

very wet place. You name it and they were doing it there." ("Greenwich Village: A Gay History," www.huzbears.com/nychistory/gv.html, accessed August 30, 2011). R. Nemo Hill, with whom Eastman lived for a time, states that Eastman was "into S and M." Eastman told Sublette that he preferred "vicious sissies."

135. Hilton Als, "A Pryor Love," in *Life Stories*, ed. David Remnick, 382–402 (New York: Modern Library, 2001).

136. Sublette interview.

137. Arthur Russell died of AIDS in 1992, at age forty.

138. Gerald Eastman interviews.

139. Tim Page, interview with the author, February 14, 2011.

140. The Brooklyn Philharmonia records indicate, however, that it was premiered on December 10, 1977, at the Brooklyn Academy of Music.

141. Thomas Putnam, "Romp in Violins," *Buffalo Courier Express*, February 12, 1979.

142. John Dwyer, "Performances of New Music Worthy of Best," *Buffalo Evening News*, February 12, 1979.

143. Julius Eastman, program note, *If You're So Smart, Why Aren't You Rich?* Evenings for New Music, February 11, 1979.

144. Peter Gena, interview with the author, May 21, 2000.

145. George Lewis, interview with the author, December 28, 2009.

146. Ibid.

147. R. Nemo Hill, interview with the author, March 6, 2009.

148. The Brooklyn Philharmonia's community concert series began in 1977 and lasted for almost a dozen years, but, according to Tania León, Eastman lost interest after three years or so and left. "He had a lack of tolerance for things he didn't like" (León telephone interview).

149. Hill interview. Ananda is a principal disciple and devout attendant of the Buddha.

150. Gerald Eastman interview.

151. Joseph Kubera, "Recollections of Julius Eastman and His Piano Music," June 14, 2012 (unpublished manuscript). See chapter 9.

152. Ibid. Joseph Kubera's recording of *Piano 2* is available on *Book of Horizons*, Joseph Kubera, New World Records CD 80745, 2014.

153. George Lewis to the author, December 29, 2009.

154. Benjamin Hudson, interview with the author, March 23, 2007.

155. Gerald Eastman interviews, numerous telephone conversations, and less formal visits.

156. Thomas Sokol, telephone conversation with the author, September 16, 2011.

157. Ibid.

158. Patrick Will, "Cayuga Orchestra Breaks a Tradition with Bach and Gusto," *Ithaca Journal*, December 6, 2003.

159. Sokol telephone conversation.

160. Sokol interview, October 1, 2009.
161. Gerry Eastman interview.
162. Frances Eastman interview.
163. Ibid.
164. Burkhardt interview.
165. Lewis interview.
166. Molissa Fenley telephone communication with the author, February 24, 2009.
167. David Gibson, telephone communication with the author, May 18, 2011.
168. Ford telephone conversation.
169. Paul Tai, telephone conversation with the author, April 2, 2009.
170. Burkhardt interview; e-mail to the author, May 15, 2011.
171. Singletary interview.
172. Frances Eastman interview.

CHAPTER TWO

UNJUST MALAISE

David Borden

The earliest most of us heard about Julius Eastman's death was in January of 1991, when Kyle Gann wrote an obituary in the *Village Voice*. At one point, Gann called me to ask if Julius had died from AIDS. I didn't know, and didn't feel comfortable asking Frances, his mother. Cardiac arrest is the official cause, but evidently he was also on the verge of starvation. It has been said that when he was in his last days at the Millard Fillmore Hospital in Buffalo, New York, the nurses asked him what family members or close friends they should contact. He replied that he had no family or friends, and he died alone in May 1990. In fact, Eastman gave Karl Singletary's name to the staff, and the hospital notified Singletary when he died. It was Singletary who called Julius's mother with the dreadful news.

Almost immediately, I felt the urge to compose a piece in his memory. I decided to compose it for two pianos, because his friend Edmund Niemann was half of the duo piano team Double Edge with Nurit Tilles. They premiered the piece at Lincoln Center Out of Doors in July 1991. The title, *Unjust Malaise*, is an anagram of Julius Eastman, and is part of my Anagram Portrait series. In 2005, New World Records released a three-disc set of Eastman's music under the same title, with my blessing. In fact, I'm proud to say that I had a small part in making the release possible.

I first met Julius in the spring of 1967 in Ithaca, New York, a few months after his New York Town Hall debut piano recital. He was twenty-six and I was twenty-eight. There was no inkling then of how self-fulfilling his anagram would become. He had returned to Ithaca to sort out his options, and volunteered to give a piano recital for the students at DeWitt Middle School in Ithaca, which he himself had attended. According to the music teachers, it was supposed to inspire kids from modest economic backgrounds to work hard toward their dreams, no matter what the circumstances of their lives. As it happened, I was at DeWitt as a recipient of a Ford Foundation grant, and was the composer-in-residence for the Ithaca City Schools. I had a studio on the top floor of the DeWitt building, which had been condemned as too dangerous for classrooms. I had just returned from a Fulbright student year in Berlin; Julius had graduated from the Curtis Institute of Music in Philadelphia a few years before.

What I remember from that first meeting was his friendly smile and the deep resonance of his voice. It was as if a large concert hall had been buried deep within his voice box, and some record producer was adding reverb. This speaking voice brought to mind a broadcaster of some kind: radio commercials, voiceovers, announcements. It served both as an attention getter and as a layer of protection. It added a psychic distance not unlike performers have with their audiences. The friendly smile did not mean he was forthcoming or that he revealed much about himself. It meant he was willing to know you better. Growing up in mid-century America as a gay African-American male no doubt made one very guarded around almost everyone. Many white Americans of that era, regardless of their geographic background, were openly hostile to blacks. As for homosexuality, not only was it not tolerated by almost everyone outside the arts, but it was illegal as well. In addition, he was an intellectual and a creative genius on multiple levels, which added to the professional complexity and social intensity of it all.

After his recital, which was a repeat of his Town Hall program, with maybe a bit more improvisation, we had lunch together. We talked about various things in music, about how repressive the atmosphere in academia was, with its emphasis on serial and cerebral techniques, the recent rebirth of Charles Ives, and our backgrounds in jazz and how important improvisation was. At various times in our lives we had both worked as accompanists for dance classes. Our conversation was just a pleasant getting-to-know-you kind of thing. Nothing momentous. When we finished our lunch, we parted friends. Julius was a beautiful, multifaceted powerful enigma. He drifted in and out of my life sporadically for the next twenty-two years.

Several months later, at Cornell in November, he sang the bass part in Igor Stravinsky's *Oedipus Rex*, which Tom Sokol, the Cornell choral director, conducted. Sokol, who also prepared the chorus, told me that when it was time for Julius's entrance in his role as the messenger, he turned on his music stand light to reveal his face, which he had covered in silver paint. Sokol said it was a theatrical masterstroke, although it had never been done in rehearsal. This kind of spontaneity can be disconcerting to conductors, and this would not be his last experience with Julius in this regard.

Three years later, in the summer of 1970, I saw Julius again, when I took part in a concert of his music at Cornell University, in a series of summer concerts that Sokol arranged for and conducted. Julius had moved to Buffalo by then, and was part of the Creative Associates program at the university there. In the meantime, I had befriended Robert Moog, who had generously given me the run of his electronic studio in the evenings. I was incredibly busy working on a film score for Ed Emshwiller. Moog's company was in Trumansburg, which was a twenty-minute drive north of Ithaca. I was also working on pieces intended for live synthesizer performance. It was during that summer that Steve Reich came to visit for a couple of days, and Gordon Mumma was around most of July and August. I had been composer/pianist for dance at Cornell since 1968, and was accompanying dance classes given by Barbara Lloyd of the Merce Cunningham Dance Company for Cornell's Summer School. Yvonne Rainer also showed up for about a week. So it was a busy and exciting summer.

Initially, I was reluctant to take part in Julius's concert because I had so little time to prepare. But it was soon obvious that my piano part consisted of segments that were to be improvised based on some simple ideas provided by him. I don't remember much about the performance, but I remember a few performers playing disparate musical phrases from the corners of the foyer as the audience entered. Julius was striking some kind of chime every once in a while. We performed his *Thruway* and *The Moon's Silent Modulation*. *Thruway* was performed with flute, trombone, percussion, piano, small vocal ensemble, and string quartet. Gerry Eastman, Julius's brother, and an outstanding jazz musician, is listed as the sound technician, but all this meant was that a microphone was set up backstage for Julius to interject phrases and various vocal sounds during the performance. None of the instruments were amplified. Sokol remembers that during *Thruway* one of the phrases Julius yelled out was "See the USA in your Chevrolet!" All of this was a total surprise to the performers, including Sokol, because during the rehearsals this aspect of the piece was never mentioned.

The Moon's Silent Modulation used much the same instrumentation, but with a double bass instead of a trombone, and a few more voices. The main difference was that this piece also used three dancers. The piece began with a chamber chorale entering from the rear of the auditorium in the same way that a gospel choir usually enters a church. There was a lot of improvisation, and it was interactive as well, using various noises from the audience as cues. Julius wrote the libretto, composed the music, and choreographed the dance. I remember some beautiful lighting also, but the lighting designer is not included on the program. Years later, Frances Eastman, Julius's mother, mentioned this piece on several occasions as her favorite.

In the 1970s I averaged about two trips to New York City every month. In 1974 or 1975, Julius hitched a ride with me from Ithaca. We discussed several things, among them the use in our music of steady tempos, repetition, and simple chord progressions, like those found in pop music. He mentioned his piece *Stay On It* (1973), which contained these elements, but slowly changed from a persistently intense steady, but loose jazz feel, to a kind of quiet exhaustion at the end. We had both played in jazz groups in our teens. I told him that my *Frank Sinatra* piece (1971) and another one called *Music* (1972), had the same kind of elements, but used actual taped segments from recordings (which would now be called samples and loops) that morphed into other things while performers played along. His music was for acoustic instruments, mine for electronic ones. The word "minimalism" was not mentioned, because the term was not yet in common use for music, only in the visual arts. Julius mentioned several composers whom he found interesting, but I don't remember the names. However, when Philip Glass's name came up, he got very agitated and burst out, "What kind of music is that? It sounds French!" I didn't ask what he meant, but simply laughed for a while, and so did he. I think he meant that Glass's music didn't reflect any kind of assimilation of the constant bombardment of pop and jazz that we all heard growing up, even though his father owned a record store.

We also talked about how not living in New York City made it more difficult to pursue a career in new music. He said that he eventually planned to move there, but as yet hadn't found a way to sustain himself financially. I had no desire to live in the city, and loved Ithaca. I was lucky to be represented by Performing Artservices.[1] Julius had no such support, but was already notorious for his performances and Nonesuch recording of *Eight Songs for a Mad King* by composer Peter Maxwell Davies. He told me that he had received generous offers for help in his career without enumerating them. He also spoke of some not so generous offers, including commissions in return for sexual favors from white men who were either wealthy or well-connected. He turned them down. When it came to his art and profession, Julius was a man of honor.

The next time I saw Julius was in the spring of 1981. He gave a concert of music by Federico Mompou at the Statler Auditorium on the Cornell campus. He was assisted in this by a young male singer, whose name I can't recall, but who I think was from South America. By this time in his career, Julius was known for his sometimes outrageous behavior, but this concert had none of that, except I noticed he played the concert in bare feet. Otherwise, his attire was completely normal. I took it as a bit of eccentricity. Later he told me that he felt more comfortable being able to touch the piano pedals directly. All through the concert he was totally engaged and energetic, conveying the music beautifully, both as a piano soloist and as an accompanist to the young singer.

After the concert I took them to a local restaurant, Old Port Harbor, which no longer exists. Julius went on and on about how he loved Mompou's music, and couldn't understand why there weren't more performances of his work. As for me, the music made hardly any impression at all. It struck me as a kind of watered-down Satie. But it was great seeing Julius so enthusiastic and full of energy. The evening was full of laughter. Sadly, it would be the last time I saw him truly happy.

Thanks to the late Jane Yockel, who had close ties to Meredith Monk, I saw Julius sing with her ensemble in Midtown Manhattan in the fall of that same year. I think it was a private concert of some kind. The venue was a strange basement space in the afternoon, a very unlikely place and time for a concert of any kind. Nonetheless, I got there on time and heard the entire presentation. They performed selections from *Dolmen Music*. This was either just before or just after they had recorded it for the ECM label. Julius was very professional, and we talked briefly, but he seemed preoccupied and somewhat removed from the whole undertaking.

What was certain was that he had finally made the move to New York City. He lived on the top floor of a building on Second Avenue and East Sixth Street. The young actor, Donna Sliby, lived a few floors below. They ran into each other once in a while, exchanging pleasantries. By then, Julius was wearing his motorcycle boots, black leather, chains, and looking strikingly handsome. Soon, he began leaving little "presents" outside Donna's door. Among the small items was a metronome. Donna and Julius became friends. She was dating Edmund Niemann, a pianist long associated with Steve Reich and Musicians, who taught at the Third Street Music School Settlement. Edmund and Donna were married soon after, and Julius remained their friend throughout the 1980s.

By 1983, it was becoming obvious that Julius was drinking heavily and experimenting with drugs. One possible reason is that what he assumed was a promised job in the Cornell Music Department did not materialize. After several years of living hand-to-mouth, he was evidently looking for some kind of steady employment, even though he had never been able to acclimate himself to such a regimen. I was employed by Cornell at the time, but was not aware of any of this. My affiliation was with the Department of Athletics. In fact, the Music Department had, since 1973, banned me and my synthesizer ensemble, Mother Mallard's Portable Masterpiece Company, from performing in their concert hall.

During this period one of the vice-provosts of the university received funds to institute an affirmative action program to help remedy the racial imbalance among Cornell's faculty members. Professor Sokol, a longtime advocate of Julius and his music, made inquiries and was able to find Julius some work as a vocal coach. Sokol told me that, although he assured Julius that he would lobby on his behalf in order to find him some kind of steady work, he never promised him a full-time position. It was simply not in his power to do so. Maybe there was some kind of miscommunication. I don't know.

Edmund Niemann gave his debut recital in New York City at the Abraham Goodman House (aka Merkin Concert Hall) in late May 1984. I attended, partly because he included one of my pieces on the program, and also because he had become a friend of mine. After intermission and right after he had walked out onstage to begin the second half, Julius walked down the aisle in a beautifully flowing white toga. He approached the stage, shook hands with Niemann and uttered a few words that none of us could hear. Niemann smiled and proceeded to sit down at the piano while Julius disappeared backstage, not to be seen again. In his review for the *New York Times*, Tim Page omits any mention of this strange interlude. Later I learned that Julius was simply asking Niemann for some money to buy wine. He agreed, and after the concert, while still backstage, the transaction occurred.

I saw Julius only two more times after this, and the dates are a bit hazy in my mind. I remember visiting him in Tompkins Square Park, where he lived after he was thrown out of his apartment for not paying the rent. He looked harassed, frustrated, and a little embarrassed. His eyes were fiery, yet resigned. I was with Jane Yockel, who helped me find the park. I think I gave Julius some cash and talked with him for a short while. He said he was not at the park all the time, but the people in the adjacent spaces kept his place for him. It was all very sad and surreal. I was at a loss. We said goodbye. It would be a couple of years before I saw him again.

In the meantime, somehow, after the park episode, he was back in Ithaca at Cornell. This was around the mid-eighties. Tom Sokol says that he appeared as the bass soloist in a performance of Bach's *Christmas Oratorio* for orchestra and chorus, conducted by Pulitzer Prize-winning composer Karel Husa. The soloists were sitting in a row, to the side, in front of the orchestra, waiting their turn to stand up, and then move to center stage to sing. When it was Julius's turn, he got up early and moved to his center-stage spot in a slow choreographed stepping movement, in sync with the music, so that when he reached the appointed spot, he sang his first note. The aria he sang was not Bach's (although the words were the same) but a vocal melismatic riff on the harmonies in a style somewhere between John Coltrane and Bobby McFerrin. Other performers in the concert said he looked really high on something. Afterward, backstage, no one had ever seen Husa so stunned. He was wide-eyed and speechless. I wish I had been present at this event.

Edmund Niemann tells me that in the period between 1986 and 1989, Julius would show up unannounced at his and Donna's apartment on Central Park West. The time was usually late evening, and his arrival would sometimes wake them up at 2:00 A.M. They always let him stay there for the night and, on occasion, for days at a time. Julius was always gentle and kind with their young daughter Anastasia. Sometimes he came not to stay, but to borrow money, and he would never go away empty-handed.

The last time I saw Julius was in early December of 1989. He was back in Ithaca. By this time, I was the director (and founder) of the Digital Music program at Cornell. My ensemble and I had been reinstated, and we gave concerts with the department's blessing. Professor Sokol was now Music Department chairman. I was working late one evening when he came into my studio. He asked me to check on Julius, who was in one of the basement practice rooms. He wanted to make sure that everything was OK, considering Julius's past behavior, which could be unpredictable. I went downstairs and found him playing on one of the new upright pianos. He was smoking. I had never known him to smoke before. He had put the cigarette on the wood panel, just below the lowest bass note. It was beginning to burn the wood. I said nothing about it. It was also against university policy to smoke in the building. I kept my cool, and asked him how he was, what he was doing, and so on. I eventually talked him into going someplace to get something to eat and drink, and left him off at his mother's house on Plain Street. Five months later he was dead.

From 1985 to 1989 he had managed to alienate those who loved him most: his brother, his mother, his lovers, and his closest friends. I think it was hardest on his mother, because sometimes he behaved cruelly to her, when he was at his weakest. But she never stopped loving him, and always gave him a place to stay, as long as she was there to keep tabs on him. No one knows what he did from January to May 1990. we can only speculate about whatever took its toll on him. Being a genius, and knowing it, must be both fulfilling and frustrating, because who else can you confide in, and think that the other person fully understands you? And, let's face it, there is racism in our society that I, as a white person, cannot possibly understand, but have seen all around me. Plus, being openly gay is still a problem for so many straight people in our society. "Don't ask, don't tell?" How stupid is that? Julius could do almost anything connected to music, dance, and theater, both as composer and performer. He was also deeply articulate. In the end, he just couldn't put it all together. He couldn't find a home. He had to somehow give up on his feeling of supreme confidence. Maybe, at the end, he was teaching himself humility on his own terms.

Notes

1. Performing Artservices, a nonprofit organization, produces, presents, and facilitates the work of artists working in contemporary forms of music, theater, and dance.

CHAPTER THREE

THE JULIUS EASTMAN PARABLES

R. Nemo Hill

With perfect sincerity and a suitable amount of head wagging, a musician acquaintance of mine, reflecting on the death of Julius Eastman, lamented: "What a waste of talent." At the time I found the remark so astonishingly beside the truly tragic point that I could scarcely speak. The very idea of tallying the talent, and then separating it from the life and the death, seemed nothing short of blasphemous. And yet I was soon to hear that sentiment echoed over and over again in one form or another: a *waste* of talent, an *abuse* of talent, a *persecution* of talent—the permutations were endless, whether the thief was conceived of as an internal or an external one. But where in all this lamentation and accusation was the sense of marvel at a talent and a life so perfectly and maddeningly attuned; so deliberately and defiantly crafted? Where was the respect that this man, who so fearlessly controlled his own surrender to his own fate, demanded of us with such infuriating consistency? *What a burden of talent*—that seemed the more fitting lamentation. Indeed, in the relatively short but intense period during which I knew Julius, he seemed more than anything else intent on shedding that burden of talent—and not out of laziness or irresponsibility, and not out of plain orneriness (although it may have seemed that way to many of us at the time)—but in order to test it, subjecting it to a series of alchemical tortures in order to purify its coin of all counterfeit, ultimately dragging what was left of the gold in it all the way from hallowed halls to mean streets, for one final trial.

Perhaps it is not absolutely necessary for someone listening to a performance of Julius Eastman's *If You're So Smart, Why Aren't You Rich?* to know that he chose to spend one autumn afternoon at the men's shelter on East Third Street in downtown Manhattan giving pedicures to some of the residents there—not under the auspices of any particular organization, mind you, but on his own highly eccentric initiative—and with, I would not be at all surprised, no more than a pair of kitchen scissors. For those interested in the "profit" of the music alone, such an activity might seem one of talent's unfortunate detours. But to anyone unwilling to compartmentalize that talent, to anyone taking the broader view of just what it means to "practice one's instrument," such acts, touched as they are with both humility and arrogance, tend to take on the weight of religious parable. Julius took a highly dramatic view of his own life, often casting himself in a sometimes Luciferian, sometimes Messianic light, which gave many of the outlandish situations by means of which he managed to martyr himself a profoundly theatrical quality.

Aha—! No sooner do I debunk the claptrap of one myth of the artist, than I set to work mythmaking on another. Guilty as charged. But surely we owe it to our understanding of any individual artist to at least view his or her life through the myth that they constructed for themselves, rather than to impose others' outworn mythic templates upon them. Myths of talent, moreover, needn't be divorced from or at war with reality, needn't be a sanitization of the regrettably messy details of a life, needn't be reduced to an absurd balance sheet of profits and losses. Perhaps it is not absolutely necessary for someone listening to a recording of Julius Eastman's *The Holy Presence of Joan d'Arc* to know that the original score for those ten cellos was among the papers and clothes that lay in a filthy heap on the floor of a closet from which I scraped who-knows-how-many months of dried cat shit, when cleaning and painting his apartment on East Sixth Street. Nor that this original score was among the articles that were, a year or so later, stuffed unceremoniously into black plastic trash bags and hauled curbside by duty-bound city marshals. Yet I contend that cat shit and eviction were, and always will be, as integral a part of that *Holy Presence* as the ten bows that dragged this divinely infernal music out of those ten growling and wailing cellos, under the stern directives of a talent in which nothing whatsoever was wasted.

One thing was apparent to all who knew Julius, whether casually or intimately, whether professionally or (like myself) personally—his attitude toward authority was utterly uncompromising. Indeed, it was through his often harshly dogmatic claims of adherence to a kind of "higher authority" that one constantly slammed up against, both theoretically and practically, the stunning arrogance of his particular brand of humility. One thing is certain: this higher authority was by no means merely an artistic one, certainly not in the narrow sense in which artistic calling has come to be interpreted in our age of increasingly efficient commerce. Thus the "make-it-easy-on-yourself" agenda, as exemplified by advantageous career moves, held little or no power over him.

I did not know Julius in his youth—he was fifteen years my senior. I met him in The Bar on East Fourth Street and Second Avenue shortly before he celebrated his fortieth birthday in 1980. The first exposure I had to his career as an artist was visual rather than musical: an afternoon open house he held at his apartment in order to raise some quick cash by selling (at thrift store prices) a series of epigrammatic illustrations he had rendered in pastel and crayon. Whether, as some have claimed, a series of professional disappointments or betrayals had by then hardened his attitude toward so-called success, I am thus unqualified to say. I only know that his deeply held beliefs about such mundane matters immediately impressed me as passionately self-imposed rather than externally inflicted, more of a head-on cocksure collision with (rather than a reaction to) adverse circumstances.

And no detail was too small to elicit the symbolic act of resistance; no taboo was too tiny to be broken. A rehearsal room complete with tuned piano at the Third Street Music School Settlement, a great resource, was eventually barred to him, due to the fact that he simply refused to lock the door, despite repeatedly well-intentioned warnings. Likewise, he refused to lock the door to his own apartment, which resulted in the theft of what little I owned at that time, a theft perpetrated by a homeless man who had been offered, now and again, the rare gift of no-strings-attached sanctuary. For Julius, the often disastrous practical consequences of such unorthodox behavior were but minor irritations that had to be dealt with—and not, as they are for less disciplined souls like the rest of us poor mortals, the projected fears that keep us in line with social norms. If circumstances seemed to offer no mercy to him, I posit that this was because he flatly refused the mercy of mere circumstances—choosing instead the delayed gratification of a sort of mercy more ultimate in nature—one that ordinary circumstantial luxuries are entirely impotent to impart. Faced with the loss of a piano to practice and compose upon, his reaction was one of defiantly dismissive adaptation. "I can compose music sitting down on the sidewalk on Second Avenue," he drawled, in a tone of voice that might have seemed boasting in anyone else, but that, when followed by one of his unrestrained howls of laughter and that Holy Roller stomping of his black engineer boots, seemed simply an admission of the strange fact of his power over those petty inconveniences of a life in poverty, which, to paraphrase Rilke from one of his letters, afflict only those who allow themselves to be distracted from vaster concerns.[1]

Such attitudes seem far more brutal, of course, and less defensible, when their consequences are felt by others who had not bargained for such harsh life lessons. The gatekeepers of the Third Street Music School Settlement judiciously retrieved the key to their practice room before any material damage could be done. In the meantime, confronted by the wholly avoidable theft of a precious portable typewriter, the very last thing that I, a twenty-five-year-old writer, wanted to hear was a flippant "What are you whining about? Some people have nothing. You call yourself a writer? Then go get yourself a pencil and paper."

"Incorrigible prick," I must have muttered to myself, or something to that effect.

And yet I stuck around.

I stuck around, yes. And though I did soon learn to protect myself from an increasingly dire quest not necessarily my own, and though I eventually did lose touch with Julius in the years preceding his death, I am still in a way sticking around even after all these years—still haunted. The day to day with Julius, well, that could not last long. Saddled as I was by a petulantly introverted temperament, I was unable to withstand the constant petty public penury, the virulent arguments, the frustrated emotional expectations, and serially unreasonable demands. As exalted as my foray into mythmaking may here appear, this was no mythic picnic. No one, I think, could make the case that Julius's psyche was a smoothly running, well-oiled machine. Pathology rather than passivity is really the whole point.

I found my own apartment eventually, several buildings down the street, and moved on with my own life. After his inevitable eviction, I adopted one of his many displaced cats when it fled across the roofs and fire escapes of East Sixth Street, and wandered in through my open window. Yet my attempts to accommodate Julius, a stray himself by now, were ultimately a failure. At the time it seemed to me that he deliberately sabotaged such attempts. Callow youth that I was, even then I was beginning to understand that I would never become adept at the peculiarly heroic form of surrender that he himself was so painfully mastering.

Right from the beginning there *was* this dynamic of master and disciple. The difference in our ages made such a tension inevitable, I suppose. And yet Julius's archetypal take on situations, as well as his exalted view of his own mission, often led him to cast himself in a role that went far beyond the patterns of paternal affection that tend to develop between an older and a younger man. Like all other aspects of his life, the *master/disciple* drama was one he insisted on enacting without restraint, turning its tension upside down and inside out, and then stripping it bare so as to miss none of its ramifications. Restraint would have been capitulation to societal tomfoolery, would have cramped transcendence. On one end of the spectrum, the *teacher/student* end, there was his annoying habit of christening me *Ananda* to his *Buddha*, a notion that embarrassed me no end, and that I disabused him of as vociferously as possible. On the other end of the spectrum was the more provocative and harder to resist *master/slave* paradigm. I suppose I should defend myself in advance against charges of gratuitous salaciousness that may well be leveled against me for my wide-openness in matters of deviant sexual conduct. Yet, with all due apologies to the offended modesty of more reticent friends or family members, there seems to me to be no honest way to gloss over the details of such blatant transgressions against prescribed codes of behavior, without doing harm to the core of Julius's uncompromising legacy. The very first night I found myself in Julius's apartment he proffered me his boot—holding it up between us as if it were a sacred object of some sort—to which each of us in turn applied lips and tongue, meeting sometimes at the toe, sometimes at the heel. My willingness to submit so soon to such a brazen ritual (and to disclose its details in this context) speaks volumes about the sort of trust that I placed in Julius's boldness right from the start. And Julius was constantly inventing new forms of submission, both for himself and others—and not just privately, but publicly as well. Ask any of those good citizens appalled at Northwestern University in 1980 by the scandalous titles (*Evil Nigger*, *Crazy Nigger*), which he insisted they submit to if they wanted to hear his music. Far from superficial theatrical sensationalism, the antics of this *Gay Guerrilla* were highly deliberate choices, often made at great cost to his own comfort and well-being. Right from the get-go I knew the stakes of this game would be high. The errors would be monstrous. The rewards unimaginable.

And so it is that many of the experiences I shared with Julius take on, in retrospect, such a parable-like quality that I am stunned at times to find that I am living out their merciless lessons even now; stunned to find that these experiences, preserved intact in memory, come more and more to resemble works of art themselves—so uncanny is their ability to bear witness to the trail blazed by one highly individual man in his prodigious passage through time and the world—despite the fact that time and the world seem (perhaps until now) to have paid him little heed, and to have lost all track of him. What's more, I know that I am not alone in this feeling: so many of those who knew Julius, even peripherally, were so affected by him that he can be conjured in heart and mind by the recollection of one vivid instant.

The crucial question remains as to whether such "personality problems" (as they have been referred to in print) were the symptoms of some sort of psychological delusion that interfered with what might otherwise have proved a smooth artistic trajectory. Sounds rational enough. And yet to wrench the work out of the personality that gave birth to it still seems to me the unkindest blow of all. Likewise, protestations of a hostile environment, either racial or otherwise, while undeniable in their own right, seem to beg the question of the use to which Julius put every aspect of every dilemma. What such dislocations of man-from-work or man-from-environment do not take into account is the essentially *religious* nature of the program Julius set for himself, and thus the use to which he put the various givens of his very existence. None of us can choose *who* we are, but we are certainly given some say over *what* we become once we stop whining over what we cannot control and get down to business—to "that which is fundamental," as he himself expressed it. That what Julius became is viewed with such a mixture of pity and horror by so many people, says much about how heroism is defined in the current cultural and spiritual milieu from which he struggled to carve out some transcendent meaning for his life. Instinctually devout, with an eclectic scriptural playbook, I am not sure whether Julius was literally familiar with San Juan de la Cruz's "dark night of the soul," but he was certainly fond of quoting (and at the darnedest moments) one of his favorite maxims of the prophet Mohammed: "Die before you die."

In a largely secular society such as our own—one beset increasingly since Julius's death by the sort of religious fanaticism that in theory threatens its very foundations—it is perhaps unpopular and dangerous to defend the sort of religious pathology that I think holds the key to understanding Julius Eastman's life and work. And yet it is perhaps only the proverbial Madness of the Saints that can account for the combination of Quixotic drive and fanatical iconoclasm with which he battled both inner and outer demons. Fanaticism is dangerous, to be sure—every crusader is a terrorist on some level—and the notion of an artist as a religious fanatic seems more medieval than modern. And yet, it was a practitioner of the very modern art of filmmaking, Andrey Tarkovsky, who avowed that the aim of art is to harrow the soul for death.[2] There is no denying the awe, grudging or otherwise, that Julius's fundamentalist challenges to the surface of the contemporary quotidian engendered in others. His categorical refusal to play by any rules he suspected of even the slightest infraction of his core principles, his refusal to obey any authority other than that which he had identified *in his own conscience* as the Law—this program was carried out with all the solemnity of a full-blown heresy against prevailing doctrine. If that meant throwing the money changers out of the temple, so be it. If that meant throwing dirt onto the keys of a venerable institution's piano before playing it, perhaps destroying it in the process, perhaps being thrown out oneself as a result, so be it. The distinction between act of courage and act of madness was immaterial. Such a standard of judgment was no longer applicable. This superimposition of such a lack of restraint and such a severity of etiquette is one of the central paradoxes of Julius Eastman's life and work. This is the pathological opera of the religious life played out in its starkest form.

Sometime in 1981, I believe in the cold winter months, Julius took me up to the bathroom of the 125th Street subway station, and while we were about to engage in a sexual escapade with several other men parked in a line at the urinals, a policeman entered and threatened us with arrest. I was scared stiff and immediately tried to dart out through the doorway. And I might even have escaped in the confusion—had not Julius, blithely ignoring the cop, howled out in his best booming baritone—"Wheeeere the hell do you think you're going? Get back in here and face it like a man!" So irreparably diminished was the supposed authority of this officer of the law by such a combination of fearlessness and fearsomeness, that we escaped with nothing more than a reprimand. After a few drinks at a local gay bar, however, Julius insisted that we return to the scene of the crime, where we resumed what had been interrupted, albeit with a different set of partners. Telling and retelling this story in the years that followed, I was convinced that what made it so memorable was the colorful detail that I had, as a coda, performed fellatio on a man who was holding a large birdcage with two parakeets in it. But as the years have passed, and I have had time to reflect upon it, it is that battle between the law and true authority—as well as my somewhat cowardly position as the catalyst for the moral of the tale—that have reverberated most powerfully for me. Having called upon the saints for succor, whether onstage or at the urinal, this fortress was well nigh impregnable.

The New York City of the early 1980s was, of course, a far more sympathetic stage for the performance of such gleefully sociopathic *coups de théâtre*, be they devotional, demented, or just frivolous in nature. I shudder to think of what might have become of Julius in present-day New York—transformed as it has been, by an easily justifiable paranoia, into a more tightly controlled cityscape in which any threat to stability and order is dealt with as criminal, as the political or viral barbarian at the gates. There seemed to be a tacit tolerance on the streets of the city in those days, a space allocated on the margins of the metropolis for the violence of experimentation so necessary to a thriving avant-garde. Those days are long gone, and far too many to count are the players who, having once graced its cracked and tilted stages, have left the now renovated theater for good—by any one of a number of exits. Perhaps it is this sociocultural whitewashing that so impels me to defend not just those portions of the JE oeuvre that are concert hall worthy, but also those other parts that are less so—those cantankerous biographical details that seem intent on clashing with and undermining the rest: those that frustrate, those that contaminate and corrupt, even those that cut short. Thus I cleave firmly to the alchemical dictum of the *putrefactio*, insisting that "our gold is not the common gold" and that its value is to be measured more by the green or the rust upon it, by the imperfections within it, those we work with and through, than by any ultimate outward luster.[3] The degradation of the mystical goldsmith, a commonplace enough trope from the romance of the fairy tale to the exotic lore of the bodhisattva, is perhaps less palatable when made more palpable by that strange but brilliant man right there on your doorstep or on the crooked street where you live.

That a rose may arise from the dung heap is the grandest of all paradoxes, and as such not so difficult to embrace in the abstract. But other less exalted paradoxes are piling up here, the many sharp thorns of that rose, the unpleasant odor of that miraculous fertilizer, a host of minor irritations whose pearls are harder to locate and identify—the bothersome burden of the oxymoron that is a human life. There is that arrogant humility. That wide-open closed-mindedness. That mastery of submission. That heretical fundamentalism. That pious depravity. That ostentatiously selfless egomania. Not to mention that almost obsequious deference, which could morph so unexpectedly into unreasonable defiance. For the fact remains that Julius Eastman was just . . . well . . . just impossible. Exasperating. A royal pain in the ass. Oh, it could be consummately entertaining, if you were in the mood for it, to watch him taste-testing their food straight out of the can before offering any of it to his herd of cats. The anthology of such mock-shocking anecdotes is a thick tome for anyone who spent an appreciable amount of time with Julius. But there were other, more grievous impossibilities, as well. Having lost touch with a by-then homeless Julius, I am in no position to judge the veracity of various grueling rumors that have surfaced here and there regarding his behavior as he reached what proved to be the end of his tether—rumors of drug addiction, crack cocaine, that sort of thing. I do, unfortunately, have it firsthand from a close mutual friend of ours that this man-of-highest-principle, after being graciously offered a free meal in a local East Village restaurant, took the opportunity of his host's use of the toilet to swipe from the table the money left to pay both bill and tip—before vanishing out the door. Far be it from me to make excuses for such a crude insult, but the sort of morals drawn from what appear to be the final stages of such an exemplary pageant of degradation cannot be the same as those drawn from the slow and steady stream of bourgeois life. Certain abominations simply come with the territory. One of the last things I remember Julius saying to me, after an interval in which I did not see him for some months, was in response to the simple query, "How are you?" "I think I have suffered enough," he said clearly, shaking his head calmly from side to side, "I don't think I can suffer anymore."

And yet, even through the occluding clouds of this vexing degradation, there shine forth (with a clarity almost equally as vexing) these recollected parables; from out of the distress of the awful chaos of situations are shot these razor-sharp arrows of revelatory light. Why is it that I recall most acutely not my feeling of disdain, when one summer morning I discovered Julius brushing his teeth with Comet—because "it whitens and brightens"—but rather my own pathetically comical outrage that he had somehow ruined my toothbrush, my precious toothbrush.

When we were still living together at 314 East Sixth Street, Julius returned home one summer day in visible pain, scarcely able to lie down on our bed without assistance. When I asked him what was wrong, he told me that he had been enjoying the afternoon of bright sunshine on East Third Street, a block that at the time was pretty much dominated by a local chapter of the Hells Angels, who had purchased their own building there. He had spent this idle afternoon with a homeless acquaintance, a man whose name I think I remember as Jamie (to give society's chronically anonymous their due). I had never been particularly fond of Jamie, probably due to the inconveniences his sporadic presence caused me at home, where the door was never locked, and the privacy I often craved was in short supply. Apparently they had been drinking a bit, and Jamie had become somewhat aggressive with several of the bikers on the block. Despite their desire for him to leave, and despite Julius's attempts to persuade him to withdraw, Jamie had unwisely become more and more confrontational—until the bikers, presumably never too far from spoiling for a fight, finally attacked him physically. The precise details of the situation were not forthcoming, but no doubt the general air of machismo at work would not hold up well in any court of law. The problem was, for Julius, that he could not abandon his friend to his fortune, despite the no doubt objectionable behavior with which he had courted its slings and arrows and fisticuffs. Julius, lean and mean, though mostly lean, was compelled by his own code to defend his imprudent companion, even though dangerously outmatched physically by the violence thus unleashed upon him. No doubt he gave Jamie a haughty tongue-lashing on the way home, and I don't recall his ever seeing him again. At the time, my reaction was one of concern for his health, for what was most likely a broken rib or two—but also one of anger, anger that he repeatedly allowed himself to get into these situations from which there was no painless escape. Yet now, in the razor-sharp light of recollection, that escape route really isn't the point of the parable—is it?

On the title page of an abandoned draft of Julius's Eastman's *The Faithful Friend: The Lover Friend's One For The Beloved: Symphony II*, in hand-lettered script, is inscribed the following:

Parable

> On Tuesday, Main and Chestnut at 19 o'clock, the Faithful Friend and his Beloved Friend decided to meet. On Monday the day before, Christ came, just as it was foretold. Some went up on the right, and some went down on the left. Trumpets did sound (a little sharp), and electric violins did play (a little flat). A most terrible sound. And in the twinkling of an eye the earth vanished and was no more.
>
> But on Tuesday the day after on Main and Chestnut at 19 o'clock, there stood the Lover Friend and his Beloved Friend, just as they had planned, embracing one another.

I am sitting here, as I write this, in the very same apartment on East Sixth Street that I moved into in 1981, when I vacated my cramped quarters with Julius down the block, the same apartment beneath whose desk this rolled-up unfinished symphony has been safely tucked away for the past eighteen years. The wall opposite my bed still bears traces of the hole punched through it when, in the heat of one of our final arguments, I pushed Julius across the room in a rage and then tossed him, holy books and all, down the stairs of the building. The doorsill may still bears traces of his body as well, less legible traces, traces of that night I came home, with my present boyfriend, to find Julius curled up in the hall at the top of the stairs—a night of melancholy rather than rage, that winter night that I escorted him down and out, and somehow found the inhuman strength within myself to send him off into the cold and the dark. Carefully decorating the title page of *Symphony II*, just above the parable of the two friends, the Faithful and the Beloved, are the following words, the same words that Julius chanted as he stomped off to their rhythm into the heavily falling snow: "Hail Mary full of grace, blessed are you among women, and blessed is the fruit of your womb, Jesus."

One might have wished that Julius could have found for himself a more Buddhistic middle way, rather than the awful majesty of that crown of thorns that, as goddammed fucking fate would have it, fit him like a glove. One might have wished for him that the text engraved in his very bones had been not *The Imitation of Christ*, but something more along the lines of *The Imitation of Chuang-Tzu*. And yet, to pity him?—that would seem an insult to a man of such strength, and I cannot find it in my heart to do so. Rather I shall exalt, and exult. And meet him, of course, as he ordained with characteristically exasperating prescience, for one more heartfelt *Hosanna!* of-the-lowest-in-the-highest, here, on this page, at the corner of Chestnut and Main.

19 o'clock, May 9, 2009—New York City

Notes

1. "What can who wants a great deal say of this wanting without betraying it and becoming a boaster? Here every word involves a false note and an affront to what it means. One can only say that one comes more and more to protect this wanting which goes toward deep and important things, that one longs more and more sincerely and wholeheartedly to give it all one's strength and all one's love and to experience worries through it and not through the little harassing accidents of which life in poverty is full." Rainer Maria Rilke, "Letter of June 25, 1902," in *Letters: 1892–1910*, trans. Jane Bannard Greene and M. D. Herder (New York: Norton, 1940).

2. "The aim of art is to prepare a person for death, to plough and harrow his soul, rendering it capable of turning to good." Andrey Tarkovsky, *Sculpting In Time*, trans. Kitty Hunter-Blair (New York:. Knopf, 1986), 43.

3. "Our gold is not the common gold. But thou hast inquired concerning the greenness, deeming the bronze to be a leprous body on account of the greenness it hath upon it. Therefore I say unto thee that whatever is perfect in the bronze is that greenness only, because that greenness is straightaway changed by our magistery into our most true gold." Zadith Senior (Mohammed ibn Umail), translator unknown, tenth-century alchemical treatise.

CHAPTER FOUR

JULIUS EASTMAN AND THE CONCEPTION OF "ORGANIC MUSIC"

Kyle Gann

The astonishing thing about Julius Eastman, for those of us who knew him, is that his music rose from the dead. When he died, in May 1990 at the age of only forty-nine, no one in the music world knew about it for eight months. His friends had lost touch with him. He hadn't performed for years. The rumor was that he had been evicted from his Manhattan apartment and was living in Tompkins Square Park, his possessions scattered to the winds. I forget who mentioned to me they heard he'd died, but I researched and confirmed it, and wrote his obituary for the January 22, 1991, *Village Voice*. When I called to tell his friends, some were skeptical, because rumors of his death had circulated before.

Those of us who loved Eastman's music despaired that we would never hear it again. But thanks to the miracle of modern musicology, his music is back, recorded, and being played, and he has a place in history.

Eastman was a wiry, gay, African-American man with a sepulchral voice incommensurate with his slim figure. A phenomenal pianist and singer, he attended Ithaca College and the Curtis Institute, and was discovered in 1968 by Lukas Foss, who recruited him for the Creative Associates at the University at Buffalo. There was an amazing avant-garde energy in the Buffalo music scene at the time, coalesced around Foss, Morton Feldman, Petr Kotik, and others.

The first that most people outside of this scene heard of Eastman was through his electric 1973 recording of *Eight Songs for a Mad King* by British composer Peter Maxwell Davies, in which Eastman sang the part of King George III descending into dementia. Eastman was on his way to becoming an underground legend. I first saw him in 1974, when he and Kotik, a flutist and composer, played at Oberlin (where I was a student) as the S.E.M. Ensemble. Kotik played slow, randomized melodies on the flute, with Eastman singing a perfect fifth below, using long, mesmerizingly repetitive texts of Gertrude Stein. (Years later, Kotik told me that he started playing parallel fifths with Eastman to keep him in tune, and decided he liked the sound.) I was enchanted, but it was too much for a couple of my music student peers, who tried to disrupt the concert by banging on the doors from outside.

In 1975 I saw Eastman again, at the first June in Buffalo festival, a subsequently annual event directed by the inimitable Morton Feldman. John Cage, Christian Wolff, and Earle Brown were the invited composers. Eastman participated in a performance of Cage's anarchic theater piece *Song Books*, and, in the realization of a direction to "Give a lecture," presented a lecture about sex, during which he undressed a young man he had brought onstage, and tried unsuccessfully to undress a young woman. The next morning, people there saw Cage furious for the only time in their lives, as he banged his fist on the piano and stormed, "the freedom in my music does not mean the freedom to be irresponsible!"

It is a sign of how far Eastman's reputation has boomeranged since he died in complete obscurity, that recently two students of mine, born after Eastman's death, regaled me with the notorious story of this crazy Julius Eastman character who undressed a young man onstage during a performance of Cage's *Song Books*. I let them finish, and then said, "Yeah, I was there."

Scandal followed Eastman around, but not always because he was irresponsible. My next contact with him was in January of 1980, when my teacher Peter Gena brought him to Northwestern University, where he performed a concert of his music with the school's new music ensemble. There was an uproar on campus about the titles of the pieces: *Evil Nigger*, *Crazy Nigger*, and *Gay Guerrilla*. The acceptable compromise Gena and Eastman finally made, was to not print the titles in the program. When Eastman came onstage, however, he gave a wise, calm speech about his pieces that made his seeming outrageousness a noble part of his advocacy for African-American and gay causes. The concert of his high-energy multiple piano works was phenomenally powerful. I participated in a performance of one of them later that year, at the New Music America festival in Minneapolis.

From that point, I didn't see Eastman again for several years. In 1981 he toured with Meredith Monk, singing in her production of *Dolmen Music*. Foss conducted his music with the Brooklyn Philharmonia. The 1981 New Music America festival featured Eastman's *The Holy Presence of Joan d'Arc*. The Creative Associates toured his *Stay On It* in Europe. Always in search of financial security, and somehow torpedoing it when he found it, he set his goals on teaching jobs. For a while he became an assistant professor of music at the University at Buffalo, and conducted and directed the Brooklyn Philharmonia's Community Concert Series, but he was not good at organization or paperwork. In 1983 a hoped-for job at Cornell University failed to materialize, and his life started falling apart. He drank heavily and smoked crack. He took a job at Tower Records in New York, hired by Paul Tai (who would later run New World Records, the label that has released Eastman's music on CD), but one day he just disappeared. The sheriff kicked him out of his Manhattan apartment at Sixth Street and Second Avenue, and confiscated his belongings, his scores doubtless included. He did end up living, at least part of the time, in Tompkins Square Park.

Nevertheless, I saw Eastman one more time, around 1989, standing in line for a concert at the Brooklyn Academy of Music. He looked good, we spoke briefly, and I started hoping that I would be able to write about his music soon in the *Village Voice*. The next thing I knew, months later, he had died alone, in a hospital in Buffalo, officially of cardiac arrest—brought on possibly by insomnia, tuberculosis, dehydration, starvation, exhaustion, or depression. (The suspected culprit, denied by the family, was AIDS.)

After his death, more than a decade went by in which Eastman existed only in the memories of his friends. Before leaving Northwestern, I had made a tape of *Evil Nigger* and *Gay Guerrilla*, and I carried that music with me. In 2004 I played them on an Internet radio station I had started—possibly the first time since Joseph Kubera's performance of *Piano 2* in Merkin Concert Hall in 1991, that Eastman's music had been heard publicly since his death. In 2006 I directed a student group in an electric guitar ensemble version of *Gay Guerrilla*. Since then, performances of his music are becoming less and less rare. He has found his niche in history.

That niche was initially placed in the minimalist world of the late 1970s, whose epicenter was Downtown Manhattan, but Eastman was never content with being only a card-carrying minimalist. At the time, his music seemed an exciting and eccentric part of what was going on, but looking back today, his pieces sound particularly distinctive, as though he had not only absorbed minimalism, but could see into its future. His *Stay On It* of 1973 used repetition and additive process in a way that Steve Reich and

Philip Glass had made familiar, but it may have been the first minimalist piece to appropriate pop rhythms and harmonies. Its repetitions of a syncopated cadence were not so much for the purpose of minimalist process, but rather as a kind of framing device to create both unity and surprise, and to allow improvisation—which, in 1973, the avant-garde music world had not yet started warming up to. It is amazing to think that at that time Glass had not yet written *Music in Twelve Parts* nor Reich *Music for Eighteen Musicians*. Minimalism was still in its austere, two-dimensional phase, conceptual and concerned with abstract pattern, but in one step Eastman started mixing genres and forecasting techniques that would be tried in postminimalism fifteen years hence.

The three works Eastman was touring in 1979–80, which I heard at Northwestern, were intended for any group of identical instruments with up to eighteen players, but they are so dependent on fast repeated notes that there are really only a few potential instruments that could work—pianos, guitars, mallet percussion, and strings. He explained at the time that they were written in an attempt to create a paradigm that he called "organic music": "That is to say, the third part of any part has to contain all of the information of the first two parts, and then go on from there. . . . They're not exactly perfect yet. There's an attempt to make every section contain all the information of the previous sections, or else, taking out information at a gradual and logical rate."[1] It's not quite literally true, and Eastman relies on a little more dramatic contrast than he allows to here, but in general, each section of each piece repeats what was in the previous section, adding one more element. This in itself was a concept familiar to the minimalists, but what Eastman did with it went beyond minimalism altogether. *Evil Nigger*, *Crazy Nigger*, and *Gay Guerrilla* each start out repeating a single pitch, and for quite awhile the pieces sound statically tonal in a familiar minimalist way. But as Eastman keeps organically adding in new pitches, they crescendo in density to the point that they sometimes have all twelve pitches being played at once, and even the same tonal melody being played in all twelve keys at once, an unprecented idea at the time—and I don't know an example of anyone else doing anything similar since.

Eastman's last "organic music" pieces we know of are his *Prelude to Joan d'Arc* and *The Holy Presence of Joan d'Arc* (1981), consisting of a long, meditative vocal introduction (*Prelude*) followed by an "organic" continuum for cellos. In his introduction, Eastman calls the work:

> a reminder to those who think they can destroy liberators by acts of treachery, malice, and murder. . . . Like all organizations, especially

> governments and religious organizations, they oppress in order to perpetuate themselves. Their methods of oppression are legion. But when they find that their more subtle methods are failing, they resort to murder. Even now in my own country, my own people, my own time, gross oppression and murder still continue.[2]

The *Prelude* shows off Eastman's commanding vocal prowess with a recitative that proceeds minimalistically adding phrases wherein a litany of saints exhort the Maid of Orleans, "Joan, speak boldly, when they question you." The piece for cellos opens with a vigorous ostinato, to which dissonant melodies are added one after another until we hear a dissonant continuum in which we can hardly distinguish the elements—and yet that simple, rhythmic ostinato keeps going in the background, keeping the music focused. It is remarkable the extent to which Eastman could build a gradual continuum between utter simplicity and cacophony; it is the key to his distinctive aesthetic. The use of dissonance in a minimalist context would return among other composers as part of the totalist movement of the late 1980s and 1990s, but not with the kind of accumulating transcendence that is so unexpected in Eastman's best works.

Sadly, no score survives for *The Holy Presence of Joan d'Arc*; we have only the recording. Eastman's scores are peculiarly and loosely notated (something he had in common with other Downtown Manhattan composers of the time, such as Rhys Chatham and Glenn Branca); without the recordings as guides, it would be very difficult to figure out what he intended. An intriguing-looking *Symphony No. II* survives: can we put it together? Will it be heard posthumously? That remains to be seen. It is enough of a miracle that Julius Eastman's music, which we spent years thinking of as tragically lost, is now back in the repertoire, an exciting highlight to our total picture of late twentieth-century music.

Notes

1. Julius Eastman, spoken introduction to the Northwestern concert, *Unjust Malaise*, New World Records CD 80638, 2005.

2. This is from the text that was printed in The Kitchen program of April 1–5, 1981, for the premiere of *The Holy Presence of Joan d'Arc*.

CHAPTER FIVE

JULIUS EASTMAN SINGING

John Patrick Thomas

The last time I saw Julius Eastman was in London. He was touring in 1974 with the Creative Associates from the State University of New York at Buffalo; they performed in the Queen Elizabeth Hall on the South Bank, and Julius was playing the piano in Morton Feldman's *For Frank O'Hara*. That was just one of his activities. The ensemble also had a piece by Julius, *Stay On It*, in their repertory for the tour. Julius seemed fine. He was then thirty-four years old.

Julius's name came up more recently, now many years later, in Essen, Germany, when my colleague at the Folkwang University of the Arts, Patricia Martin, loaned me the multi-CD recording of Julius's music that she had just received.[1] She had played one of the pianos in the famous 1980 performance of his music at Northwestern University in Chicago. To hear the music on the CDs (as well as the spoken defense of his work that is included) is to wonder at his mastery as a composer, singer, and articulate polemicist.

It is sometimes said that certain artists lack discipline. Julius Eastman was often accused of that. Nonetheless, he had enough discipline to develop his abilities to a professional level in several areas: as a pianist, dancer, singer, and composer. Of course, the task of organizing these various talents is always difficult for anyone with such gifts. Being black and gay cannot have made things easier for him, but it may have given him the impetus of anger, fear, and defiance that he needed to pursue such a range of ambitions. I think I should mention, as well, the love he had for so many things, and his humor. If he was provocative, it was because he lived in a prejudiced and repressive time, place, and society, where art can be trivialized, black people cruelly discriminated against, and gays censored, not for what they do, but for who they are.

I am primarily concerned here with Julius's work as a singer. Singing for him, of course, was simply another area where he excelled. He was not a tall person—physically he was rather spindly—but in singing he seemed to spread out. His voice was big; he had an enormous vocal and expressive range, and as his career developed he never held back or played safe (the same could be said for his life). He was, finally, both generous and dangerous as a performing artist, willing to make whatever sound was necessary for the moment and for the piece.

Being intelligent can be inhibiting for some singers, but Julius's impressive intelligence never caused him to censor himself in his work, or to resist The Impulse. He seemed, by nature, empowered to do the right thing as a performing artist on the stage, even though some of his choices were controversial. This decisiveness made him a compelling singer, and especially interesting for composers and for music theater. It must be said that such a range of intensity is difficult for some artists to sustain. In a recording of R. Murray Schafer's *Requiems for the Party Girl* (available only in the archives of the Center for the Creative and Performing Arts at the University at Buffalo [UB] Music Library), one can hear Julius's voice in the course of this more than twenty-minute piece—which requires a vocal range from a tenor low D to a soprano high B♭—begin to tire somewhat, but the recording is from a performance that no doubt followed a series of strenuous rehearsals. For the most part, I believe Julius Eastman's vocal technique was more than sufficient to realize his intentions.

A composer himself, he had a quick understanding of whatever vocal music he encountered. He was a twentieth-century kind of artist, made for, and well-equipped to deal with, the many challenges inherent in the music of our time. This spontaneous kind of musical understanding was something he had in common with Lukas Foss, one of the founders and a mentor of the Creative Associates program at UB. I think it made Foss particularly sympathetic toward Julius Eastman. I remember Foss saying that as a composer/performer, he tried to perform music he had written as if it were by someone else, and to approach music by other people as if it were his own. Julius also tended to appropriate the music he performed.

Julius had a certain reluctance, even resistance sometimes, to practicing and rehearsals, as if he thought such situations were more necessary for "other people" than for him. He tended to be most interested in, and perform best, pieces that engaged him as a composer (or that invited his provocateur's impulses). He was not as interested in things less compelling or less relevant to his own work. He permitted himself the luxury of choosing what he would devote himself to and what things he would deal with in a passing manner, if not with outright resistance (his encounter with Hans Werner Henze's *El Cimarrón*, for instance).

Of Julius Eastman's vocal training, I know very little; I have heard he never had voice lessons as such. I understand he sang as a boy (which suggests that he kept singing to some extent during puberty, which accounts for the impressive "falsetto" vocal register he retained, a situation common to many countertenors). Julius came out of a high school music program in Ithaca, New York, where the vocal work was both constructive and supportive. That kind of background gave an instinctive artist like Julius an advantage, in that it shielded him from the clichés of much so-called classical voice training. It freed and equipped his vocal instrument to respond to, and to realize, almost any kind of vocal intention, his own or that of others—provided it interested him. In any case, the initial development of his voice (at school and in choirs where he did solo work) was essentially healthy. Julius had the technical means by the late 1960s to take on a wide range of extremely difficult vocal works: the *El Cimarrón* project in Buffalo and, more important, Peter Maxwell Davies's *Eight Songs for a Mad King*, to mention only two examples.

Julius, of course, had a natural talent as a singer. Some people are born and grow up being able to do it. Regardless of what other problems may be involved, such singers come through the identity crises and physical changes of puberty and adolescence with a sense of their singing voice intact. They accept who they are, the person they have become, love what they can do, and get on with it. They are wonderful to teach, and exciting performers. Julius was that kind of singer: vocally he knew who he was.

Natural singers can go a long way and do remarkable work—for a while. The problem for them is that the life of a professional singer is very difficult. You can sing any old way for a certain period of time, but if you have professional intentions, you need to know what you are doing, how, and why, in order to maintain your voice and sustain a career. Professional singers have to rescue themselves daily from the stress and strain of the profession, and of their everyday lives, in order to appear on the stage in optimal condition. They need to find their way—via healthy exercises, yoga, meditation, good diets, good hours, good partners, good friends, additional good teaching, good coaching, or whatever else works for them—to a state that will allow them to do their best work when they show up for a rehearsal, walk onstage to perform, or go into a studio to record. This requires some sacrifices, some degree of renunciation, and choices to be made. That was difficult for Julius, whose own interests were so broad. But I think it is also important to remember that he grew up situated between two poles in America: on one hand prejudice, and on the other hand, privileges arranged by the majority white culture and distributed, formally and informally, to selected members of minority groups—a clear example of mixed signals and a recipe for inner conflict.

If you listen to the body of recorded material that documents Julius Eastman's singing, many things become apparent. For example, on the CDs devoted to his work, there is a piece of his called *Prelude to The Holy Presence of Joan d'Arc* (1981), for solo baritone, which Julius sings himself. It is an eleven-minute aria without accompaniment, a particularly naked demonstration of his work. The text consists of a series of repeated and varied admonitions to the saint ("speak boldly," etc.), sung to a repeating series of pitches, which range over two octaves, gradually extending downward to a low bass E♭. The recording itself was made privately, on short notice, in his tiny apartment, so the glossy perfection of an edited studio production is missing. Nonetheless, the brilliance of his instrument, his musicality, and the conviction he brought to almost all his interpretations, are obvious. The voice is perhaps a bit on the "singerly" side, which suggests—if it is true, as is said, that he never had serious vocal training—he at least paid attention to models who were "classically" trained; Julius seemed to admire that kind of vocal resonance and color. Then again, his speaking voice (also present on the above-mentioned recording) was also extraordinarily resonant; he was the rare example of a person whose singing voice was closely related to the timbre of his speaking voice; his singing had qualities naturally that other singers spend years to acquire.

Julius's work as a speaker and reciter can be heard (again, in the archives of the UB Music Library) in Frederic Rzewski's *Coming Together*, as performed on October 20, 1974. This work had profound significance for Julius as a person: it deals with the racially charged uprising at the Attica prison in upstate New York in 1971, in which twenty-nine prisoners and ten hostages were killed after the state police were called in. Attica was a facility in which 54 percent of the total prison population was black, whereas all the guards were white (no evidence exists, however, to indicate that the prisoners were in any way responsible for the death of the hostages). Julius's reading of a letter from Sam Melville, an antiwar activist and convicted bomber, who was one of the inmates killed during the police attack, has a remarkable intensity. You hear in Julius's recitation, in his speaking voice, the same color and resonance characteristic of his singing voice. It is a performance never forgotten by those who heard it. Rzewski's work, with its additive structures, may also have had an important influence on Julius's later development as a composer.

The best-known recording of Julius Eastman's singing currently on the market is, of course, his performance of *Eight Songs for a Mad King* (music by Maxwell Davies, text by the Australian writer Randolph Stowe).[2] Written for the actor/singer Roy Hart in 1969, the work has always been a tour de force. When Julius was first asked to undertake the piece—as Hart had withdrawn from the project—he was uncertain; many advised him, however, that it could be a rare professional opportunity. Julius's agreement to learn this extremely difficult and unusual piece was one of his best decisions.

The vocal writing in *Eight Songs for a Mad King* is based on the teachings of a German voice teacher, Alfred Wolfsohn, who advocated a close connection between singing and psychology (he will be recognized by some as the Amadeus Daberlohn figure in *Life? Or Theater?* a series of artworks by the tragic Charlotte Salomon, regarded by some as the Anne Frank of the graphic arts). Hart had discovered Wolfsohn in 1947 in London after the war; his charismatic influence caused Hart to abandon his promising acting career to spend some thirteen years devoted completely to studies with Wolfsohn. This teacher believed that the normal human voice should encompass eight octaves, that singing should have the fundamental imperative of a baby crying, and that it should emerge from the deepest parts of a singer's psyche—much the way many actors seek to function. Hart worked to achieve that. In the 1960s, he sent a demonstration tape to six composers (among them Maxwell Davies, Karlheinz Stockhausen, and Henze) introducing the vocal work he had evolved through his studies with Wolfsohn. The rest is history.

In 1970, *Eight Songs for a Mad King* marked the beginning of Julius's engagement with "extended vocal techniques," an experience that made him aware of a much broader range of vocal expression. In this work, the conventional aesthetic borders between singing and all the other capabilities of the human voice are essentially erased or crossed over. Crying, speaking, screaming, the overtone resources of the voice, vocal multiphonics, register extremities—all these sounds, both expressive and abstracted as pure sound or noise, became available to Julius Eastman as material both for performance and for composition. The work called into play extensive use of Julius's high, so-called *falsetto* (the *whistle* register for women), a perfectly natural high register of the male vocal instrument. *Eight Songs for a Mad King* employs all these resources in an extremely expressionistic and parodistic manner, and Julius rose to the occasion, as if he had been waiting since the moment of his birth for this complete engagement of his talents. From the opening crash and screams, Julius Eastman embodies the full range of the character, George III, as the disintegrating monarch sings fragments of period songs, bewails his fate and crumbling sanity, and tries to train his pet canary (represented by the flute) to repeat particular musical phrases. The vocal part extends over five octaves and requires the most extreme and subtle resources of an exceptionally talented singer/actor. Several recordings have been made of this work since 1970. Julius, in his recording, is said to "sing" the role to a greater extent than do the later performers, but his dramatic intensity is nonetheless impressive. It is, however, a typically cruel irony in Julius's career that this recording of his spectacular performance includes biographies of everyone involved—except Julius Eastman, an inexplicable editorial omission.

Other examples of Julius Eastman's singing are available, as mentioned before, in the archive recordings at the Music Library of UB. Julius can be heard there performing works by an enormous range of distinguished composers; among them Pauline Oliveros (*Crow*), David Del Tredici (*Night Conjure-Verse*—for countertenor), Luis de Pablo (*Berceuse*), Henze (*El Cimarrón*), and Schafer (*Requiems for the Party Girl*—an extreme performance, both in range and character, not least because the solo role was conceived for a female mezzo-soprano and not for a black countertenor in drag).

When I moved to Europe in 1971, I lost contact with Julius. Later, I heard troubling news: the controversial performance of John Cage's *Song Books* at the June in Buffalo festival in 1975; the erratic choir job in New Jersey; drugs and alcohol; and so on, and so forth. In America, in our increasingly commercial and marketed age, it is not enough to be an artist doing an artist's work. Most have to have a "second job" or major promotional skills, since there is pressure for everything in life to be run as a business, for the artist to produce whatever is fashionable at the moment, and to generate significant capital through this work for publishers, recording companies, performing institutions, and so on. I fear Julius was as little interested in business and marketing as he was in the mechanics of choral conducting or institutional teaching (it should be noted that his methods as a teacher were unorthodox, but he was very popular with students during the period he was an assistant professor in the Music Department at UB, 1971–75).

Julius did have exceptional opportunities, which he deserved, and of which he took advantage to the extent he was able. Nonetheless, one worry

I have is that perhaps the extent of Julius's abilities was, for whatever reason, beyond what he himself really believed he was capable of doing. Or, I worry that Julius knew all too well what he had in him, and suffered that the world offered insufficient place and understanding for what he had to offer. These problems tend to exist in a pendulum situation, where the person concerned swings between feelings of great competence and deep feelings of inadequacy. If the reasons for doing things, the hopes and expectations, are too loaded, nothing that happens can ever be enough. I also worry that he may have had the problems many gifted people acquire: being praised, but, because it is so easy, not understanding why; being criticized, but not knowing what else to do. In the end, sometimes, a vision simply has no alternatives. And Julius was a visionary.

I cannot fully know the pressures he lived under and suffered as an avant-garde artist who was gay and black. I know some of these pressures intellectually, some I feel in my heart, but I cannot know such things as I would if I had experienced this combination of problems on the front line, all the time, as he did. Julius Eastman was born living at the edge of several frontiers, where life is sometimes wild and raw; he sang the way he lived his life. When I think of him now, I have a lingering anxiety that many artists must have: a fear that the Gods of Art can desert us. I think of Julius, so brilliant and so gifted, lost and helpless in the Big City, where you have to "make it" no matter what. As I was remembering Julius recently and listening to his music, I was reminded of lines from Constantine Cavafy's great poem "The Gods Abandon Anthony":

> . . . listen with emotion, but not
> with entreaties and complaints of the coward,
> as a last enjoyment listen to the sounds.[3]

Notes

1. Julius Eastman, *Unjust Malaise*, New World Records CD 80638, 2005.

2. Peter Maxwell Davies, *Eight Songs for a Mad King*, The Fires of London, Julius Eastman, baritone, Peter Maxwell Davies conducting, Unicorn-Kanchana CD DKP 9052.

3. Constantine Cavafy, *The Complete Poems of Cavafy*, trans. Rae Dalven (New York: Harcourt, Brace and World, 1961).

CHAPTER SIX

AN ACCIDENTAL MUSICOLOGIST PASSES THE TORCH

Mary Jane Leach

It all began in 1998, when I tried to find *The Holy Presence of Joan d'Arc* (*Joan*), a piece for ten cellos, by Julius Eastman. What started off as a simple search for one composition, gradually broadened into a search for all of Eastman's music, one that continues to this day. Initially I didn't think of this as performing musicological research—I was just trying to find pieces by a composer whose music I liked. As the years have passed, though, what I once considered to be a simple search fueled by stubbornness, has turned out to be an important act of musicology—recovering music once thought hopelessly lost.

I met Eastman in early 1981. We were both hired to be vocalists in a theater piece by Jim Neu, for which Hugh Levick was writing the music.[1] At the first rehearsal, at 10 A.M., Eastman breezed in, dressed in black leather and chains, drinking scotch! That was my introduction to the outrageousness of Julius Eastman. Soon after this meeting, I attended the premiere of *Joan*, at The Kitchen in New York.[2] Its energy and sound left a big impression on me.

In the fall of 1998, I was asked to teach a course in composition at the California Institute of the Arts (Cal Arts), for "real" instruments (i.e., acoustic instruments), since many of its courses focused on electronic and computer music. I thought an interesting approach would be to focus on music written for multiples—pieces composed for four or more of the same instrument—as a concentrated way for students to absorb the character and sound qualities of each instrument. One piece that I wanted to include was Eastman's *Joan*.

Shortly after trying to find a recording of *Joan*, I learned that composer Lois V Vierk had a tape of it, but when she went to make a copy for me, she found the cassette box empty, the cassette left in some unknown tape machine. This was the first of many obstacles that I was to encounter while trying to find Eastman's music. Vierk put me in touch with C. Bryan Rulon, who had originally given her the copy of *Joan*, made from a cassette that Eastman had given him. While Rulon was making a copy for me, we talked about Eastman's music and life, and that was when I learned that much of his music had been lost.[3]

I now had a tape of *Joan*, but I wanted to have the score as well, since it would be very useful for the students to see it. Pieces for multiples are much more complicated aurally than they appear to be on the page, due to the many sound phenomena (combination, difference, and interference tones) that are created—sounds that are heard, but not notated or played. Also, because of the uniformity of sound, it is difficult to differentiate who is playing what. For these reasons, being able to see a score is very helpful. The recording had been made for a radio broadcast, and it had spoken credits naming the performers and sound engineer at the end of the tape.[4] I reasoned that if the engineer, Steve Cellum, had the master tape, I would have a good chance of finding the score. I had worked on recordings with Cellum in the past, and knew that he is meticulous, always including an annotated score with the master tape, as well as noting other pertinent information. He did have the master, but there was no score. And no details, other than the title and tape speed. I should have interpreted this out of character sloppiness as an omen of similar inconsistencies and difficulties to come, while trying to locate Eastman's music.

Without the spoken credits, I never would have been able to track down all of the performers, as everyone involved had slightly different memories of who had played on the recording, when (not even the year), and where it was recorded. These cellists were the only people I have ever contacted about Eastman who didn't have strong impressions or colorful anecdotes about him. It had been a fly-by-night recording with freelance musicians, and most only had contact with him for the few hours that it took to record the piece. Ironically, they were fairly easy to locate. I found all of them and heard back from nine, which is remarkable, since so much time had passed from the time of the recording. But still, no one had the score.

Example 6.1. First system of *The Holy Presence of Joan d'Arc*. Reproduced by permission from the Estate of Julius Eastman.

I also contacted the cellists from The Kitchen performance, but none of them had the score, either. To date I haven't been able to find it, even though it has been performed by three different sets of performers.[5] All I have is a fragment of the first page of the score, which was printed on the cover of the program notes for its premiere.[6]

By the time I finished teaching the course at Cal Arts, I had come to realize that if much more time passed, Eastman's music would be even more difficult to find than it had already proven to be. I decided to recontact people, to see if they had any scores or recordings of his other pieces, or information about where I could find them. I hoped to find at least enough of his music to be able to release a CD. Perhaps I was being too optimistic, but in the fall of 1999, I approached New World Records about putting out a CD of Eastman's music, and they jumped at the chance, as he was a composer whom they were already very interested in.

Thus, I began what turned out to be a quixotic search for the music of Julius Eastman that culminated in 2005, with the first commercial release of his compositions.[7] I began a series of what I came to regard as a vicious circle of phone calls and letters. One person would direct me to another, who would then direct me to another, until at some point I would be referred back to the original person I had contacted, a cycle that could take a year or more (this was before e-mail, the Web, and Google were ubiquitous). Most people didn't have anything to contribute, except for a lot of interesting anecdotes. I soon became the "expert." People would tell me, "You should contact Kyle Gann" (or Renée Levine Packer, or a number of other people who had known Eastman), who, in the meantime, would be directing people to me. It was not only frustrating, but shocking, to see how quickly the work of a composer who had been such a vital member of the artistic community could disappear, falling through the cracks of communal memory.

People's memories were unreliable. Eastman had given a concert for voice and keyboard at Experimental Intermedia Foundation in 1976,[8] and although Phill Niblock, its director, swore that this was before he started to record concerts, Warren Burt had a tape of the concert. When I got a copy, though, it was very disappointing: the electronic keyboard that Eastman played had a cheesy sound, and his voice sounded as if it had been miked from a distance. I had hoped to have an example of him singing and playing piano at the same time, but this was unusable. Still, it was an example of having a recording where none was thought to exist, and that was encouraging.

Along the way, I would occasionally locate someone who did have a recording or a score, but in many cases it was either not easily accessible or it took some coaxing (to say nothing of patience) to obtain. I was confident that tapes were out there, but locating and obtaining them was proving to be more difficult than I had anticipated.

Months passed, sometimes even years, and some of the people who had tapes or scores were either unable or unwilling to look for them and send them along. Eventually, I got a complete score for the solo piano piece, *Piano 2*, from Nurit Tilles, and shortly afterward, a concert recording of it from Joseph Kubera.[9]

While Eastman had been a member of the Creative Associates at the University at Buffalo, many of their concerts were recorded.[10] Negotiations with the Music Library to listen to some of these recordings, and then later to use them for the CD, went on for a considerable period of time, complete with changing policies and decision makers. Finally, in June 2003, they sent me almost three hours of archival recordings on cassettes (their archive was not digitized at that time).[11]

At this point I had recordings of: *Joan*, a solo voice piece (*Prelude to The Holy Presence of Joan d'Arc*), some solo piano pieces (*Piano 2* and *Piano Pieces I–IV*), and a few ensemble pieces (notably, *Stay On It* and *If You're So Smart, Why Aren't You Rich?*).[12] What I really wanted, though, to complete the artistic picture and make a well-rounded CD (we expected it to be a two-CD set), was one or all of Eastman's three major pieces for multiple pianos: *Crazy Nigger*, *Evil Nigger*, and *Gay Guerrilla*. Kyle Gann had promised to send me copies of two out of three of them (*Evil Nigger* and *Gay Guerrilla*), from a concert that he had attended, in which Eastman had participated. Several years passed and I hadn't received any tapes from Gann. Meanwhile, I was making contingency plans. Even if I got the tapes, what if they were unusable, or we couldn't get permission to use the recordings? I had contacted Peter Gena in the fall of 1999, having learned that he had the scores to all three pieces.[13] In the best-case scenario, I was hoping to synchronize concert performances of those pieces with the CD release. In the worst case, we would be able to record the pieces if no usable recordings were found, although I preferred to have performances that Eastman had not only coached but also performed in. Only after the CD was released did Gena send the scores on to other people, who in turn sent them on to me. I then scanned them and posted them on a website that I set up for Eastman's music, and they have been performed regularly since then.[14]

When I finally got the tapes from Gann in June 2004, I was relieved to hear not only that they were good pieces but also that the performances were excellent, and the recordings were "clean"—they sounded more like studio recordings than concert recordings. It turned out that they were from a concert at Northwestern University.[15] New World had recently released *Music from the ONCE Festival 1961–1966,*[16] using archival tapes from Northwestern, so they had a working relationship with the university that made getting permission to use the tapes a lot easier than it might have been otherwise.

All of the recordings that I had located were on reel-to-reel tapes and had to be baked—a process that needs to be done in order for the emulsion to be reattached to the tape—before being able to play them. No one was sure whether the third piece, *Crazy Nigger*, was in the Northwestern archives. A technician there had started to play one of the tapes to see what was on it, which almost gave me a heart attack when I heard about it, as I had visions of the emulsion building up on the tape heads, and the recording being destroyed, which happens if you don't bake the tapes first. So it was an incredible relief in December 2004, when the tapes were duly baked and digitally transferred, to discover that all three pieces were there, that the recording quality was uniformly high, and that *Crazy Nigger* was fifty-five minutes! All of a sudden there was enough material for a well-balanced three-CD set.

I realized that I had been feeling anxious about the recordings, when I dreamed that I found several brown garbage bags full of Eastman's old musty clothes. After laundering them, I put one of his white shirts into my cassette deck and it played perfectly, which seemed perfectly logical in my dream state. This didn't seem any more illogical than some inexplicable occurrences that happened while wide awake. The e-mails in my folder of correspondence about the project ("Eastman") could not be opened or moved. I started another folder ("Eastman #2"). Those e-mails could not be opened or moved. I started a third ("Julius"). Those e-mails could not be opened or moved. These were the only folders and e-mails in my e-mail program with which I have ever had a problem. I began to wonder if Eastman's spirit was trying to sabotage the dissemination of his music.

After seven years of searching, a three-CD set of music by one of our most gifted contemporary composers was released. When I started trying to find Eastman's music, I only knew one piece well, *Joan*, so the high artistic quality of his other pieces was satisfying. The CD release turned out not to be the final step, though, but the beginning of a process of discovering and rediscovering his music that continues to this day.

Musicologists frequently encounter stumbling blocks when trying to research a composer or find complete manuscripts. War and fire are culprits, as with the music of Renaissance composer Heinrich Finck, much of whose music was lost in the World War II bombing of Dresden. Or unfriendly governments interfere—as in Franco's Spain, where access was denied to its archives of early music for many years. With Eastman, even though so much of his music was lost, much of it due to his own carelessness and indifference, a surprising amount has survived or has been able to be reconstructed. Where there are no manuscripts, but only recordings, performers who worked with Eastman are able to answer questions and guide new performances, as is the situation when there are scores but no recordings. Best of all, are pieces that have both scores and recordings (or, better yet, multiple recordings).[17]

With the assistance of some of Eastman's former colleagues and the enthusiasm of young musicologists, writers, and performers, his music is now being played all over the world. Students in colleges and universities are organizing performances of his music and analyzing and writing papers about it. Thankfully, most of the attention is being paid to his music, instead of his flamboyant life, as fascinating as it was. Serious musicological research is being conducted by Luciano Chessa, Ryan Dohoney, Andrew Hanson-Dvoracek, and Matthew Mendez, who have all contributed essays to this book. It has been gratifying to have so much activity and attention paid to Eastman and his music, when, just a few years ago, he was only a faint memory or an amusing anecdote.

Notes

Portions of this chapter originally appeared in Mary Jane Leach, "In Search of Julius Eastman," *NewMusicBox*, November 8, 2005, http://www.newmusicbox.org/articles/In-Search-of-Julius-Eastman/, and are reproduced with permission.

1. *Oneosaph*, written by Hugh Levick and Jim Neu, performed by Levick, and directed by Neu. Presented at The Performing Garage, 33 Wooster Street, New York, NY, May 28–31, 1981.

2. Andy de Groat choreographed his dance piece *Gravy* to *Joan*, April 1–5, 1981, at The Kitchen, 484 Broome Street (mailing address 59 Wooster Street), New York, NY.

3. Julius Eastman died in 1990. In his final years his life spiraled out of control, to the point that he was occasionally living in Tompkins Square Park in Alphabet City in New York's East Village. His possessions, including music scores and recordings, had been dumped onto the street by the city sheriff, when he was evicted from his apartment at 314 East Sixth Street, New York City for not paying his rent. The exact date of Eastman's eviction is unknown, but in a November 18, 2014, e-mail correspondence, R. Nemo Hill, Eastman's lover from that time (see ch. 3), surmises that it was either in late 1981 or 1982. Eastman made no effort to recover any of his music. Various friends, though, upon hearing about this, tried to salvage as much of his music as they could, but very little was saved.

4. This radio program, which was recorded in the auditorium of the Third Street Music School Settlement, was one of three radio programs on new composers that the Creative Music Foundation produced. From e-mail correspondence with Steve Cellum, April 28, 2014.

5. *Joan* has been performed April 1–5, 1981, at The Kitchen in New York City; recorded for radio broadcast at the Third Street Music School Settlement in New York City (date unknown); and performed June 8, 1981, at New Music America 1981, in San Francisco.

6. Two pages (which include this score fragment) of *Joan* have recently turned up at the Performing Arts Research Collections–Music Library at Lincoln Center. They had been in an exibit, "Contemporary American Composers: Photography by Gene Bagnatto," in the New York Public Library's Performing Arts Research Center in spring 1982, were never reclaimed by Eastman, and subsequently deposited in the library's archives.

7. Julius Eastman, *Unjust Malaise*, New World Records CD 80638, 2005. Pieces on the three-CD set are: *Stay On It*; *If You're So Smart, Why Aren't You Rich?*; *Prelude to The Holy Presence of Joan d'Arc*; *The Holy Presence of Joan d'Arc*; *Gay Guerrilla*; *Evil Nigger*; *Crazy Nigger*; and Julius Eastman's spoken introduction to the 1980 Northwestern University concert.

8. December 15, 1976, at Experimental Intermedia Foundation, New York City.

9. Nurit Tilles and Edmund Niemann perform as the piano duo Double Edge. Eastman was a friend, and at times frequent visitor, of Niemann and his wife, Donna (see ch. 2). Joseph Kubera was a Creative Associate at UB from 1974 to 1976. He and Eastman continued to perform together once they both lived in New York City. *Piano 2* has now been released on: Joseph Kubera, *Book of Horizons*, New World Records CD 80745, 2014.

10. Eastman was a member of the Creative Associates at UB from 1969 to 1975 (see ch. 1). See also Renée Levine Packer, *This Life of Sounds* (New York: Oxford University Press, 2010).

11. Due, in part, to the use of two of its archival recordings in the release of *Unjust Malaise*, the UB Music Library realized the importance of their collection and the need to digitize its aging recordings. Patricia Donovan, "UB Music Library to Digitize Influential Collections of New Music," December 3, 2007, http://www.buffalo.edu/news/releases/2007/12/9008.html.

12. *Prelude to The Holy Presence of Joan d'Arc* was included in the radio program with *Joan*, as well as a spoken introduction (which was printed in the program notes for The Kitchen concert). *Piano Pieces I–IV* are in the UB Music Library archive. *Stay On It* and *If You're So Smart, Why Aren't You Rich?* are also in the UB Music Library archive.

13. Peter Gena, who had been a Creative Associate graduate fellow at UB while Eastman was there, was teaching at Northwestern in 1980. He produced the January 16, 1980, concert of Eastman's three multipiano pieces, whose recordings

appear on *Unjust Malaise*. Fortunately, he was given copies of all three pieces performed in the concert, which are the only copies of them found to date.

14. Many performers have accessed this website for Eastman's scores, accessed November 25, 2014, http://www.mjleach.com/EastmanScores.htm.

15. January 16, 1980, in Pick-Staiger Concert Hall, at Northwestern University, Evanston, IL.

16. *Music from the ONCE Festival 1961–1966*, New World Records CD 80567, 2003.

17. There are multiple performances of *Stay On It* in the UB music library archives, as well as a video recording from a Creative Associates concert on February 16, 1974, in Glasgow, Scotland. A two-piano version of *Crazy Nigger* was recorded from the February 8–9, 1980, performances at The Kitchen. A performance of *Gay Guerrilla* was recorded in October 1980, in Berlin as part of The Kitchen's European tour, in which Eastman participated.

CHAPTER SEVEN

A FLEXIBLE MUSICAL IDENTITY

Julius Eastman in New York City, 1976–90

Ryan Dohoney

In a press release announcing a performance at The Kitchen in 1981, Julius Eastman provided a succinct autobiography:

> I have sung, played, and written music for a very long time, and the end is not in sight. I sang as a boy soprano and I still sing as a boy soprano 30 years later. I have played the old masters on the pianoforte and have appreciated their help and guidance. But now music is only one of my attributes. I could be a Dancer, Choreographer, Painter or any other kind of artist if I so wished; but right thought, speech and action are now my main concerns. No other thing is as important or as useful. Right thought, Right Speech, Right action, Right music.[1]

Eastman's self-assessment evinces a broad engagement with creative and expressive culture as he practiced it up to that point in his life. Eastman's autobiography speaks to a widely distributed and multiply directed aesthetic practice, one that explored networks of thought, speech, and action cutting across genres, styles, and communities. Nowhere is this more evident than in Eastman's time in New York's downtown scene in the years 1976–90.[2]

Two examples from his performing repertoire in the 1970s demonstrate this plurality. Eastman had, in the early 1970s, become the chief performer of Peter Maxwell Davies's theater piece *Eight Songs for a Mad King*, through performances with the Creative Associates and his recording with Maxwell Davies's ensemble the Fires of London.[3] This piece remained Eastman's claim to fame throughout the 1970s, and he sang it with other ensembles, including the Brooklyn Philharmonia under the direction of Lukas Foss, and the New York Philharmonic under Pierre Boulez. Yet at the same time, Eastman could also be heard singing avant-garde disco at The Kitchen. His recording with the group Dinosaur L, a loose dance music collective organized by composer-performer-producer Arthur Russell, extended the reach of Eastman's voice beyond high culture institutions to downtown's mostly gay dance clubs. Within Dinosaur L, Eastman's keyboard work was a powerful force, holding down the groove, as well as inflecting the songs with out-there improvisations on record. Eastman's voice, though, with its multi-octave range and expressive resonance, was his strongest contribution to Dinosaur L's music. Pushed into the front of the mix on remixes of the tracks "In the Corn Belt" and "Go Bang," Eastman's voice resonated in the cavernous discotheques of Manhattan such as the Paradise Garage and the Loft, as much as it was heard in the genteel trappings of Lincoln Center.

The aesthetic gulf separating the late-modernist theatricality of Maxwell Davies and the libidinal excess of Dinosaur L's mutant disco, may at first seem insurmountable. Stylistically, they have little to do with one another. However, what they do have in common is the voice of Julius Eastman. In this essay, I compose an account of the so-called downtown scene from forgotten performances, outrageous improvisations, and intimate collaborations all marked by the voice of Julius Eastman. My focus on Eastman and his collaborators gives a view on life in downtown New York City that accounts for a wider variety of social groups than has been included in narratives of its history.[4] In particular, Eastman shows how experimental music, the radical black tradition, and post-Stonewall gay sexuality were components in a cultural assemblage that is today usually celebrated for the creativity of mostly white punk rock, the minimalism of Philip Glass and Steve Reich, and the performance art of Laurie Anderson and Robert Wilson.

By recovering the voice of Julius Eastman, we can understand the multiplicity of associations that sustained vibrant musical communities in New York City, from the emergence of the gay liberation and black power movements in the 1960s, to the devastation of the AIDS epidemic in the 1980s.[5] Eastman's communities performed a complex cultural shift in American musical life—the reworking of a high art/low art dichotomy acted out in an urban landscape marked by racial, ethnic, sexual, and political concerns.

This reworking was lived as the transformation of a state-funded high-modernism into a do-it-yourself scene hybridizing pop, improvisation, and experimental performance that has had, and continues to have, direct effects on musical lives in the twenty-first century. With the composer Mary Jane Leach having made a strong case for Julius Eastman as a composer through her collection of Eastman's recordings, I want to argue for Eastman's importance as a performer and nodal point for his varied communities in New York City's music scenes.

Downtown New York City was a primary geographical site of Eastman's musical practice from 1976, and this scene has, since the early 2000s, become a focus of music and cultural studies. As described by curators and scholars such as Marvin J. Taylor, Bernard Gendron, and Kyle Gann, the geographical area of Manhattan below Fourteenth Street was, from the late 1960s to the early 1980s, a teeming artists' colony.[6] Low rents and expansive lofts provided space for performances and studios, and the concentrated physical proximity of numerous artists working in distinct media provided unparalleled opportunities for collaboration. The musical genres and modes of performance fostered in the downtown scene include loft jazz, various types of musical performance art, disco, new wave, no wave, punk rock, experimental music of many kinds, and various fusions of all of the above. Important venues hosting this plethora of styles included experimental arts venues such as The Kitchen, Environ, and Experimental Intermedia Foundation. Dance clubs were also important sites and among them were venues such as The Loft, Paradise Garage, the Mudd Club, and Danceteria; there were also punk and new wave clubs such as CBGB and Max's Kansas City. Another key arts presenter, the Brooklyn Academy of Music, could be considered downtown's outpost across the East River.

Beginning with sociologist Samuel Gilmore in the 1980s, downtown has been contrasted with other sociocultural locations in New York City—the midtown of Lincoln Center, the Juilliard School, and Carnegie Hall, and the academic uptown of Columbia University, the Manhattan School of Music, and the Columbia-Princeton Electronic Music Center.[7] More recent writers, like Taylor and Gann, have strongly delineated the aesthetic and structural distinctions between downtown, midtown, and uptown—perhaps more than is necessary. Eastman's movement among these various sites troubles such firm demarcations, and also demonstrates how the diminishment of academic, philanthropic, and governmental funding sources for modernist and experimental music in the 1970s required practitioners to adapt modes of production and collectivity from pop and jazz to ensure their continued viability. Eastman's development of his musical networks in downtown culture gives a sense of how support systems changed and institutional hierarchies transformed, as well as what the personal costs were for those who wanted to live musically.

Five episodes in Eastman's life exemplify the varied communities in which he participated along with the mutability of his musical identity: first, Eastman's role in the experimental classical scene and the turn toward extended vocal techniques and theatrical performance; second, his role in the Brooklyn Philhamonia's Community Concert Series; third, his improvisational practice of melding experimental forms of sexuality with his improvisational practice; fourth, his borrowings from punk rock as a way of rethinking racial politics in the downtown scene; and, finally, Eastman's collaborations with composer-producer Arthur Russell, which served as a model for the coexistence of human and musical difference. Throughout what follows, I will also describe Eastman's performance aesthetic, one that was, as he described in the autobiography quoted above, concerned with "Right thought, Right Speech, Right action, Right music." This rightness was figured as a musical and political orientation inflected by his identity as a black gay man working in a mostly white, straight musical scene.[8] Even as I make an argument about the importance of Eastman to his collaborators, I also want to show how he held himself apart from them in important ways. As his friend Ned Sublette remarked to me in an interview, Eastman, "didn't run with anybody" and his participation in the downtown scene reflected an agonistic community whose tensions animated the aesthetic and human assemblies that formed within it.[9]

Eastman's first appearances as a professional musician in New York City began at the end of his Curtis days and continued sporadically until 1968, when he began working with the Creative Associates at the University at Buffalo. Eastman then began to perform regularly at major midtown venues.[10] His numerous concerts with the Creative Associates took place at Carnegie Recital Hall (now Weill Recital Hall) in a series called "Evenings for New Music." Like Cathy Berberian, with whom he shared a concert program in the early 1970s, Eastman was an important contributor to the vocal turn in late-modernist musical performance that began to treat human voices as dynamic, flexible instruments that allowed experimentation with timbre, resonance, and expression. Composer Ned Rorem remembers that Eastman was one of a handful of singers active in the 1970s "who could always do anything."[11]

This new vocal virtuosity was put to use in new forms of music theater that explored extended techniques, multimedia, and the radical juxtaposition of musical styles. Maxwell Davies's *Eight Songs for a Mad King* exemplifies these traits, especially with its campy lounge-music version of Handel's aria "Comfort Ye," extracted from *Messiah*, as well as the vocal multiphonics required of the singer. Eastman's performance aesthetic also drew from his interest in modernist gay theater, particularly the work of Jean Genet, whose play *The Blacks* he performed in while living in Buffalo.[12] In the early 1970s Eastman performed Hans Werner Henze's *El Cimarrón: The Diary of a Runaway Slave*, which marked his encounter with Marxist critiques of race that would affect his later sense of "right action." Explicit concern with sexuality and race marked his work as a performer, and became the basis for his compositional and improvisational aesthetic.

After leaving the Creative Associates and the S.E.M. Ensemble in 1975, Eastman relocated to New York.[13] The professional networks he had established in Buffalo ensured his continued presence in New York's musical life. Lukas Foss, who had left Buffalo to become music director of the Brooklyn Philharmonia, engaged him as a featured soloist and composer with the orchestra throughout the 1970s. On a more ad hoc basis, musicians and friends from Buffalo formed a collective that reassembled the experimental sensibility of the Creative Associates in the urban landscape of downtown. Musicians based around the performance and video venue The Kitchen became new collaborators. Eastman's status as a vocalist and his reputation as a performer preceded him, and he was actively sought out by other musicians as a hired gun. This was the case with Meredith Monk, who in an interview with me recalled:

> I knew I was going to be working on [the piece] *Dolmen Music*. I'm not sure if at the point that I met Julius that I knew the name of the piece. . . . Michael Byron and Rhys Chatham said if you want a bass, you've got to get Julius Eastman. I found out that he was doing a concert . . . at St. Mark's Church. . . . I loved him immediately . . . there was Julius in his leather vest and his keys hanging out of his jeans and his dreads. And I said, "I'm Meredith and I'm working on this piece, would you like to be in it?" and he said, "Oh, sure." You know Julius, "Of course, of course."[14]

The collaboration between Eastman and Monk resulted in the piece *Dolmen Music*, an important early ensemble composition for her, and one whose recording garnered much critical acclaim. Monk also recalled that Eastman gave her lessons in theory and counterpoint, and helped her hone her skills as a composer of large-scale works.

Eastman's work with Meredith Monk and Vocal Ensemble was only one of the many communities that he maintained in the late 1970s. His ties to Lukas Foss afforded him regular performances with the Brooklyn Philharmonia. Through Foss's support, he also became codirector of a new multicultural community initiative sponsored by the orchestra. Like many arts institutions in the 1970s, the Brooklyn Philharmonia, as it was then known, developed an outreach program featuring the music of non-white composers in hopes of building new audiences. Eastman, along with composer-conductor Tania León and composer Talib Hakim, organized a three-concert series for the 1977–78 season, performed in the then-predominantly black Brooklyn neighborhoods of Fort Greene, Bedford-Stuyvesant, and Boerum Hill. This Community Concert series, as it was called, was initially conceived as a series featuring only black composers, though it broadened its programming to "reach new audiences and feature the works of ethnic composers."[15] Consolidated Edison and Philip Morris provided seed funds that allowed the series to continue until the 1981–82 season, when it was merged with the Philharmonia's family concert series. Apart from his administrative duties, Eastman participated as conductor, pianist, vocalist, and featured composer in the series. His vocal performances on an early concert in the series were provocatively described as "weird incantatory chants" by critic Jon Ciner.[16]

The Community Concerts mobilized a long-established network of composers that had, since 1968, organized themselves as the Society of Black Composers.[17] Many of their members were featured on the concert series, including Hale Smith, Dorothy Rudd Moore, Omar Clay, Noel DaCosta, Carman Moore, Oliver Lake, and Arthur Cunningham. Writing soon after the society's organization, Carman Moore connected the aims of the group explicitly to the black radical tradition, noting especially the date of its formation. In one of his many articles for the *New York Times*, Moore stated that "suddenly the number of black American composers has become sizable, and, as testimony to this sudden blossoming (and certainly as an outgrowth of the Black Revolution), an organization called the Society of Black Composers was born in May, 1968."[18] Up to the time of the Community Concerts in the late 1970s, the society had mostly held its performances in venues in Harlem and Columbia University's McMillan Theater (now Miller Theater). Their increased presence in Brooklyn, with occasional Community Concerts at the East Village's Third Street Music School Settlement, shows a fluid mobility between uptown and downtown among other participants in New York musical life, one much less circumscribed by aesthetic divisions. Both the Community Concerts and the Society of Black Composers offer alternate models for thinking about the relationship between downtown and uptown that work against rigid distinctions. The Society of Black Composers' activities and the Community Concert series show a more flexible community less concerned with the discursive, stylistic, and geographical categories of white downtown musicians.

As evinced by his "weird incantatory chants" and vocal improvisations displayed on the Brooklyn Community Concerts, Eastman was an active improviser drawing on both experimental music and jazz for his unique vocal displays. It was through his improvisations that he forged a connection with the politics of a depathologized post-Stonewall gay sexuality. He had long improvised as a pianist while living in Buffalo, and played in a jazz combo with his brother Gerry Eastman, an accomplished bassist and guitarist. Eastman's chamber music compositions from the early 1970s, such as *Stay On It*, *Joy Boy*, and *Femenine*, have sections requiring extensive improvisation among the players or are structured improvisations with some given musical material. While he continued working with brother Gerry in New York, Eastman mostly performed solo vocal and keyboard improvisations in the jazz and experimental music venues in the city.[19]

In the fall of 1976, Eastman performed an evening-length improvisation titled "Praise God from Whom All Devils Grow" at the Environ (Loft) space in SoHo.[20] This performance's title is an example of Eastman's aesthetic of blending the sacred and profane. He twists the hymn title "Praise God from Whom All Blessings Flow" into something much more sinister, and reviews emphasized the more threatening aspects of his performance. Joseph Horowitz, a reviewer from the *New York Times*, reported "Eastman speaks of his music in terms of 'black forces'" and that his performance was "intense and astringent, often demonic."[21] His vocal improvisations also explicitly explored a transgressive gender-bending erotic sensibility. Part of the text Eastman improvised with was reported by Tom Johnson, former critic for the *Village Voice*: "Why don't you treat me like a real woman?" and "Open, open wider."[22] Johnson also compared Eastman to improvisers Cecil Taylor and Keith Jarrett, hearing similarities in their respective piano techniques.

The following December, Eastman performed another evening-length improvisation at composer Phill Niblock's Experimental Intermedia Foundation loft. That night, Eastman projected homemade Super 8 films simultaneously with his vocal and keyboard improvisations. This performance made explicit some of the more ambiguous erotic themes in the

Julius Eastman's childhood home, South Plains Street, Ithaca, New York. Photograph by Renée Levine Packer.

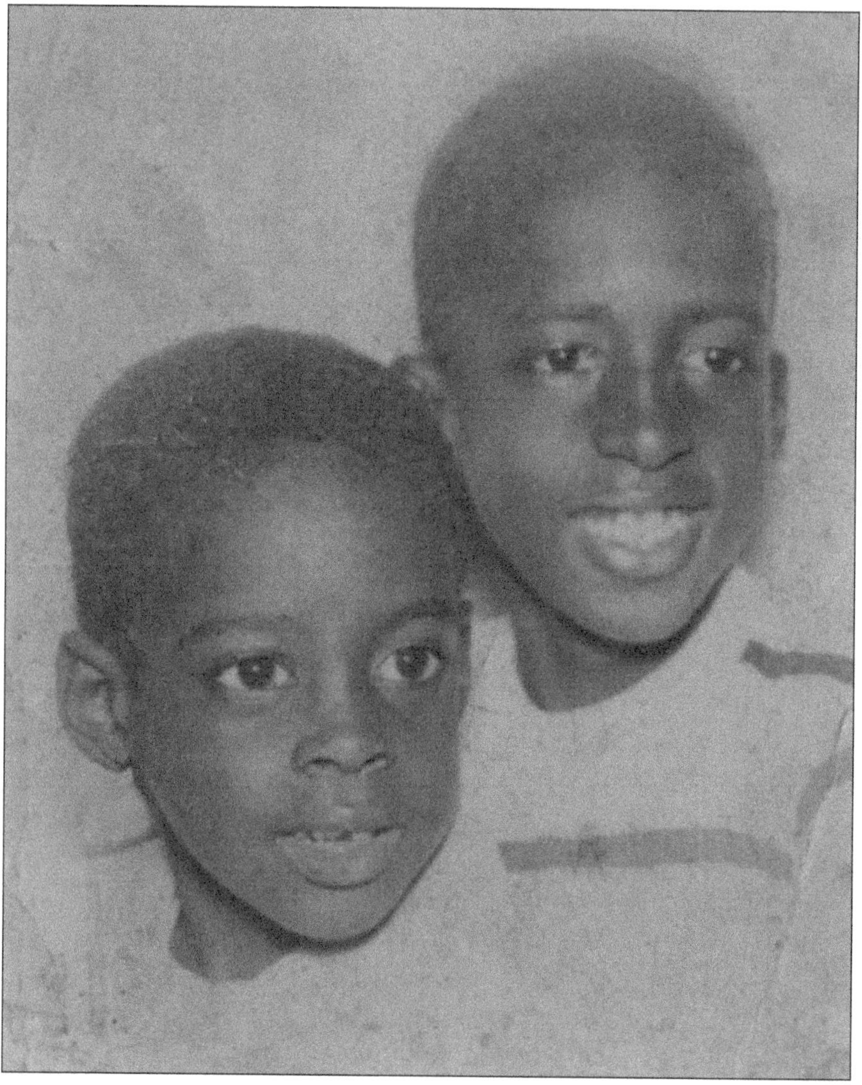

Gerald (Gerry) and Julius Eastman. Photographer unknown. Reproduced by permission of the Estate of Julius Eastman.

Julius Eastman in front of the Ezra Cornell statue on the Cornell University campus in Ithaca, New York. Photograph by D. W. Burkhardt.

From left to right: Frances Eastman, Janice Eastman, Gerry Eastman, and Julius Eastman. Photograph by D. W. Burkhardt.

Karl Singletary and Julius Eastman, spring 1973. Photographer unknown. Courtesy of Karl Singletary.

Julius Eastman and Lukas Foss, April 1972. Photographer unknown. Courtesy of the Music Library, University at Buffalo.

Julius Eastman performing his *Piano Pieces I-IV* at Albright-Knox Art Gallery, December 1968. Photographer unknown. Courtesy of the Music Library, University at Buffalo.

Julius Eastman performing Peter Maxwell Davies's *Eight Songs for a Mad King*, Artpark, 1975; also shown: Mark Sokol (violin) and Petr Kotik (flute). Photograph by Chris Rusiniak. Courtesy of the Music Library, University at Buffalo.

S.E.M. Ensemble 1971-72. *From left to right:* Julius Eastman, Roberto Laneri, Jan Williams, and Petr Kotik. Photograph by Jim Tuttle. Courtesy of the Music Library, University at Buffalo.

From left to right: Donald Burkhardt, Julius Eastman, James Fulkerson, Mary Fulkerson (with baby), Roberto Laneri, and unidentified friends, at 18 Plymouth Street, Buffalo, 1972. Photograph by D. W. Burkhardt.

Rehearsal of Morton Feldman's *Pianos and Voices*. Morton Feldman seated at piano; *from left to right:* Julius Eastman, Jan Williams, William Appleby, and David Del Tredici, Baird Hall, October, 1972. Photographer unknown. Courtesy of the Music Library, University at Buffalo.

Julius Eastman's Bird Avenue house, Buffalo. Photograph by Renée Levine Packer.

Creative Associates at Dartmouth College. *From left to right:* Morton Feldman, Dennis Kahle, Amrom Chodos, Renée Levine, Peter Gena, Eberhard Blum, Julius Eastman, David Gibson, Jan Williams, David Sussman, Benjamin Hudson, and Ralph Jones, January 1974. Photograph by Stuart Bratesman Jr. © 1974 Stuart Bratesman Jr. Courtesy of the Music Library, University at Buffalo.

The Black Composer Series in the Brooklyn Philharmonia Community Concert Series. *Standing from left to right:* Talib Hakim, Hale Smith, Carman Moore, Julius Eastman, Oliver Lake, and Dorothy Rudd Moore; *sitting from left to right:* Tania León, Noel da Costa, and Arthur Cunningham, 1977. Photograph by Marbeth. Courtesy of Tania León.

The Brooklyn Philharmonia Community Concert Series personnel, outside of the Brooklyn Academy of Music. *From left to right:* Corrine Coleman, program director, with composer/coordinators Tania León, Talib Hakim, and Julius Eastman. Photograph by Marbeth. Courtesy of Tania León.

Julius Eastman and R. Nemo Hill in front of the St. Marks Bar & Grill, New York City, 1981. Photographer unknown. Courtesy of R. Nemo Hill.

Frances Eastman, 2006. Photograph by Renée Levine Packer.

Portrait of Julius Eastman. Photographer unknown. Courtesy of R. Nemo Hill.

previous show at Environ. His text sung that evening alternated between romantic effusions and the enjoyment of what he euphemistically called "the right wrong." Ned Sublette recalls Eastman adding an intermedia element to the performance and improvising to his own Super 8 films showing close-up shots of dog waste on the street, intercut with shots of a long, slow pan up the body of a drag queen, whose face appears frozen in horror. Such juxtapositions of base materiality and the transgressively sexual, place Eastman in the company of other avant-garde gay artists active in downtown, namely, David Wojnarowicz and Jack Smith, whose art reveled in abjection, homoeroticism, shock, and camp. The juxtaposition of vocal improvisation and abject film imagery marks Eastman's particular contribution to downtown gay aesthetics.

Both of these improvised performances exemplify what I have identified in Eastman's work as an aesthetic of abjection. Eastman's performances transformed societal refuse (excrement, homosexuality, drag performance) into something highly valued, ritualized, and sacred. His critical engagement with abjection through his performance extended to his compositions, as well. One of the most salient examples is Eastman's multi-piano piece *Gay Guerrilla* from 1979. Toward the final third of the composition, Eastman's repetitive, ecstatic sound world coalesces into a canon pounding out the Lutheran chorale tune "A Mighty Fortress Is Our God." *Gay Guerrilla*'s provocative title and overt quotation call to mind not only ecclesiastical tradition but also the lineage of European "old masters" he valued, including J. S. Bach, Felix Mendelssohn, and Giacomo Meyerbeer. *Gay Guerrilla* has been described by Kyle Gann as a type of manifesto, though one that gains its force not only through its sonic power but also from this musical borrowing and its reinterpretation as the sound of gay martyrdom. To borrow a description from historian of sexuality David Halperin, "Humiliation turns into defiance. Abjection discloses a secret grace that saves him from contempt."[23] The profane aspects of deviant sexuality are recuperated through a dynamic process of resignification and creative juxtaposition of musical signs.

While Eastman's improvisations explored the edges of sexual and political self-fashioning, his concern with race engaged the unlikely world of mostly white new wave. His relocation to the Bowery area of New York's downtown in the late 1970s exposed him to punk rock at nearby CBGB and he took from it an attitude toward the redefinition of hate speech that became a crucial component of his aesthetic of abjection. While living on the Bowery, Eastman shared a loft with the new wave band Su-Sin Schocks.

At a party hosted by the band and attended by Eastman and his friend Ned Sublette, the hosts played records, including Patti Smith's recently released "Rock N Roll Nigger" from her 1978 album *Easter*. Sublette recalls being put off by Smith's song and was surprised when Eastman took to it:

> It was at this party, that was the first time I heard "Rock N Roll Nigger," and I was actually appalled because I'm from the South. To hear a white person going "nigger nigger nigger nigger nigger nigger nigger" was to me just across the line. You just fuckin' didn't do that. I saw it as not too different from what it purported to lampoon. Julius loved it. It was a very important record for Julius. I remember the subject of the n-word came up and I said, this was often a little rhetorical device, you would say something and somebody would say it back to you confirming it. "So Patti Smith used it correctly?" "Patti Smith used it correctly."[24]

Smith had been, and continues to be, criticized for her song; however, it resonated with Eastman's own repurposing of hate speech, both racist and homophobic. Smith's use of the racist epithet attempted to transform it into a proud marker of otherness and artistry. Eastman was indeed so taken with her song that a portion of it, the rhythmic repetition of "nigger" in the song's bridge, became what Eastman called "the cantus firmus" in his work for ten cellos, *The Holy Presence of Joan d'Arc*. The figure, the repetition of thirteen sixteenth notes followed by a dotted eighth, pervades the composition and does indeed provide the rushing, intense backdrop for aching and astringent melodies that emerge from the texture.[25]

Eastman often refunctioned hate speech in the titles of his instrumental compositions such as *Nigger Faggot* and *Evil Nigger*, part of the series of pieces that Sublette mentions in the excerpt above. Eastman elaborated on his politics of piece titles in a preconcert talk at Northwestern University in 1980. "And what I mean by 'niggers' is that thing which is fundamental, that person or thing that attains to a basicness, a fundamentalness, and eschews that thing which is superficial or, can we say, elegant. So that, a 'nigger' for me is that kind of thing which is, attains himself or herself to the ground of anything."[26]

For Eastman, such words had a "basicness" to them, and he spoke of his glorifying the words or the words glorifying him. Such an attempt at controlling meaning, of glorifying the abject, exemplified an attitude toward unequal power relations that cut across a number of musical practices that attempted to reverse value systems and redefine terms of condemnation.[27] Moreover, this approach to music and politics extended Eastman's use of abjection, attempting to transform historical oppression into strength. Yet the actual efficacy of such an approach was often called into question, as Eastman's titles were occasionally omitted or altered on concert programs, as was the case at the premiere of *Nigger Faggot* on the Community Concert series. There it was simply listed as *NF*. The suppression of the titles of *Evil Nigger* and *Crazy Nigger*, as well as *Gay Guerrilla*, at his Northwestern University concert in 1980, prompted Eastman's explanation cited above. The tense race relations that had persisted on the Northwestern campus since the late 1960s provided a fraught situation for Eastman's music, and protests against his titles came from African-American students and faculty, precipitating the removal of the titles from the printed program. Audience reactions to Eastman's music indicate the limits of his recuperative aesthetic projects; they can, and did, fail. It is crucial that any historian dealing with these musical moments understand that attempts to salvage the abject may be doomed to such failure, that abjection's ability to be recuperated might always have a limit. There might always be a grace irredeemable, because the freight of history remains too strong.

While Eastman's compositional and improvisatory practices evinced a transgressive sensibility, his collaborative projects with the queer artists Meredith Monk and Arthur Russell provided new forms of progressive networks, inclusive of racial and sexual difference. In particular, his work with Arthur Russell brought together his personal constellation of interests, namely, the experimentalist, gay, and black aesthetics that he cultivated. Such aesthetic multiplicity, as I discussed earlier, had been part of his improvisational practice, and flourished within the multiethnic and pansexual collective mobilized by Russell. As his biographer Tim Lawrence has detailed, Russell was, like Eastman, a musical polymath. After studying composition with Charles Wuorinen at the Manhattan School of Music, Russell immersed himself in the downtown scene, serving for a time as music director for The Kitchen and working closely with Philip Glass. Much of Russell's work moved between genres, yet focused on disco as an important site for experimentation. While Eastman had not participated in making disco music before his work with Russell, he had long frequented dance clubs in both Buffalo and New York.[28]

Eastman and Russell met through Ned Sublette, and The Kitchen became the main setting for their work together. Initially, Russell enlisted Eastman as a conductor for his orchestral music. As director of the Community Concert series with the Brooklyn Philharmonia, Eastman could marshal a number of musicians. Many such performers were funded by the Comprehensive Employment and Training Act, a governmental program that provided work for underemployed musicians in the city. Eastman enlisted members of the so-called Comprehensive Employment and Training Act Orchestra for a performance of Russell's mammoth piece titled *Instrumentals* in February of 1978. Besides their orchestral collaborations, Russell invited Eastman to participate in his disco-chamber-music performances as vocalist and organist. An early incarnation of the group, Dinosaur L, performed at The Kitchen in 1979. The performance was described as "an evening-length piece for trombone, 'cello, keyboards, electric bass and drums."[29] Though calling the performance a "piece" obscures the fact that Russell's music was largely a structured improvisation, and each musician brought his own musicality and style to the performance. The recording sessions for *24→24 Music* that followed are an example of the sort of experimental assemblages Russell and Eastman participated in. Russell's inclusion and advocacy of both human and musical difference allowed for radically individualistic performers like Eastman to bring their sonic identities to a performance and create a pluralist aesthetic, one also found in jazz and improvisational music of downtown.

Eastman in particular brought his amazing voice to Dinosaur L, contributing his experimental vocal techniques. From the unhinged utterance of the song "No Thank You," to the operatic energy of "In the Corn Belt," Eastman's voice emerged as a performance of erotic exuberance. Situated among the other musicians of Dinosaur L, Eastman also contributed his organ playing, keeping his improvisational style largely intact. Isolating Eastman's participation in Russell's work with Dinosaur L highlights an important moment in the creative practices of these musicians. Russell was an essential mediator for Eastman's voice, moving it from the largely experimental music scene into the dance music communities that moved to the sound of Dinosaur L's biggest hit "Go Bang." Through their collaboration, Eastman and Russell created a radically open community that afforded spaces for experimentation in the musical sites of downtown.

Ned Sublette recalls that Eastman was for him "the convergence of a lot of things."[30] As I've traced here, Eastman's convergences moved through a number of scenes, and he participated in diverse world-making explorations. Following Eastman from the Brooklyn Community Concerts to experimental music at The Kitchen, from improvisation at Environ to the avant-disco spun at the Paradise Garage, he has revealed a flexible musical identity that opened up new possibilities and musical relations. He practiced a type of musicianship that George Lewis has, in another context, described as "a form of boundary-blurring resistance to efforts to restrict the mobility of black musicians."[31] With Eastman's voice as a guide, musical identity in the downtown scene is perhaps best thought of as outward-directed and capable of bringing together diverse networks, similar to what Tim Lawrence has described as "rhizomatic musicianship."[32] To no small extent, Eastman's life maps a counterhistory of downtown culture, one not bound to a history of style and genre, but one open to attachment, affect, and empathy. Indeed, the dizzying speed with which genres, styles, institutions, and performances were combined, networked, and reconfigured requires modes of inquiry and historiography sensitive to actors whose traces remain.

Notes

Versions of this chapter were presented at the 2009 meeting of the American Musicological Society in Philadelphia, the 2009 Meeting of the Society for American Music, Columbia University, and Portland State University. I am grateful for the comments of those audiences, as well as the insightful suggestions of Walter Frisch, Bernard Gendron, Karen Henson, Tim Lawrence, and George E. Lewis.

1. Julius Eastman, press release for "Humanity and Not Spiritual Beings," January 30, 1981, The Kitchen clippings file, New York Public Library for the Performing Arts. The first piece, *Humanity*, was a vocal solo, perhaps largely improvised; the second piece, *Not Spiritual Beings*, is described as "a written work for Pianos and Instruments, based on nothing else than Harmony and Melody. Harmonies and Melodies that build step by step, conclude, and then begin again."

2. This date range indicates the years in which Eastman lived in New York City after leaving Buffalo and the Creative Associates. As the time line indicates, he was an active presence in the city's musical life prior to 1975, as a performer with the Creative Associates and as a solo pianist.

3. Eastman was a Creative Associate at the University at Buffalo from 1969 to 1975.

4. My methodology for this project draws on the microhistorical work of Carlo Ginzburg, as well as the sociology of association developed by Bruno Latour. The minoritarian and rhizomatic theory of Gilles Deleuze and Félix Guattari has served as an important influence as well. For an introduction to Ginzburg's thought see his "Latitude, Slaves, and the Bible: An Experiment in Microhistory," *Critical Inquiry* 31 (Spring 2005): 665–83. See also Bruno Latour, *Reassembling the Social* (New York: Oxford University Press, 2005). For the relevant work of Deleuze and Guattari, see especially their *Kafka: Toward a Minor Literature*, trans. Dana Pola (Minneapolis: University of Minnesota Press, 1986). In addition, the ethical orientation of this project has largely been guided by the late work of Paul

Ricouer. In his ultimate philosophical reflection, *Memory, History, Forgetting*, he states, "I continue to be troubled by the unsettling spectacle offered by an excess of memory here, and an excess of forgetting elsewhere, to say nothing of the influence of commemorations and abuses of memory—and of forgetting." Such reflections on history and memory have profoundly shaped my attempts at thinking a history of cultural production in downtown New York City. See Ricouer, *Memory, History, Forgetting* (Chicago: University of Chicago Press, 2005), xv.

5. Lauren Berlant and Michael Warner have advocated for modes of history and description that "promote radical aspirations of queer culture building; not just a safe zone for queer sex, but the changed possibilities of identity, intelligibility, publics, culture, and sex" that they have described as the production and maintenance of "queer counterpublics" as world-making projects. It is in this spirit that my work on Julius Eastman is also a political project. See Lauren Berland and Michael Warner, "Sex in Public" in Michael Warner, *Publics and Counterpublics* (New York: Zone, 2002), 187–208; here 187 and 198, respectively.

6. See Marvin J. Taylor, "Playing the Cultural Field," in *The Downtown Book*, ed. Taylor (Princeton, NJ: Princeton University Press, 2005), 17–39; Bernard Gendron, *Between Montmartre and the Mudd Club* (Chicago: University of Chicago Press, 2002), 227–316; Bernard Gendron, "The Downtown Music Scene" in Taylor, *The Downtown Book*, 41–66; Kyle Gann, *Music Downtown: Writings from the Village Voice* (Berkeley: University of California Press, 2006); and Tim Lawrence, *Hold On to Your Dreams: Arthur Russell and the Downtown Music Scene, 1974–1992* (Durham, NC: Duke University Press, 2009).

7. Samuel Gilmore, "Schools of Activity and Innovation," *Sociological Quarterly* 29, no. 2 (1988): 203–19.

8. I explore issues of race and sexuality in greater depth in my essay, "John Cage, Julius Eastman, and the Homosexual Ego," in *Tomorrow Is the Question: New Approaches to Experimental Music*, ed. Benjamin Piekut, 39–62 (Ann Arbor: University of Michigan Press, 2014).

9. Ned Sublette, interview with the author, February 18, 2009.

10. Eastman graduated from the Curtis Institute of Music in 1963 with a degree in composition.

11. Rorem writes, "The past years have seen a crop of American singers—not properly a recital singer—skilled to deal with current vocal concepts. These concepts stress words as sound no less than as sense, and inevitably enmesh the voice in a jungle of instrumental hues. The parent work is Boulez's *Le Marteau sans Maitre* (1954), and the spinoff interpreter in America is Bethany Beardslee, who could always do anything, as could Julius Eastman, Cathy Berberian, Jan de Gaetani, and Phyllis Bryn-Julson. The pieces are not songs, because they do not restrict themselves to piano and lyric poem. They are shows—narrational, terrifically up to date, yet still using texts from another time and place, like George Crumb with Lorca, David Del Tredici with Lewis Carroll, or, from abroad, Peter Maxwell Davies' *Mad King* and Henze's *Runaway Slave*. But these paragraphs were

not meant to evaluate the decade of the 1970s." Ned Rorem, "The American Art Song 1900–1960, a Personal Appraisal," liner notes to *But Yesterday Is Not Today: The American Art Song, 1927–1972*, New World Records 80243, 1996.

12. Renée Levine Packer, *This Life of Sounds: Evenings for New Music in Buffalo* (New York: Oxford University Press, 2010), 92.

13. Biographical information is derived from my interviews with Petr Kotik, Mary Jane Leach, Renée Levine Packer, Meredith Monk, Jeffery Nussbaum, and Ned Sublette conducted in 2008 and 2009. Eastman was a member of Kotik's group, the S.E.M. Ensemble, during his time living in Buffalo.

14. Meredith Monk, phone interview with the author, January 14, 2009.

15. Carol Lawson "Weekender Guide," *New York Times*, January 19, 1979, C1.

16. Quoted in Maurice Edwards, *How Music Grew in Brooklyn: A Biography of the Brooklyn Philharmonic Orchestra* (Lanham, MD: Scarecrow Press, 2006), 99.

17. Zita d'Azalia Allen, "Society of Black Composers in View," *New Amsterdam News*, June 7, 1969, 38.

18. Carman Moore, "Does a Black Mozart—or Stravinsky—Wait in the Wings?" *New York Times*, September 7, 1969.

19. Petr Kotik and Ned Sublette indicate that Eastman was an active jazz musician in Buffalo. Kotik, Sublette, interviews with the author.

20. The two reviews that give accounts of the performance do not give a title for the performance. However, Ned Sublette remembers the title as such. Ned Sublette, interview with the author, February 2, 2009.

21. Joseph Horowitz, "Julius Eastman Sings, Plays Piano at Environ," *New York Times*, October 12, 1976, 35.

22. Tom Johnson, *The Voice of New Music* (Paris: Editions 75, 1989), 144. Ned Sublette, interview.

23. David M. Halperin, *What Do Gay Men Want?* (Ann Arbor: University of Michigan Press, 2007), 84.

24. Ned Sublette interview.

25. The first system of the score is reproduced in chapter 6.

26. Julius Eastman, Introduction to the Northwestern University concert, *Unjust Malaise*, New World Records, 80638, 2005.

27. Sublette suggests that Eastman had a cutting sense of humor that involved "laughing at power" and attempted to undo the traditions of subjection and violence done through racist and homophobic hate speech. This is certainly not an easy project to pull off, and philosophers and queer theorists have noted the continuing difficulty in repurposing hate speech. See Judith Butler, *Bodies That Matter* (New York: Routledge, 1993), 223–42, and Butler, *Excitable Speech* (New York: Routledge, 1997).

28. Ned Sublette interview.

29. The Kitchen press release announcing "Arthur Russell, 24→24 Music." Kitchen clippings file, New York Library for the Performing Arts.

30. Ned Sublette interview.

31. George E. Lewis, *A Power Stronger than Itself: The AACM and the American Experimental Tradition* (Chicago: University of Chicago Press, 2008), 370.

32. See Tim Lawrence, "Connecting with the Cosmic: Arthur Russell, Rhizomatic Musicianship, and the Downtown. Music Scene, 1973–92," *Liminalities: A Journal of Performance Studies* 3, no. 3 (November 2007): 1–84.

CHAPTER EIGHT

EVIL NIGGER

A Piece for Multiple Instruments of the Same Type by Julius Eastman (1979), with Performance Instructions by Joseph Kubera

David Borden

My approach to dissecting Julius Eastman's *Evil Nigger*, in this case for multiple pianos, is in the form of an interpretation and description, rather than a strictly theoretical analysis. I also refer to Joseph Kubera's "General Instructions" (which may be found at the end of this chapter), that he put together as performance notes for the pianists with whom he has performed the piece.[1]

Overview

In general, the piece has many elements associated with the minimalist genre. It has short tonal phrases, played in a steady tempo, that are repeated many times. Its overall structure and harmonic language, however, are too quirky to completely fall into that mold. It contains very dramatic harmonic passages, which eventually lead to a nontonal disparate arrhythmic pointillistic texture of pitches of long duration that seemingly lead nowhere. It uses minimalist gestures and gradually abandons them for a free-floating ambient atmosphere. The piece proceeds in precisely notated clock time and takes twenty-one minutes and five seconds to perform. Each player needs a stopwatch, or some mobile device, showing the passing time in large numbers so that the changes happen precisely. Although it is not absolutely necessary, the piece should have a conductor in order for it to proceed smoothly. The recording of the piece on New World Records (Julius Eastman, *Unjust Malaise*) employs four pianos, but as Eastman has explained elsewhere, it could be performed by any group of instruments of the same type, such as strings or clarinets, but would take more players—anywhere from ten to eighteen.[2]

Structural Segments

Musically, the piece proceeds with almost constant sixteenth notes played at quarter note = 144 throughout, until the last few minutes. There are twenty-nine sections in all. Kubera's excellent set of instructions for performers encompasses most of the issues discussed below.

Many sections are subdivided into shorter time segments, so the numbering of events can be confusing at times. The note events can be played in any octave, and are not limited to the range of the written note. This implies that the performers can decide ahead of time which octave they will play in any given section.

The first segment lasts from zero to thirty seconds, the second segment from thirty seconds to one minute and five seconds. The third segment is from one minute and five seconds to one minute and thirty seconds. The fourth and final segment of section 1 is from one minute and thirty seconds to two minutes and ten seconds. The scanned copy of the original manuscript often omits the section numbers, so it is difficult to figure out when some sections begin and end, although the time segments are fairly (but not absolutely) clearly delineated.

Harmonic Language

The piece starts out in D-natural minor, although C♮, the seventh note of the scale is not heard until after four minutes have elapsed. The opening motive (hereafter called OM) of F–E–D as it looks in Eastman's notation is shown in example 8.1.

Example 8.1. Opening motive from *Evil Nigger* (original score). Reproduced by permission from the Estate of Julius Eastman.

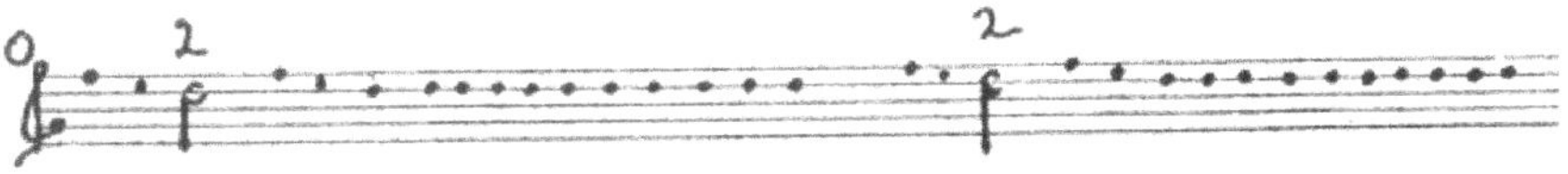

Which translates in conventional notation to that shown in example 8.2.

Example 8.2. Opening motive from *Evil Nigger* using conventional notation.

The first figure comprising three notes can be repeated more than once before continuing on. The number of repetitions of the final D is up to the player within the restraints of the allotted time.

Written in standard notation, what Kubera calls the "Continuo figure" (CF) is shown in example 8.3.

Example 8.3. The "Continuo Figure" in *Evil Nigger.*

When played in unison on cue, CF acts as a recurring point of reference during the first third of the piece or so. The CF and the OM are also interspersed with other melodic figures throughout most of the piece. The pianists play this in octaves within the octave range of their choice.

The CF is played once in unison at 1:30, 2:40, 4:55, 6:30, and 8:30. After that point, the gravitational pull of D-natural minor gets weaker and weaker. Even so, it does not entirely disappear until after the eighteen-minute mark.

Evolution of the Pitches

1. All the pitches in the natural D-minor scale (aeolian mode) are introduced during the opening minute and a half of the piece except C♮, the seventh: D–E–F–G–A–B♭.
2. After the CF is played once in unison at 1:30, no new pitches are introduced, but the triad of G–B♭–D is emphasized in arpeggiated form, with each pitch being repeated many times sequentially (i.e., not as chords).
3. Following the CF unison at 2:40, no new pitches are introduced until finally C appears at 4:10, forty-five seconds before the next unison CF at 4:55. During this segment, new pitches are introduced, going up the circle of fifths with F♯ and C♯.
4. At 5:40 the circle of fifths continues, but this time going down, starting at E♭, then down to A♭ and D♭ taking us further away from D minor.
5. At 6:10 the OM returns to superimpose itself on other repeating pitches that suggest A-flat major, creating tonal ambiguity.
6. The CF begins the 6:30 segment, followed by the OM to remind us of D minor and a brief sense of "return."
7. The CF and OM continue at the 7:00 segment, only the CF is now in D-flat minor, not in unison, but free, while the OM continues in D minor. At the same time, four other pitches are played that outline a D-flat-major seventh plus ninth (D♭–F–A♭–C–E♭), so the whole segment is centered on a D-flat tonality but is distracted by the OM in its original key.
8. At 7:30 more pitches from A-flat major appear, but the OM stays in D minor. The CF is not present.
9. This continues more or less at 8:00 but with the addition of the CF in D-flat minor.
10. Time 8:30 marks the last time the CF is heard in unison, once, in its original key of D minor, followed by all twelve pitches of the chromatic scale in constant steady repetitive figures accompanied now and then by the OM in its original key.
11. The next change, at 9:35, contains the OM in all twelve keys simultaneously, thus removing all remnants of a tonal center.
12. At 11:00 both the OM and the CF are presented in all keys.
13. From 11:45 to 12:15, the players return to the CF in the original key, but not in unison or necessarily in the same octave.
14. The next three segments (until 13:15) return to the pitches of D minor, this time with a C♯ instead of a C♮. Then, at 13:15, there is a return to

the OM in D minor only, but not in unison. From here on, the piece takes on a floating quality and gradually floats away.

15. Then, at 13:25, appear the first repeated half notes (instead of sixteenth notes as written above). At first, these half notes are equal to four black noteheads (or four sixteenths), but later, at 13:50, they become equal to two black noteheads (quarter notes). This is indicated by the only recording we have in which Eastman is playing one of the pianos. This procedure continues until 16:45 with a D "minorish" feel, although at various times, depending on which pitches in the D-minor scale receive prominence, it can be rather vague.
16. At 16:45, even longer sustained notes are introduced, and they gradually drift away from any tonal center. The OM and CF are indicated now and then, but appear to be optional. The long notes become farther and farther apart and the half notes disappear until, at the very end, the piece seems to disappear from view and out of earshot.

Overall Structure

I found a graphic representation of this piece in an unlikely place: the Indian Space Research Organization. Although it is not an exact diagram of *Evil Nigger*, it comes very close. The Chandrayaan-1 was a lunar probe spacecraft launched in October of 2008. For the sake of comparing it to Eastman's piece, simply eliminate the lunar orbit from the picture, and substitute instead, that the spacecraft simply kept on going into deep space (fig. 8.1).

Earth is D natural minor, the home key.

The IO is the initial orbit.

The EBN orbits are akin to the "Continuo figure" played once in unison (returning to Earth) with the interim sections developing farther away from D minor.

EBN-5 is like the introduction of very long notes, and instead of attaining another orbit, simply breaks away and continues on into deep space.

I like this graphic because it makes the overall structure simple to understand. I think it fits. As I said above, it is not exact, but very close.

Conclusion

But Julius, what about the title? *Evil Nigger* is not something one sees on a classical music program very often. At Northwestern University, he was

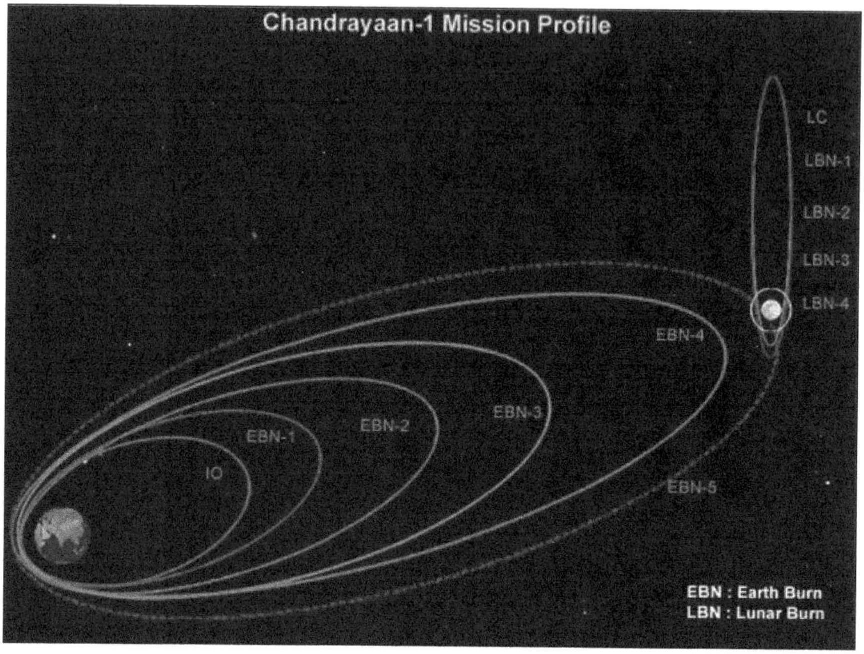

Figure 8.1. Chandrayaan-1 Lunar Probe Mission Profile. Reproduced by permission from Indian Space Research Organization.

called upon to explain his use of *nigger* in his titles (there is a *Nigger* series) because some black students and a faculty member found the use of the word offensive. He spoke eloquently about the word, saying among other things, that to him, "nigger" means "that which is fundamental." That is, the foundation of many things. He alludes to field niggers as the basis of the American economy. He avoids discussing the obvious derogatory meaning of the word.

Since Eastman was African American, he could use the word with a certain freedom that is not appropriate for the rest of us. The word connotes racism, lynching, slavery, injustice, unimaginable suffering, and so on, and so forth. I used to think that since African-American rappers used the word often, it would lose its power over time and become just another word. I was wrong. Even Richard Pryor stopped using it. Hate words have a seemingly indestructible quality, so that no matter how many times they are used in a comedic way, to point out how ridiculous and corrosive they are, their original negative meanings remain intact. Julius knew perfectly well what the word invoked and used it to make audiences come face to face with it. After all, he had to every day. But at the same time, through his art and creativity he attempted to transcend and transform it, to go beyond its obvious flash points of condescension and irrational hatred. I think he was trying to heal the word and us.

Now, when I listen to *Evil Nigger* and follow its beautiful and powerful journey through the unfolding of pitches, rhythm, and varying textures, I am transported to a new level of consciousness every time. And when, finally, during the last few minutes when it achieves an otherworldly weightlessness, I cannot help thinking that Eastman has delivered us from evil.

General Instructions for Julius Eastman's *Evil Nigger*, by Joseph Kubera

The tempo is about MM 144, four black noteheads equaling one beat. We may decide to take it a little slower if necessary. Every musician must have a stopwatch to follow the progress through the piece.

There is usually a sense of pulse except in long lines of uninterrupted strings of black noteheads. No rests or separations between time-delimited sections.

Lines consisting of black noteheads continue to the end of each staff. Occasionally pitches change midstaff (as at 3:40). If several lines have note changes mid-staff at about the same time, the pianists should not change all at the same time.

The general rule is that any of these lines may be played in any octave, high or low. I did note some places in the recording where players seemed to play only in the written octaves, but this may have been only coincidence. Toward the end of the piece, there are regions where there are distinct treble and bass areas (starting 16:45).

I will assign pianists specific staves within time-delimited segments, so that most, if not all, the notated pitches get played. (The piece as written is designed to be played by a varying numbers of pianists.) Where the number of staves (lines) within a system become great (as at 4:55 and beyond), pianists must use both hands to execute two lines at once (I will specify these). In an ideal situation, one might surmise this could be left to the performers' discretion, but with our limited rehearsal time I will have to make choices.

Also, sometimes the pianists can jump from one staff to another within the same time segment (this can be heard on the recording in the sections starting at 3:10 and 4:10). When doing so, do not leave rests between one series of notes and the next. Listen carefully to one another to hear what lines you might wish to contribute to the texture. And sometimes the register you choose can fundamentally alter the group sound, as in playing repeated notes in an octave lower than any other being played.

There are two prominent melodic fragments that constantly recur. One is the figure beginning with the descending "F–E–D" and then a string of repeated Ds (opening of the piece). In the first three notes of this figure, the D is written as a half note with a "2" above it. This means the D has the value of two black noteheads. What is intended, but not written, is that the F–E–D sequence of three notes may be iterated one, two, three, or four times at will, before settling on the repeated Ds. This is all up to the individual performer. It may be played in any octave. It is important to keep the pulse strongly in mind when playing this figure. Either the F or the first D may come on the strong part of the beat.

The other melodic fragment is what I call the "Continuo figure," which sounds like a figured bass pattern, and can be seen best at time 1:30. It always has the same notes and always eight iterations of each note in the sequence. It is usually played in octaves (chosen by the pianists), only once, with the last repeated D continuing until the end of that time segment. The Continuo figure is usually begun upon cue from the leader (this is the shouted "one, two, three, four" in the recording). It could have been conducted, but since Julius was one of the four pianists, he was busy playing, and so had to shout out the "bar for nothing." We will probably do the same.

Be aware that later in the piece (around 16:00) both these melodic figures are transposed by the pianists into different keys, at the pianists' choice of key. They are uncoordinated in some of these later occurrences. Please practice them in different keys to be ready for them. Of course, they are also played in various octaves of your choice.

The "Continuo" and F–E–D figures are written in very often but are not always played. So, they are "semi-optional." When two or more pianists happen to be playing them optionally, they are not coordinated, but the overall pulse must be kept in mind.

Repeated half notes first appear at 13:25. At first, a half-note equals four black noteheads, but (in the recording) a half note becomes equal to two black noteheads, and so it remains until the end of the piece.[3]

Notes

1. Joseph Kubera was a Creative Associate at the University of Buffalo from 1974 to 1976. He and Eastman continued to perform together once they both lived in New York City.

2. Julius Eastman, *Unjust Malaise*, New World Records CD 80638, 2005.

3. Joseph Kubera, "Recollections of Julius Eastman and His Piano Music," 67–68. Unpublished essay. Reprinted with permission.

CHAPTER NINE

A POSTMINIMALIST ANALYSIS OF JULIUS EASTMAN'S *CRAZY NIGGER*

Andrew Hanson-Dvoracek

No one can deny that Julius Eastman had a unique voice, both literally and compositionally. Figures such as Kyle Gann, Mary Jane Leach, and Diamanda Galas have all singled out Eastman's music as being inimitable and unforgettable.[1] However, until recently there has been little study of what distinguishes his voice. At first glance, an openly gay African-American composer, championed by the likes of Morton Feldman and Lukas Foss, would provide ample avenues to explore his work both analytically and hermeneutically. But his erratic career, the dispersion of his scores, and the cryptic nature of those scores that have been found, make the performance or even cursory knowledge of his works, much less intensive analysis, tremendously difficult. The work of Leach, Joseph Kubera, and Cees van Zeeland constitute a concentration of materials concerning Eastman's late 1970s work *Crazy Nigger*.[2] Several of the techniques Eastman used in this work are salient to the listener, such as his bracing dissonance and the obscuring of minimalism's omnipresent pulse. Through analysis, the origins of these qualities reveal themselves to be extended tonalities more akin to Stravinsky and Bartók than the French symbolists, ragas, and modal jazz that informed earlier minimalists, as well as a larger overall additive process Eastman called "organic music."

My analysis is based on three sources. The first is a facsimile of an autograph score from Mary Jane Leach's online compilation of Eastman's scores. The second is a live recording available on the New World Records CD set *Unjust Malaise*. This recording dates from a concert given at Northwestern University as part of his residency there in January 1980, which featured Eastman as one of four pianists performing *Crazy Nigger*, along with two identically scored works: *Evil Nigger* and *Gay Guerrilla*. Like many contemporary minimalist composers, Eastman's scores were never intended for transmission as much as they were mnemonic reminders for his own performances. Thus, either a recording or the memories of performers are vital for the resolution from the score into sounding music. The third source is a schematic in Eastman's hand from a February 1980 performance at The Kitchen in New York City. Classification of this document lies somewhere between a sketch and program notes. The schematic provides invaluable insight into Eastman's compositional process and the overarching form of the work, but this is a document intended for public consumption. It should be noted that the schematic is not an exhaustive diagram of *Crazy Nigger*'s processes, and thus further illustrates which processes Eastman chose to highlight to his audience.

Eastman's schematic divides *Crazy Nigger* into ten sections, each demarcating a change in process.[3] The entire work is based on a vertical additive process, in which new parts are added and removed as others continue, resulting in increasingly dense harmonies. Once each process has reached its "logical conclusion," according to Eastman, it resets to a single repeated note resulting in a sawtooth motion of harmonic complexity.[4]

The work is scored for any number of instruments of the same family, so each part is notated on its own staff with stemless noteheads. Although the attacks by the different players are not necessarily aligned, the most obvious aural perception is that of a steadily evolving progression of chords. Eastman suggests this in the schematic by referring to figuration and other motion in the individual parts as appoggiaturas.

I have divided *Crazy Nigger* into four larger segments, also by process, but on a more general level than Eastman. A chart comparing my divisions to Eastman's is shown as table 9.1. The first segment comprises sections 1–6, each of which builds toward a particular mode or chord. The second segment encompasses sections 7 and 8, which construct even larger chords by thirds and seconds, respectively. Sections 9 and 10 use idiosyncratic processes and will be discussed individually.

Table 9.1. *Crazy Nigger* organizational chart

Eastman's divisions		New divisions
Section 1	Initial process (B♭)	Segment 1, "Intro"
Section 2	Transition/reduction	
Section 3	New key (A)	
Section 4	Melody in A	
Section 5	Arpeggio in B♭	
Section 6	Melody in B♭	
Section 7	Addition in thirds	Segment 2
Section 8	Addition in seconds	
Section 9	Nonpulsed	Segment 3
Section 10	Harmonic series	Segment 4

The term "key" appears five times on the first page of the schematic. Eastman seems to have considered *Crazy Nigger* to be tonal, although obviously not in a functional sense. The tonal center is established at the beginning of each additive phrase, by a single repeating note. Examining only the first three additive phrases, the first and third have a tonal center B♭, whereas the second occurs on a tonal center of A. Of these three, only the first concludes in a recognizable functional chord, a dominant ninth-flat five, whereas the other two more fully realize their modality through melodic and arpeggiated figures.

Eastman began all three of these additive processes with whole-tone movement, and each takes three measures before adding parts, which settle them into a particular mode. These figures include transitional phases between processes that Eastman discarded from the remainder of the work. In the first Bb area, this consists of a simplification of the previous chord's figures. Eastman labels this single measure as section 2 (illustrated in ex. 9.1). Eastman removes C♯ and D♮ appoggiaturas, and transforms the diminished fifth (E♮) into an augmented fifth (F♯).

The A tonal area ends after three minutes, in contrast to the first B♭ area, which lasts ten and half, and does so with a descending melodic figure followed by ten seconds of silence. The second B♭ area ends with this same melodic figure, enharmonically transposed to the key. This is the first example of a technique Eastman referred as "organic music." In his introduction to the recorded recital at Northwestern, he describes "organic music" as:

Example 9.1. Simplification of parts in section 2 in *Crazy Nigger.*

simplified to:

> The third part of any part, so the third measure or the third section, the third part, has to contain all of the information of the first two parts and then go on from there. So therefore, unlike Romantic music or Classical music, where you have different sections and you have these sections, for instance are in great contrast to the first section or to some other section in the piece, these pieces, they're not exactly perfect, but there is an attempt to make every section contain all the information of the previous section, or else take out information at a gradual and logical rate.[5]

In this introductory segment, the three parts that Eastman refers to are the three tonal areas. From the first area, the third inherits its tonal center and its mixolydian mode, while from the second, it receives the melodic figure and the addition of ascending whole tones.

This first segment also includes the first hints in this work of Eastman expanding upon the minimalist aesthetic of nonfunctional tonality by incorporating bitonality. Although C♮ lies within the key of B flat, in the final two measures of section 1, a C indicated in "long note + octaves" is added. In his schematic, Eastman explicitly states the purpose of this is to establish two keys, C and B flat.

In the second segment of the work, sections 7 and 8, we come to a new tonal area of F minor, and several changes are made to the additive process. Rather than establishing a tonal center with a single repeated note, section 7 begins with an F-minor triad. Starting with a much less ambiguous kernel than before, Eastman uses an additive process by ascending thirds similar to the first section. Instead of using whole tones as a tonally evasive maneuver, this process is firmly in F Dorian. Once all the notes in the mode are exhausted, the process begins to fill in ascending seconds.

Just as section 2 is a simplification and alteration of the process for section 1, Eastman treats section 8 similarly in relation to section 7. Instead of beginning with addition by thirds before resorting to seconds, Eastman begins the process with seconds, and descends rather than ascends. This section begins with a single B, which would have been the next added note according to section 7's process had Eastman allowed it to continue.

The motion in seconds quickly eliminates any sense of B as a tonal center, as this process continues until all twelve pitch classes are sounding. Rather than progressing downward by means of a single interval, Eastman uses a pattern that is symmetrical around a C/D♭ axis, which is shown in example 9.2.

Section 9 is by far the longest and most complex of the entire work (see ex. 9.3). While each of the previous sections consists of either a part of or an entire additive phrase, this section has six complete additive phrases, each resulting in a different final chord. This point also coincides with a radical shift in the notation of the score.

Throughout the majority of the score, Eastman notated the parts with unmeasured repeated noteheads. In section 9, however, a new aspect of rhythmic complexity is introduced. Rather than sharing a pulse, each

Example 9.2. Symmetrical nature of section 8 in *Crazy Nigger*.

Example 9.3. Excerpt from section 9 of autograph score of *Crazy Nigger*. Reproduced by permission from the Estate of Julius Eastman.

player is now free to choose between any of a specific set of pitches and multiples of the pulse. In addition, the suggested duration of each measure is reduced from ninety seconds down to fifteen. The first eleven measures (34:00–36:45) of section 9, encompassing the first two iterations of the additive process, are written as whole notes on a grand staff. After this, he simply notated the pitch classes by name. Both methods are accompanied by either a range or discrete set of permissible durations.

A third notational system is used in the schematic. Eastman highlighted the additive process that forms the basis of *Crazy Nigger* by labeling each part individually, though he does not label every part within the schematic. The totality of each measure is the sum of all the component figures linked with carats, using plus signs to divide each measure. He described each figure on its first appearance and sometimes reasserts it in subsequent appearances.

The labeling system follows a logical, if opaque, method. Returning to the introductory segment, in the B♭ tonal area, the parts are labeled A and given a subscript index based on order of appearance. When these parts are later simplified, a sub-subscript of 1 is added. The two parts added in the A tonal area are labeled differently, as BA and BA1. All subsequent parts return to the previous labeling system.

It is fortuitous that this change in labeling occurs in the same place that best exemplified Eastman's ideal of organic music. With one exception, every measure in section 9 consisting of three or more notes, contains both A- and B-labeled figures. By intentionally using notes from both the B♭ and A tonal area, section 9 is the largest example of Eastman's organic music, and likely the inspiration for this labeling system.

This is not the only way that section 9 expands upon prior material. Within this section, there are six complete additive phrases. Each of these results in a chord that refers to a previous section and is illustrated in example 9.4. The first additive phrase results in a D-major pentatonic scale, recalling the Mixolydian mode of the introductory segment.

The next three phrases of section 9 all result in symmetrical cells revolving around an axis that rises in semitones. The first of the three is based around a G/A♭ axis, the second is an incomplete cell around A♭, and the final cell centers on an A♭/A axis. These all look back to the symmetrical nature of section 8, the process built on descending seconds. The fifth process of section 9 builds a chord that is similar to, although not exactly, the "transitional chord" from the introductory segment. The final process of this section is truncated one note shy of becoming an octatonic scale, OCT(0,1)B, specifically.

The final note to complete this octatonic scale would be a C♯, which is the note that inaugurates the final section of this piece. Beginning with the C♯ below the bass staff (C♯2),[6] the added parts climb up the harmonic series to the E above the treble staff (E6) as the time between entrances shrinks from thirty seconds to only one. In this section, Eastman continues the rhythmic notation of section 9, beginning with forty pulses for the low C♯, and increases the temporal frequency of each part by the same ratio as its pitch frequency.

The use of the harmonic series within minimalist works was already well-established by La Monte Young a decade before *Crazy Nigger*. But the direct mathematical correlation with temporal and pitch frequency is most associated with Estonian composer Arvo Pärt, particularly his 1977 work *Cantus in Memoriam Benjamin Britten*.[7] However, it seems unlikely that Eastman was aware of Pärt's work, because the 1984 ECM New Series recordings, which brought Pärt fame in North America, had yet to be made.[8]

Eastman's choice to base the harmonic series in section 10 on a C♯ makes sense (see ex. 9.5); he has already used one transition, where the next step in one process is then used as the first note of the next one. However, the appearance of C♯ is also meant to be dramatic, given that he took great pains to avoid using the pitch class anywhere else in the piece.

There are three instances in *Crazy Nigger* where the purposeful exclusion of this particular pitch class is obvious. First, of the three tonal areas used in the first half of the work, only A Mixolydian by definition includes a C♯. While in this tonal area, all the notes of the mode are used except for C♯. Second, in section 7 where the process is based on thirds and then seconds, Eastman resets the process when it reaches a B. If it had been allowed to proceed an additional step, it would have resulted in a C♯. Finally, if all the labeled parts from the schematic are assembled as a list as in example 9.4, C♯ is notably absent.

One conclusion that could be drawn from the last example is that it was not given a label in the schematic because it did not appear in any part. However, this is not the case. In section 8, when the process is built on descending seconds, one of the parts is a repeating D♭. This evades the schematic, as Eastman describes that section only by its process, rather than an explicit list of parts.

Of course, a D♭ is not the same thing as a C♯. At 9:00, the last measure of section 1, however, a seventh and lowest part added remains mysteriously absent from the schematic. This part doubles the low C that was added in the previous measure, and also adds a C♯ appoggiatura. I believe

Example 9.4. Beginning notes and resultant chords of additive phrases in section 9 in *Crazy Nigger*.

Example 9.5. Penultimate page of *Crazy Nigger*. Reproduced by permission from the Estate of Julius Eastman.

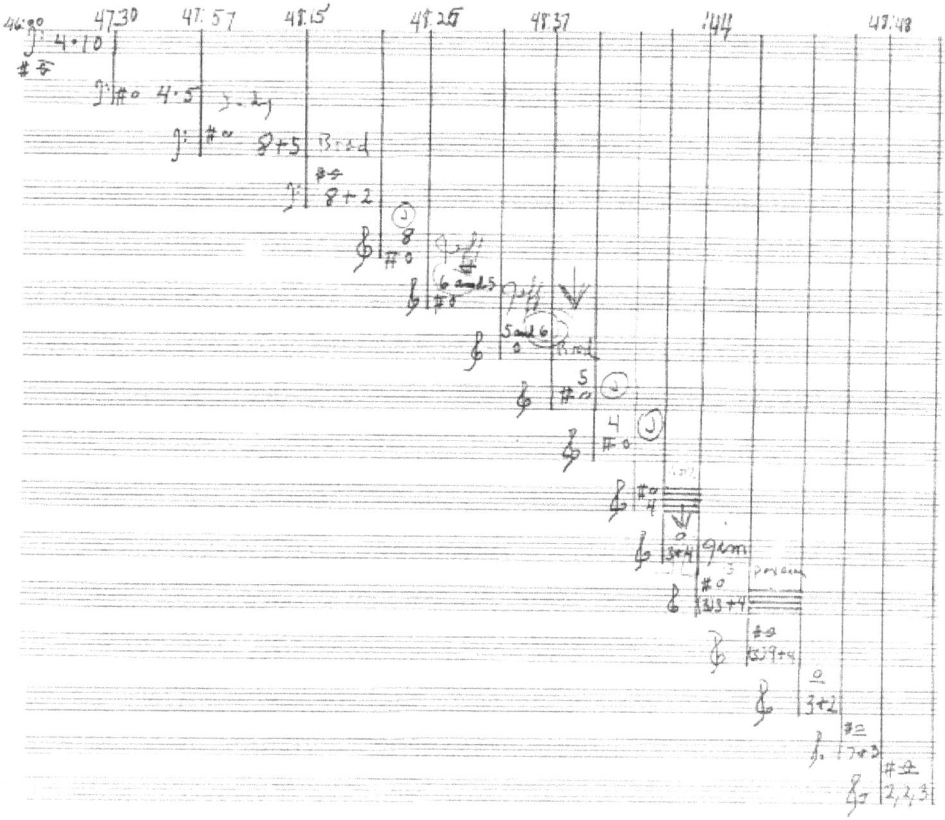

the bookkeeping that obscures them is greater proof that the scarcity, if not absence, of C♯s is a deliberate architectural decision.

By the late 1970s, when *Crazy Nigger* and the other pieces performed at Northwestern were written, the first wave of minimalist composers, such as Steve Reich and Philip Glass, had themselves moved away from strictly ideological compositional processes.[9] So it would seem that the schematic represents the rigorous precompositional process, which would certainly be of great interest to an audience comprising composers and new music enthusiasts. On the other hand, the appearance of C♯s before that pitch class's "proper entry" indicates that Eastman did not conclude his composition with these processes, but felt free to make note-by-note changes for aesthetic reasons.

The use of extended tonality such as octatonic scales and symmetric cells in *Crazy Nigger* is another one of the ways that the minimalist aesthetic mutated into the postminimalist style. This particular innovation is often credited to European composers, particularly Louis Andriessen and his group Hoketus, who strove to make their own personal statements within a largely American conversation.

It may be even more dangerous to refer to this harmonic palette as "uptown" rather than European. Nevertheless, Eastman did spend time at academic institutions, such as the University at Buffalo and the Curtis Institute of Music, while maintaining a philosophy that embraced minimalism and managed to infuriate even John Cage. Therefore, Eastman's work could be seen as an alternate history. While it seems unlikely that he intended to broker a détente between the two warring factions of Manhattan, it does appear that he was attempting to reconcile these two conflicted sides of his own compositional style.

Eastman's harmonic language can also offer insight into his use of controversial titles. The reasons for and ramifications of Eastman's titles are discussed to much greater effect elsewhere in this volume, but they do demand that even a highly analytical discussion of the work confronts the complications of race. In his introduction to the Northwestern concert, Eastman claims that his use of "work nigger" is meant to convey a sense of "basicness," and "that thing which is fundamental." This idea seems to run in opposition to the highly intellectualized and academic harmonic vocabulary he uses in the work. Conversely, if this work had been titled "Four Pianos" or "Music in Seventeen Parts," that same academic language would make it profoundly easy to divorce it from its composer. Instead, the musicologist, the performer, and the listener must deal with Julius Eastman himself, or at least the conversations he wanted us to have. This is not a work for a committee to give an award to and then place onto a shelf.

So it seems that in this work Eastman has managed to suggest a different path minimalism may have taken—subvert the narrative of both African-American and academic composers, and make everyone profoundly uncomfortable in the process. Nonetheless, the music would not have survived the staggering odds against it, if it were not also engaging, searing, and unforgettable.

Notes

1. See Thomas Avena, "Interview: Diamanda Galás," in *Life Sentences: Writers, Artists, and AIDS* (San Francisco: Mercury House, 1994), 178; Mary Jane Leach, "In Search of Julius Eastman," *NewMusicBox*, November 8, 2005, http://www.newmusicbox.org/articles/In-Search-of-Julius-Eastman/; Kyle Gann, "That Which Is Fundamental," in *Music Downtown: Writings from the Village Voice* (Berkeley: University of California Press, 2006), 289.

2. In an annotated score by Cees Van Zeeland, he dates the work at 1978, which is written on the autograph score, but is cut off on the score posted online.

3. Julius Eastman, *Crazy Nigger*, schematic, accessed January 30, 2015, http://www.mjleach.com/EastmanScores.htm.

4. Julius Eastman, *Crazy Nigger*, facsimile score, accessed August 18, 2009, http://www.mjleach.com/EastmanScores.htm.

5. Julius Eastman, spoken introduction to Northwestern concert, *Unjust Malaise*, New World Records CD 80638, 2005.

6. Using the scientific pitch notation system, where middle C is C4, and octave numbering goes from C to C.

7. Daniel J. McConnell "Ringing Changes in Schoenberg's *Klangfarbenmetapher*: Music by Schoenberg, Arvo Pärt, and Brian Eno," presented at the annual meeting of the Society for Music Theory, Nashville, TN, November 7, 2008. Since this essay was written, it has come to the attention of the editors that *Spectral CANON for Conlon Nancarrow* by James Tenney, conceived in 1972 and realized for player piano in 1974, works precisely with canonic forms for both pitch and rhythm, whereas Eastman worked with this same process in the last section of *Crazy Nigger* in a more intuitive manner.

8. ECM, "ECM–History," accessed August 18, 2009, http://www.ecmrecords.com/About_ECM/History/index.php.

9. Timothy A. Johnson, "Minimalism: Aesthetic, Style, or Technique?" *Musical Quarterly* 78, no. 4 (Winter 1994): 749.

CHAPTER TEN

"THAT PIECE DOES NOT EXIST WITHOUT JULIUS"

Still Staying on *Stay On It*

Matthew Mendez

Com'on now baby, stay on it.
Change this thread on which we move
from invisible to hardly tangible.
. . . .
This is why baby cakes, I'm ringing you up
in order to relay this song message
so that you can get the feelin
O sweet boy
Because without the movin and the groovin,
the carin and the sharin,
the reelin and the feelin
I mean really.

—Julius Eastman's program note for *Stay On It* (1973)

Since the new music community's rediscovery of Julius Eastman with the 2005 release of *Unjust Malaise*,[1] *Stay On It* has quickly rushed to the head of the pack in listener popularity sweepstakes. Among critics, Mark

Swed hails the music as "intensely personal" and "radically ahead of its time."[2] Steve Smith deems it a "potent metaphor" for the virtues of "cross-pollination and collaboration."[3] And most colorfully of all, Paul Muller affectionately likens the piece to "a slightly out of control street party."[4] Nor has Eastman's resourceful fusion of relentless pulsation and elements of free improvisation failed to catch the imagination of young, open-eared performers. Captivated by the archival recordings in *Unjust Malaise*, the artistic directors of the experimental ensembles thingNY and Ne(x)tworks have independently undertaken to "realize" the music in live performance.[5] Without their efforts, it is hard to imagine that *Stay On It* would have been selected as the representative Eastman composition on the Los Angeles Philharmonic's second Minimalist Jukebox festival in April 2014—the first "official" recognition of Eastman's belated entrée into the minimalist canon.[6] All mighty impressive for a piece whose score is lost.

Yet the task of reconstructing *Stay On It* is hardly as straightforward as all that. For starters, the piece was not originally rehearsed in traditional "new music" fashion. Following the example set by the composer-led ensembles of the 1960s (such as those of Cornelius Cardew and Steve Reich), and anticipating the techniques soon to be favored by the so-called downtown movement, Eastman's working methods were marked by forms of what Walter J. Ong has termed "secondary orality."[7] Though Eastman provided the *Stay On It* players with scores, they were piecemeal and highly approximate, far more akin to jazz lead sheets than the notational hyper-precision of the "official" avant-garde. Instead, he worked hands-on with the instrumentalists, directing their interpretations verbally, as well as by example (Eastman usually did double duty on *Stay On It*, singing from the piano with the assistance of a boom microphone).[8] So in his absence, Eastman's precise musical intentions can be identified only in consultation with his former associates. However, some of these have since passed away, and the rest are spotty when it comes to details—understandably so, given the forty-year interval.[9]

This is far from the only obstacle. The open-ended nature of the score was designed to allow for considerable variation from performance to performance. As Eastman put it during his spoken introduction to a February 1974 performance in Glasgow, Scotland, *Stay On It* was primarily concerned, "without using notes," to "use the musicians' innate musical abilities."[10] He was, he said, investigating the very basic question, "How can we hear music?" and he clearly aspired to some of the spontaneity native to jazz and other improvising traditions, with the scores functioning as more or less disposable mnemonic devices. After all, *Stay On It* was performed on nearly twenty occasions during its first year, plenty of time for the musicians to put their stamp on the final product. Yet archival audio was not produced for every performance, and in most of the cases when it was made, it has not yet been located. The upshot is that it is difficult to assess the scope of the flexibility originally permitted between renditions, and to base a performing score on a single—or even a handful of—recorded documents is a dangerous proposition. Contemporary reviews and eyewitness accounts can fill in some of the gaps, though these too are patchy. Likewise, one could try to make deductions from Eastman's approach to compositions from the same period, but at present we know even less about what went into rehearsing those than we know about *Stay On It*. All in all, between the missing scores, the primacy of secondary sources, and the need to draw conclusions based on limited evidence, it is difficult to avoid the strange verdict that the Eastman situation is rather more akin to what early music scholars regularly face than to any twentieth-century precedents. That, however, is not likely to inspire much confidence, if Alex Ross's words are anything to go by: "Musicians who specialize in performing works of the deep past . . . eventually have to face up to the impossibility of their task."[11]

The following represents an attempt, foolhardy and very likely "impossible," to collate everything we currently know about *Stay On It*. The work's position in Eastman's oeuvre, his aesthetic proclivities at the time of its composition, the cultural backdrop against which the music was conceived, its performance history and reception during his lifetime, the rehearsal process and "performance practice" imposed by Eastman, and his difficult relationship with the traditional Western notion of the "musical work": all are vital pieces of the *Stay On It* puzzle. What emerges is a cautionary tale, one sure to become more urgent with the graying of the "downtown" generation. When it came to the transmission of his music, Eastman was representative of a movement audacious enough to revert to old, "unreliable" word-of-mouth techniques prevalent among traditional, preliterate cultures, while also embracing the modern innovation of mechanical reproduction. Yet no matter how many stylistic cobwebs they blow away, such maneuvers generally have the downside of shunning the very distribution networks put in place to ensure that artworks will outlive their creators. This is particularly true when it comes to a man composer Peter Gena characterized by saying: "There are composers who are 95 percent promotion; I don't know that he [Eastman] was 5 percent."[12] Not to say the undertaking is a fait accompli. Perhaps a few readers will be moved to check their attics for dusty manuscripts, the proprietors of various studios and concert venues their archives for old reel-to-reel tapes, and, with their assistance, we will be a few steps closer to piecing together the music Julius Eastman once called *Stay On It.*

* * *

At the time of Eastman's 1968 entrance into the Center of the Creative and Performing Arts orbit, it would have been difficult to predict the stylistic turn he would take with *Stay On It.* After "modal," lightly "syncopated" apprentice works with apparent "rhythmic delicacy" and "use of large musical space," the *Piano Pieces I–IV*, written the year Eastman began his association with the University at Buffalo (UB), showed him grappling with well-established avant-garde paradigms—"John Cage jostles Karlheinz Stockhausen," in the words of one reviewer.[13] Yet as Thomas Putnam of the *Buffalo Courier-Express* also quickly recognized, "The piano is not enough to express what Eastman wants."[14] Ensuing works for larger forces were correspondingly chaotic, polyglot, even "maximalist," all very much in the syncretic collage-oriented vein of the day. For example, the jazz-tinged *Thruway*, written in 1970 for youth chorus, instrumental ensemble, and magnetic tape, pertained to no less than "the history of the worlds."[15] It was, Eastman continued, "how I vision the beginning, the development of the world, wars, the death of planets, reincarnation," all grand notions necessitating his first experiments with nontraditional notation.[16] Meanwhile, other works from the period mined a heady brew of theatricality, montage, and sonic saturation, in service of a distinctly campy gay aesthetic.[17] Even some of the music produced concurrently with *Stay On It* occupied decidedly different territory.[18] Still, if any one thing carried over from the pre-1973 work, it was the earlier music's juxtaposition of "incongruous" elements, Eastman's mix of frank sexuality and "acoustical garbage."[19] Undoubtedly, the wild textures of *Stay On It*'s middle section have roots in these investigations.

Nor, in retrospect, did Eastman's catalog want for precedents of a different sort. A case in point is *Trumpet*, a bracing 1970 study in heterophony and protominimal ostinati inspired by big-band sonorities.[20] Different, but no less important, was 1972's *Mumbaphilia*, which constituted an attempt to fuse music and dance. According to Eastman, the performers were "not performers, but realizers. They are given movements, music, and rules; they take their materials and make their own dance; their own music."[21] Sound and choreography were part of a single conception, a tendency Putnam had already identified in *The Moon's Silent Modulation* and *Thruway*: "Eastman is interested in making dances that can be done by musicians."[22] Most pertinent of all, however, was *Wood in Time* (1972), Eastman's gloss on György

Ligeti's *Poème symphonique* for one hundred metronomes.[23] Joel Chadabe, a sympathetic colleague from the Buffalo years, recalled that Eastman

> put a little motor on a piece of wood and connected it to a maraca-like instrument so that it moved back and forth as if someone were playing it in a very mechanical way for about ten minutes without any nuance. . . . At that time, the idea of mechanical kinds of repetitions, as in many of Steve [Reich's] pieces, as well as Philip Glass's work, had become a musical paradigm, and I thought that Julius's motor piece was a comment on that, actually a parody.[24]

Eastman would fine-tune the contraption in 1974's *Femenine*, an hour-long piece built on ideas first explored in *Stay On It*, employing "four curious instruments that mechanically shook sleigh bells quickly back and forth."[25] More significant, though, is that Chadabe linked *Wood in Time* to what would become *Stay On It*, indicating that well before Eastman wrote any music under the minimalist moniker, his take on the genre was already hard to pin down: arch, and not a little tongue in cheek.

Those close to Eastman, however, would not have been surprised that he was ready to move on to new stylistic ventures by 1973. Thinking back to the emphasis his composition teacher Constant Vauclain had placed on technical bona fides, Eastman had already served notice: "The only trouble is that you master something so well you get tired of it."[26] In the meantime, a smorgasbord of composers with ties to what eventually came to be known as minimalism (David Bedford, Harold Budd, David Burge, and Michael Sahl) had their work lovingly produced by the Creative Associates (CAs). The landmark March 1968 recording of Terry Riley's *In C* was a key institutional acknowledgment of the stripped-down sound's staying power.[27] (An "encore" of *In C* was even mounted at UB in 1971.)[28] And then there were Eastman's activities with the S.E.M. Ensemble, established in 1970 by Petr Kotik. Eastman was an early member of the group, performing La Monte Young's drone music with them at least as early as 1972. It quickly rubbed off: his *440* for voice and three strings, an austere slab of static microtonal textures from the next year, was clearly written under the spell of the *Dream House*.[29] No less formative, though, was the work of Kotik himself, with whom Eastman shared a "very mutual and close understanding of music."[30] Particularly significant was Kotik's cycle *There Is Singularly Nothing*, begun in 1971. Its voice part was composed especially for Eastman,[31] and the score's quietly meandering, "minimal" sonorities arise eloquently from a deliberate application of Cagean non-hierarchical form.

But it was the music of Frederic Rzewski that would have been resounding most strongly in Eastman's ears when he conceived *Stay On It* in early 1973. With S.E.M., he first performed *Les Moutons de Panurge* in September 1970, and the piece was subsequently given another performance on a December 1971 Evenings for New Music concert, during which Eastman was active as a conductor.[32] As for Rzewski's *Coming Together*, Eastman performed it as early as April 1972 (again with S.E.M.), and it quickly went on to become one of his signature pieces.[33] Indeed, Eastman had enough of an affinity with the music that Rzewski tasked him with the world premiere of his Frederick Douglass setting, *Struggle*. Eastman took precious time out of his schedule to prepare the work, which was first presented in New York City on January 27, 1974, the day before a Dartmouth College performance of *Stay On It*, mounted as a preview for the CAs' upcoming European tour.[34]

All in all, Eastman's admiration for Rzewski's work of this period makes considerable sense. If the modular structure of *In C* provided a manifest precedent for questions regarding notation and ensemble coordination, Rzewski, for whom minimalism was merely a means to an end, offered an appealingly messy approach to pulsation and repetition. In Rzewski's hands, pulse-pattern minimalism was never rigidly nonreferential. Unlike early Reich and Glass, the "outside world" of politics and the vernacular was readily embraced. David Gibson, a CA cellist who partook in a number of performances of *Stay On It*, summed up the link between Rzewski and Eastman by remarking that their compositional styles were in some respects "cast from the same die," but with the former "aggressive and hard-nosed" and the latter "malleable and sensual."[35] Of course, this is not to reduce Eastman to a simple function of another oeuvre. Hard as it is to imagine, in a day and age when erstwhile minimalists have won Pulitzer Prizes and Golden Globes, Eastman drew most of his musical conclusions by breathing the same air and feeling the same vibrations as his more commercially successful counterparts.[36]

In his brief Glasgow talk, Eastman acknowledged that *Stay On It* was part of a wider trend, one he was actively engaging with in his latest music. In particular, he made the telling statement that "there is in America now serious music—so-called—there is a school of music which tries to bring the beat back into music."[37] It is noteworthy that Eastman emphasized rhythmic continuity ("the beat") to the exclusion of the other building blocks of early minimalism, such as process, repetition, consonance, slow harmonic rhythm, and machine-like impersonality. For no matter the direction Eastman's later projects would take, the truth is that *Stay On It* stood askew from these minimalist standbys: too haphazard for "process music," too wild and wooly for "another look at harmony," too expressive for assembly-line industrial precision. Percussionist Jan Williams, the only player to participate in every performance of *Stay On It* during the composer's lifetime, granted that by making repetition part of the lingua franca, a piece like *In C* had directly paved the way for Eastman. But Williams also concluded that early pulse-pattern minimalism had only a token impact on the composer's structural and aesthetic thinking: "He was influenced to a degree by the processes involved in these pieces, but that's about it."[38] Kotik, who played flute in a handful of performances, put it in even stronger terms, insisting that *Stay On It* "has nothing to do with" minimalism.[39]

If Kotik's assessment seems a touch exaggerated, Arthur Russell, a like-minded collaborator from the 1980s, can safely speak in Eastman's stead: "The kind of repetition that comes out of me and is in dance music is somewhat different to the repetition of minimalist works of the Sixties and Seventies. Dance music is more improvisatory. It uses an extendable structure which on the one hand is recognisable, and on the other, improvisatory. It's based on hearing what you do while you do it."[40] For Russell, the tension between static, predetermined forms and unforeseeable, off-the-cuff detours was a fruitful one, and *Stay On It* plainly examines a similar dichotomy, with the opening unison F♯ Mixolydian refrain on one side, and the extempore hoots, hollers, and wails into which it gradually devolves on the other. As we will see below, repetition here is a feedback loop between creative musical actors, whose spur-of-the-moment "inputs" make possible an endless succession of microvariations. For Eastman, who spent considerably more time in his Glasgow introduction underlining his rapport with freely improvised "open" scores, than with techniques like additive rhythm,[41] repetition was not an excuse to "lock in" or "check out," nor a basis for trance-like states. It was part and parcel of the expansion of executorial responsibility explored in *Mumbaphilia* and other early works. As in Ravel's famous *Bolero*, the repetition actually heightened the difficulty, so that, as Williams recalled, the instrumentalists "had to listen very carefully to what was going on."[42] Eastman addressed the point—albeit cryptically—noting that *Stay On It* "creates a certain tension, because musicians are very slick; that is to say, when you're off one note, *you're off*."[43] Technician and horn player Ralph Jones, in turn, confirmed that the "tension" was premeditated: "It was a tough task because the individual parts used challenging, stuttering rhythmic figures and this fought with the principle of 'grooving.'"[44]

Russell's formula gestures toward another stylistic headwater converging in the *Stay On It* delta: popular music. Dennis Kahle, who played percussion alongside Williams in most performances, identified the syncopated refrain running throughout the work as a "riff," suggesting that "it was influenced almost entirely by soul/R&B music. No trying to disguise it, it was straight-ahead American 4/4."[45] Gibson was even more specific, indicating that Diana Ross was "the hot topic" of the day, with *Stay On It* violinist Benjamin Hudson seconding him: "I remember Julius asking me to play the theme from 'Stop! In the Name of Love' by the Supremes on the piano at one point in the piece, at least in some of the performances."[46] For his part, Ned Sublette recalls Ross's disco hit "Love Hangover" later being all the rage at the Hibachi Room, one of Eastman's favorite Buffalo-area haunts, a Japanese restaurant turned popular gay bar.[47] Renée Levine Packer has fond memories of dancing with Eastman: "Julius, Benjamin Hudson, and I would get up and dance to the music that was blaring from the loudspeakers. The three of us often dancing together. It was exhilarating."[48] Eastman certainly doubled down on these associations during *Stay On It*'s first performance. The premiere began with the familiar riff, prolonged Broadway vamp-style, atop which Eastman, trusty boom mic at the ready, played the role of emcee presiding over his dance floor: "I want to introduce you to our new group we have here: 'J.E. and the Sunlights.'"[49] The original *Buffalo Evening News* reviewer thought it all a piece with the music's "obvious put-on,"[50] but whether or not the mock Motown band name was meant as a leg-pull, this was a mildly subversive gesture coming on a program of string quartets and other relatively conventional new music.

In this regard, Eastman's choice of words in his Glasgow preamble is revealing. After all, he spoke not of restoring pulse to contemporary music, but "the beat"—a horse of a very different color next to something like *In C*'s "The Pulse."[51] In a Reich or a Glass performance, the pulsation will generally be like clockwork, taut and rigid, aspiring almost to the condition of a drum machine. With its automated bells, *Femenine* is unquestionably closer to this rhythmic conception,[52] whereas *Stay On It* is all about the perpetuation of a more flexible—or "malleable," as Gibson put it—groove. As with so much music with ties to the African-American vernacular, it can easily be spoken of in terms of inflection and "feeling," with the result, as Kahle asserted, that "you could dance to it."[53] To be sure, the social conventions for listening to a program of experimental music would have forestalled any dancing, but as author-critic Jaime Rosal witnessed, the audience at the CAs' Barcelona performance got Eastman's "song message" all the same: "The crowd is infected by the instrumentalists' euphoria . . . the crowd seems to have caught on and realizes that it should engage with the performers . . . at various points in the hall, a wave is spreading to other audience members jiggling their keychains and the performers alike are very pleased because they have conveyed Eastman's message and universal delight pervades the hall."[54] The Barcelona crowd understood intuitively that this was participatory music, that these were not sounds to be received in sober "concert hall" contemplation. It was a question of audience attunement, or as Putnam put it in his review of the December 16, 1973, rendition: "Julius Eastman's shunning of virtuosity is more a matter of getting with it."[55] If we follow musicologist Simon Frith's thought-provoking hypothesis that "the ideal way of listening to music is to dance to it, if only in one's head," then in Barcelona Eastman did one better than even *Mumbaphilia*, managing to transform the spectators into "dancers" too.[56]

It is hardly insignificant that *Stay On It* was written in 1973, the very year disco is generally accepted to have emerged into mainstream consciousness. Whether or not the score was intended as a statement on the newish dance trend, it is not altogether fanciful to suggest that it stands as a prototype of "avant-disco," an alloy of the experimental ethos and the pounding bass of the discotheque. We have already noted that the uproarious sonorities Eastman envisioned for *Stay On It*'s quasi-improvised "freak-outs" are fully worthy of his earlier work (to say nothing of a Sylvano Bussotti, Vinko Globokar, or Mauricio Kagel). Then there is the standard-issue disco "recipe," which *Stay On It* matches ingredient for ingredient: "The fusion of Latin rhythms, Anglo-Caribbean instrumentation, North American black 'soul' vocals, and Euro-American melodies."[57] First, Eastman's riff is a slightly ornamented variant of the Cuban 2-3 *son clave*; second, in performances of *Stay On It*, the vibraphone (close cousin to the marimba) and cabasa/maracas were constants alongside the other CAs' traditional European instruments, all of which were amplified;[58] third, there were the *senza vibrato* imitation pop stylings of Georgia Mitoff, Gwendolin Sims Warren, and Eastman himself; and finally, the voicing of the riff, with its basic parallel thirds, obviously qualifies as "Euro-American."[59] For Eastman, who once claimed in response to a song by Earth, Wind & Fire, that he had "completely lost [his] ability to discriminate between genres of music," pulse-based experimentalism and disco had simply become part of a single continuum.[60] This stance would have been consistent with the teachings of Eastman's mentor Lukas Foss, as Levine Packer indicated: "Foss was very influential in that period in Julius's life, and Lukas said, 'You should use all the techniques. The more the merrier.' . . . That was a mantra for Julius, too: use whatever you feel like using and don't let labels bother you."[61] It helps account for Eastman's qualifier, "so-called," in his Glasgow commentary on the new, pulsed "serious music."

Mitoff and Eastman's vocal contributions are a particularly compelling tie-in to the disco aesthetic. Sometimes they sang neutral syllables, occasionally Eastman intoned lines from his poem, but mostly they kept exhorting the instrumentalists to "stay on it."[62] As Walter Hughes has persuasively asserted, "The oft-noted vacuity of the lyrics of disco songs is itself a part of the medium's message: they usually strive only to translate the rhetoric of the beat into simple imperatives. . . . Language is subjugated to the beat, and drained of its pretensions to meaning."[63] In other words, the triviality of disco vocabulary was just one more means of keeping the sweat-drenched bodies gyrating. If Eastman had not already taken the title, some disco tunesmith would have been obliged to invent a "Stay On It."[64] Eastman's poem says it all: "With you movin and groovin on it, / making me feel fine as wine, / I don't have to find the meaning." We could not be farther away from mid-century modernism, where complexity and richness of signification were implicitly valorized as desirable (straight) "masculine" traits.[65] And this is to say nothing of the abstractions of early minimalism: with Hudson's Diana Ross snippet, *Stay On It* cited disco as a social entity, highlighting the genre's associations with gay and ethnic subcultures. This was, dance music historian Tim Lawrence argues, a no-no in the early seventies downtown scene, which had embraced some of the virtues of pluralism, but remained uncomfortable with ethnically coded modes of expression.[66]

Eastman's poem brings these themes front and center. There are, of course, its allusions to jazz argot ("*You dig*"), but more significant is its evocation of same-sex love ("O sweet boy"). Once again, the date is not incidental. In the wake of the Stonewall riots, not to mention the civil rights and feminist movements, gay voices in the United States in 1973 could no longer be politely (or impolitely, as the case may have been) swept under the carpet. Making provision for Ross's iconic status in the gay community, Sublette speculates that Eastman's quotation of 1965's "Stop in the Name of Love" was meant to symbolize this shift, "a still-recent memory from the other side of the '69 Stonewall divide. Gay culture had come out of the closet in the years between the Diana Ross of 'Stop!' and the Diana Ross of 'Love Hangover.'"[67] *Stay On It*'s dramatic trajectory, progressing loosely from mechanized inflexibility, to collective riotousness, to individual expressivity, can be understood in these terms. The music enacts the opposition of "objective" materials (rigidly circumscribed repetitions) and "subjective" ones (unruly quasi-improvised figures), but Eastman finds a way to reconcile them: the concluding piano solo is all repetition, and yet it is full of feeling. Gibson insisted that "in spite of the craziness, his [Eastman's] music is very personal, very exposed. When he did a piece, it was like he was laying his heart out. . . . In the end it was very quiet and very personal and very introspective. Introspective. That's what the ending of *Stay On It* was."[68] Pinned betwixt and between modernism's heteronormativity and early minimalism's apolitical empiricism, Eastman was asserting himself as an individual gay subject, death of the author be damned.

On some occasions the subtext became explicit, with the final section of *Stay On It* developing into an extended pseudoerotic meditation. Gibson has vivid memories of these episodes:

> The *Stay On It* was you stay on this melody until you just can't stand it: "Stop it!" And it was always Ben Hudson and Julius, and they just wanted to savor every moment of this thing. Especially the performance in Aberdeen I remember, it was really out there. . . . It was musical lovemaking. It got slower and it got sexier, and eyebrows and motions towards each other and flirting with each other. This piece is as much a theater piece as it is musical.[69]

While none of the known recordings of *Stay On It* features anything of this sort, it is undeniably consistent with other improvisations Eastman gave during his lifetime.[70] As with Nam June Paik, one of the persistent concerns of his creative practice was to bring the new music establishment face to face with "taboo" erotic themes. Such was the extent of Eastman's investment in this project that Gibson concluded, "If you don't bring out the sexuality of this piece then you miss the piece."[71] In this respect *Femenine*, which can be considered a follow-up of sorts to *Stay On It*, provides a suggestive sidelight. *Femenine*'s final known performances came in June 1975 at Buffalo's Albright-Knox Art Gallery, where it was given simultaneously—but in a different part of the museum—with the now-lost *Masculine* (1974).[72] Thanks to his S.E.M. work, Eastman would have been familiar with John Cage's simultaneous-performance concept of two or more unrelated activities going on at once. Perhaps an unstated protestation that the received gender binary was really just a single spectrum, this was Eastman's take on Cagean "unimpededness and interpenetration."

Whatever the case, in the absence of further recorded documentation, it is not easy to assess precisely what *Stay On It* had to say about the libido. At the very least, the picture Gibson paints can be traced back to Eastman's earlier investigations of camp. Susan Sontag's often-debated definition provides a suitable starting point: "Camp is art that proposes itself seriously, but cannot be taken altogether seriously because it is 'too much.'"[73] By Gibson's lights ("You stay on this melody until you just can't stand it"), the repetition did not facilitate perceptibility, depersonalization, or even groove. It went so far beyond the limits of the reasonable and the "serious" that it was well out of the world of conventional, consumerist straight expressivity—or its "unpopular" avant-garde obverse, serial purity—and into something rather more ambivalent. Were Eastman and Hudson sincere? Or was their "musical lovemaking" precisely calculated to fall beyond the pale of the straight mainstream? In that case, their intent may have been to establish a field for creative play insulated from nongay behavioral norms, their artifice a safe haven for its opposite, "authentic" expressivity.

The original reviewers did not interpret the music in these terms. Reporting on the Barcelona performance, Franz Walter was only able to hear the piece through the lens of the classic épater le bourgeois strategy of transgression. Offering that the incessant repetition was "intended to challenge the public's resistance," Walter saw *Stay On It* as a Fluxus-style provocation—shades of Satie's *Vexations*, as interpreted by Cage. (Corroborating Rosal's account, Walter also mirthfully added that "the very young Barcelona audience demonstrated the most extraordinary endurance, and it is the performers who—no matter how belatedly—ultimately had to admit defeat.")[74] Stephen Walsh's review of the CAs' London concert read Eastman's music similarly, adjudging it "aggressively, unpleasantly and above all unredeemedly self-assertive."[75] Even the eminent composer-critic Xavier Montsalvatge, also covering the Barcelona show, thought the music a pushy attempt to one-up the sameness of Morton Feldman's *For Frank O'Hara*, likewise performed by the CAs on their European programs.[76] The "camp minimalist" subtext went unnoticed.

Yet it seems Eastman was also comfortable setting *Stay On It* off as an "inside joke" for a primarily gay listenership. On June 13, 1973, he was slated to present the piece as part of "An Evening of Contemporary Music" for Buffalo's Gay Pride Week. For someone specializing in "difficult," "recondite" music, Eastman's reputation in this community was considerable: his is one of only two names to appear on the cover of the Pride Week preview issue of *Fifth Freedom*, the area's most prominent serial catering to the LGBT population.[77] (The other was Arthur Bell, the well-known Gay Liberation journalist.) In the subsequent issue's appraisal of the Pride Week, the editors warmly acknowledged Eastman's efforts: "Wednesday night's concert by Julius Eastman and Chamber Ensemble made us all realize why he is acclaimed as one of the best in his field. We all extend great appreciation to Julius for the wonderful performance which he undertook at his own expense and initiative as his contribution to Gay Pride in Buffalo."[78]

This was only the city's second ever Pride Week, so Eastman's participation was more than just a token gesture. It came at a significant juncture: less than a year later, on May 14, United States Representatives Bella Abzug and Ed Koch introduced H.R. 14752 (93rd Congress), the ill-fated Equality Act of 1974, a federal bill forbidding discrimination on the grounds of sexual orientation. The upbeat mood remained short-lived. As that year's Pride Week was under way, the Buffalo Police Department began an undercover sting operation designed to shutter the Hibachi Room. The result was the revocation of the Hibachi's liquor license, and it was only after a January 16, 1975, ruling by the Appellate Division of the New York State Supreme Court that the Liquor Board's decision was overturned.

Fifth Freedom covered the affair extensively. In a curious bit of serendipity, their report celebrating the reversal was printed side by side with one of the most comprehensive eyewitness accounts in existence of an Eastman performance.[79] It is a record of *Femenine*, a copy of whose score survives. Like *Stay On It*, it is based entirely on a repeated syncopated figure:

> Each musician had a single sheet of music. Each sheet was different; establishing several isolated themes. From my listening the themes were not synchronized. If they were, the relationships of sound would have repeated themselves and become immediately boring. The juxtaposition of these themes seemed such that there was no time when there was a repetition of the same relationships between themes. . . . Instead of progressions and variations of themes prearranged by the composer, chance was given free hand providing spontaneous and unplanned variations of sound. To hold the constantly varying sounds the remainder of the performance was set in motion mechanically. The duration of the sixty-minute performance was determined by a clock.[80]

Of particular interest is the claim that each part, though unique, was only a single page long. The existing manuscript spans a whole five pages: it may have been Eastman's "conductor's score" or that of the vibraphone, which plays an almost obbligato-like role in the one known recording of *Femenine*.[81] Saxophonist Joe Ford, who participated in a few performances of *Stay On It*, but had no recollection of the earlier piece, confirmed this description: "Julius placed a digital clock set at 12:00 in front of the ensemble. Each player had a part with different little rhythmic lines to be played then slowly embellished. Each line was timed 12:00, 12:03, 12:05, etc. Each player may have had different times to change to the next section. Julius conducted, mostly for volume, intensity, etc. When the clock struck 1:00, the piece was over."[82] The *Femenine* manuscript corroborates these impressions. As Ford indicated, it features the clock timings familiar from the "Nigger Series."[83] Likewise, there are all manner of melodic modules, guidelines for harmony and accompaniment, and a variety of textual indications ("unison," "displace one 16th note," "pianist will interupt [*sic*]").

According to the testimony of *Stay On It* veterans, its score was structured similarly. Hudson, for example, remarked that his part "was a handwritten collection of phrases to use in building improvisations."[84] Gibson, who likened Eastman's notation to a looser, sloppier version of Witold Lutosławski's aleatoric modules, remembered more. He indicated that the parts were multiple pages long, like the extant *Femenine* manuscript. According to Gibson, the modules consisted of various chords and melodies, while the parts were "very compartmentalized and you went from one thing to another thing to another thing."[85] Meanwhile, Williams suggested that the content of the modules was not always sacrosanct: as Ford noted of *Femenine*, they were sometimes skeletal versions of rhythmic-melodic figures to be expanded upon in performance.[86] This dynamic was evident to audiences: Montsalvatge observed that Eastman "grants considerable freedom of improvisation to the performers out of a schematic of musical sequences," while Rosal was of the opinion that Eastman hoped "to free the interpreters from the slavery of the written score."[87] Yet no parts can be made out in the Glasgow video. It is likely that by this stage in the European tour, the players were familiar enough with the piece to dispense with written instructions.[88] Either way, the ex-CAs all agreed that the parts were especially difficult to decipher.[89] For Williams, however, Eastman's "unprofessionalism" was calculated for effect: "He was very pragmatic in that he decided on a notation that gave the performers just the right amount of information to elicit from them exactly what he wanted."[90]

The instrumentation was also flexible within certain bounds. According to Levine Packer and Williams, the lineup was wholly dependent on the CA pool, whose composition varied from semester to semester.[91] Thus, the later European performances were beholden to the touring roster, and featured a guitar and cello, with Eastman taking on sole vocal duties (Mitoff was not on hand). *In C*, as the CAs had recorded it, was therefore not a model; the instrumental overlap with the *Unjust Malaise* recording (flute, saxophone, two mallet percussionists, and piano) is a red herring. But for Gibson, who eventually concluded that his cello was not an idiomatic choice for *Stay On It*, the open scoring was a shortcoming. He felt that as long as the two vibraphone players and Eastman's piano remained constant, the same basic sonority would persist.[92] (It is unclear whether Eastman would have sanctioned performances without piano and percussion.) Even so, individual personalities were also a factor, since, as Williams indicated, some of the CAs were on Eastman's wavelength more than others.[93] This pertained especially to flutist Eberhard Blum, who was scheduled to take over from Kotik, starting at Dartmouth.[94] Before he died, however, Blum insisted that he had nothing to do with *Stay On It*.[95] Gibson remembered things quite differently: "I think he played on *Stay On It* and I think he didn't like it. He was always angry about it."[96] Gibson speculated that Blum had no time for Eastman's dalliances with popular music. The piece was polarizing even for pros trained to be open-minded.

Kotik commented on the rehearsal process: "We worked like a group, not like a pickup situation, where everybody would be watching the time. . . . Many things were finalized in rehearsal. Many times Julius himself didn't know exactly how to proceed, and we tried this and we tried that."[97] Williams concurred, indicating that the run-throughs had a "workshop"-like atmosphere, while Gibson specified that much of the time was spent establishing "the kind of character and what you were supposed to do in each of the sections."[98] Echoing Kotik, Williams described the tone of these workshops:

> The rehearsals were, let's say, dynamic, but amicable. . . . When he was not totally clear in articulating what he wanted, we cut him plenty of slack and worked patiently until he got what he wanted. That was the great thing about working with him on his pieces, nothing was cut and dried, he would say things and you would look at him and think, "What is he trying to tell us, what exactly is he asking us to do?" And that's just it, he wasn't telling us, he was asking us.[99]

It was a give-and-take process, with the instrumentalists helping to shape the ways in which Eastman's initially sketchy ideas would manifest themselves. It was most emphatically not, as Eastman once facetiously referred to it, a "fast foods concert."[100] In fact, it is precisely some of this back-and-forth that is missing from the well-known *Unjust Malaise* account, which apparently constituted the only time Eastman did not participate in a performance of the work during his lifetime. This is a peculiar irony of *Stay On It*'s afterlife: even though Eastman had done the music at Carnegie Hall just a week prior, Doug Gaston is the pianist on the commercially released account. For someone who always had a hand in performances of his music, this was unusual. Accordingly, the December 16, 1973, recording should be taken with a grain of salt. Gibson judged it "too slick, too studio, too manufactured," whereas he recalled the European performances being "much cruder."[101]

Be that as it may, there was little room for debate when it came to questions of structure and duration. Williams indicated that the approximate length was consistent across all performances (twenty-four to twenty-eight minutes), as was the general trajectory toward melodic entropy.[102] The quiet piano coda before the tambourine kicks in also remained fixed.[103] It may even have been written out in some detail, since Gaston's rendering of the coda on the *Unjust Malaise* set is more or less the same as what Eastman plays on the other known recordings. (At Glasgow, Eastman actually adds an additional minute-long "coda to the coda," in a jarring, poppy D major.)[104] In this regard, Williams drew a clear distinction between foreground and background: "Julius was active in directing us on the macro level (form, duration) but gave us considerable freedom on the micro level (licks) . . . the harmonic world was pretty much laid out."[105] Without surviving parts, however, it is not always possible today to differentiate between the two categories. Take the series of startling silences that comes four minutes into the December 16 performance. In the Glasgow recording, they occur after a full nine minutes, albeit in the same succession and context (which suggests they may have been notated to some degree), while in the premiere there are no silences whatsoever. Were they part of the global structure, but shifted or omitted as was Eastman's wont, or was it up to the musicians to decide where to place them in the heat of the moment?

In practice, the interplay between the spontaneous "micro level" and the broader form was governed by visual cues. According to Kahle, "During the repetition of the riff, any instrumentalist in the group could take a 'solo' at any time, provided they signaled their intent to the group. This was usually done via some showy gesture. At the end of the solo, the soloist would signal the group to return to the riff, via a hand gesture, a leap, or whatever."[106] As for the transitions and structural pivot points, Williams provided many of the appropriate prompts. As Gibson noted, "The problem was to get from one section to the other, and that was Jan's responsibility, and he largely did that with rhythmic cues. He would either play something on the vibraphone or he would clap a rhythm or conduct something with his mallets."[107] That being said, saxophone player Amrom Chodos can also be seen contributing cues on the Glasgow video. But no matter who gave them, the instrumentalists always had to take their colleagues' musical "inputs" into account and finesse these back into *Stay On It*'s overall refrain matrix.

At Glasgow, Eastman touched upon this structure, and the means by which the musicians interacted with it: "There are certain notes which trigger certain rhythmic patterns, and these are notes which can be played by the performer at any time. . . . The others have to respond to those notes."[108] Eastman envisions a call-and-response dynamic, with predetermined musical prompts answered with elaboration and ornamentation. This is why Williams suggested that the license demanded by *Stay On It* was not improvisation so much as "digressing from the fixed riffs," with Eastman specifying that the ad-libbed sounds should arise organically out of the opening riff:

> The abrupt introduction of material that "fought" against the prevailing unison riff was always related in some way, most of the time rhythmically. Often, jarring dissonance initiated a transition, which caused things to get really out of focus. Refocusing would sometimes happen gradually, sometimes abruptly (returning to the opening riff, for example). I recall that in rehearsal, we worked on this with Julius suggesting when, and perhaps who, might initiate a change via an interjection of "foreign" material.[109]

A memorable example of "refocusing" comes about six and a half minutes into the premiere, where the ensemble is galloping along contentedly, until Williams makes a sudden attempt to reestablish the riff. Deliberately out of phase with the other instruments, his vibraphone stubbornly holds its ground, blurring the composite beat. The tension subsides only after a held saxophone tone, which prompts the ensemble to cut back to the riff with Williams.

This is one of *Stay On It*'s most suggestive aspects, its wholly nondevelopmental refrain structure. It is absolutely characteristic of the "cut" in black aesthetics, as defined by James A. Snead: "An abrupt, seemingly unmotivated break (an accidental *da capo*) with a series already in progress and a willed return to a prior series" that "builds 'accidents' into its coverage."[110] This conception of repetition, which effectively forestalls all goal-directed behavior, is essentially alien to the European "art" music tradition (the experiments of Stravinsky, Messiaen, and Stockhausen notwithstanding). With a bit of wordplay, Putnam acknowledged the "political" import of *Stay On It*'s cuts: "These cats whine, but whenever they break out some performer puts the mindless refrain back on the track. As the music develops the performers indulge their simple disobedience."[111] Unfortunately, he was the only one: as with its campy overtones, the other critics simply dismissed the music without reflecting upon what the cut might mean in this foreign territory. Covering the London performance, William Mann complained that "the relentless squeaks and clatters induced a headache."[112] At Carnegie Hall, Donal Henahan lambasted the music as "monotony in a loud variety."[113] And Montsalvatge insisted that he and a handful of like-minded audience members left before the piece concluded, teasing that as he was writing, the "friendly Buffalo musicians might still be playing."[114] Then there was the CAs' disastrous May 25, 1974, concert at Attica Correctional Facility,[115] which concluded with the last known performance of *Stay On It* during Eastman's lifetime. For a piece with such a lucky start, this was going out with a whimper. How is it that this music could have disappeared down the rabbit hole so comprehensively?

One difficulty is that Eastman never revived *Stay On It*. Like most pop musicians, he looked exclusively toward the future. *Stay On It* was only a stepping-stone, in the sense that Eastman took the lessons he learned, and applied them in subsequent projects, without pausing to preserve a particular "version" of the piece. There was no need, not when he was around to coach players and send them tapes (Ong's "secondary orality"). Kotik was particularly understanding of the predicament, noting that "when you compose for situations in which you are always going to be around, the pieces don't seem to be finished. Finished [in the sense that they could] be given somewhere by somebody that would be able to really make sense of the music."[116] But this is not all. As in *Stay On It*, all the instrumentalists who worked with Eastman were obliged to do more than simply reproduce the notes on a page. As he put it in 1970, "This 'play the violin' is going out of business [in terms] of just being able to style."[117] Consequently, the composer's role was also expanded. In a brief manifesto provocatively titled "The Composer as Weakling," Eastman linked his creative practice with the traditions of early music, calling for the abolition of the modern division of sonic labor. Rather than "birthing music in his lonely room, awaiting the knock of an instrumentalist," Eastman insisted that composers must get their hands dirty and make their own music.[118] In other words, the music should be inseparable from the composer's physical presence. This is exactly what led Gibson, finally, to conclude about *Stay On It*: "That piece does not exist without Julius."[119] Indeed: would Eastman even have wanted the work revived after he was gone?

But even to speak of *Stay On It* as a "work" is misleading. If it is a musical work, where does that work reside? In some vanished "conductor's score" à la *Femenine*? In one of *Stay On It*'s recordings? All of them, somehow "averaged" together? What about the slightly off-color capers perpetrated by Eastman and Hudson? The Diana Ross quotes? Are they to be considered part of the piece? And what of the undocumented performances? All questions without answers. Perhaps *Stay On It* is better understood in terms of nonreproducible performance art, with each iteration being part of the same "series," yet ineluctably distinct. Rosal understood this intuitively at Barcelona: "Since the music has become a bridge between composer and audience . . . music is no longer limited to a score fixed for all time, but the composition is dynamic and its potentials are infinite, because each time it is performed it will be entirely different, depending on the degree of integration between the audience and the instrumentalists."[120] In short, context always matters. If, as Rosal suspects, *Stay On It* is participatory music, it cannot be divorced from the circumstances of its performance, nor, for that matter, from the personalities that brought the music to life on any given night. And yet, to further the performance art analogy, none of these factors have stopped museum curators from reviving the works of—say—the now-deceased Paik.[121] To resuscitate *Stay On It* may be to violate the spirit of the music, but it is undoubtedly the most persuasive testament to Eastman's overflowing creativity. The alternative, alas, is silence.

Notes

Epigraph. The full poem is available on Mary Jane Leach's website, accessed July 9, 2015, http://www.mjleach.com/Eastman%20Scores/Stay%20On%20It%20Poem.pdf.

1. Julius Eastman, *Unjust Malaise*, New World Records CD 80638, 2005.

2. Mark Swed, "Music Review: Minimalism: Math with Many Variables," *Los Angeles Times*, April 10, 2014.

3. Steve Smith, "Critic's Notebook: Festival Where Boundary-Defying Musicians Mix and Mingle," *New York Times*, January 18, 2011.

4. Paul Muller, "Maximum Minimalism at Disney Hall," *Sequenza 21: The Contemporary Classical Music Community*, April 12, 2014, accessed January 7, 2015, http://www.sequenza21.com/2014/04/9713/.

5. The artistic director of thingNY is Paul Pinto. Ne(x)tworks' performances were spearheaded by Christopher McIntyre and Cornelius Dufallo, son of Richard Dufallo, a part-time CA conductor with deep Buffalo ties. Since 2005, other performances of *Stay On It* have been mounted by the Dutch Spectra Ensemble, Austin Chamber Music Center, the Juilliard School, and New England Conservatory.

6. It was performed by the Los Angeles ensemble wild Up, conducted by Christopher Rountree, in an arrangement by Rountree and sound artist Chris Kallmyer.

7. Walter J. Ong, *Orality and Literacy: The Technologizing of the Word*, new ed. (New York: Routledge, 2012), 3.

8. E-mail communication between Dennis Kahle and Renée Levine Packer, March 3, 2004. Many thanks to Renée Levine Packer for furnishing me with a copy of this valuable correspondence.

9. Guitarist David Sussman died in April 2003, percussionist Dennis Kahle in April 2008, vocalist Gwendolin Sims Warren in May 2013, and flutist Eberhard Blum in July 2013.

10. Julius Eastman, spoken introduction to *Stay On It*, video recording (33'02"), February 16, 1974, Glasgow, Scotland. Video courtesy Francis McKee, Third Eye Centre Video Archive, Centre for Contemporary Arts, Glasgow.

11. Alex Ross, "Escaping the Museum," *New Yorker* 79, no. 33, November 3, 2003, 100.

12. Peter Gena, telephone interview with author, February 26, 2009.

13. Thomas Putnam, "Review: Eastman Traces Music," *Buffalo Courier-Express*, March 19, 1969; Thomas Putnam, "Review: Three Arts Presented by Eastman," *Buffalo Courier-Express*, April 21, 1969; and Harold C. Schonberg, "Music: Of Recent Vintage; 3 Works by Americans Get Local Premieres," *New York Times*, February 5, 1969. The apprentice works in question are the *Three Pieces* for violin and piano and the *Poems with Piano Interludes*. The dates of composition of these pieces is unknown.

14. Putnam, "Eastman Traces." Even Eastman seemed to acknowledge this, observing in the same article: "I tried to use different forms, different sounds. These piano pieces mean struggle—try to get out."

15. Raymond Ericson, "5 Works in Finale of Music Evenings," *New York Times*, May 1, 1970.

16. Thomas Putnam, "Julius Eastman Works Scheduled: Composer-Choreographer Looks Beyond Earth for His Ideas," *Buffalo Courier-Express*, April 19, 1970. Eastman's first graphic score was 1969's *The Moon's Silent Modulation*, whose scope was hardly less broad than *Thruway*. It was, Eastman avowed, "almost religious," with the message that "there are no superior persons or beings"; Thomas Putnam, "Review: *Moon's Modulation*," *Buffalo Courier-Express*, April 20, 1970.

17. Ryan Dohoney, "John Cage, Julius Eastman, and the Homosexual Ego," in *Tomorrow Is the Question: New Directions in Experimental Music Studies*, ed. Benjamin Piekut (Ann Arbor: University of Michigan Press, 2014), 46.

18. This includes *That Boy* (1973) and *Joy Boy* (1974), both of which "exploited [Eastman's] singing against mostly sustained or slow-moving instrumental parts"; John Rockwell, "S.E.M. Ensemble Offers Vocal Spark in Kitchen Concert," *New York Times*, March 15, 1975.

19. The description is of Eastman's performance of his *Macle* (1971), in which he is portrayed as having been "narcissistically in love with himself"; *Die Welt*, February 7, 1972.

20. *Trumpet* is listed both for seven trumpets and "any 7 soprano instruments"; see "UB Music Department Stages Recital," *Tonawanda News*, April 7, 1972; Ad, "Composers' Showcase," *New York Times*, April 15, 1973; Ad, "Whitney Concerts," *Village Voice*, April 26, 1973; and Ruth E. Anderson, *Contemporary American Composers: A Biographical Dictionary*, 2nd ed. (Boston: G.K. Hall, 1982), 148. A March 25, 1971, recording in the archives of the Music Library at the UB employs

oboe, clarinet, tenor saxophone, and four trumpets. Petr Kotik, who considers *Trumpet* "absolutely seminal" and "one of the most important pieces by Julius," indicated that the music was notated in orthodox fashion; Petr Kotik, telephone interview with author, August 20, 2010. Yet a contemporary review describes the work rather differently: "Julius Eastman's chancey piece for trumpet choir, called *Trumpet* . . . is 11 minutes of any old thing, controlled by cue cards held up before the players"; Daniel Cariaga, "Gilbert, Sullivan Gala Fun Enough," *Long Beach Independent*, August 23, 1971. The performance in question was by members of the Los Angeles Philharmonic and the Los Angeles Brass Society, with Eastman conducting; program for "The All-American Dream Concert" at the Hollywood Bowl, Los Angeles, California, August 18, 1971. A write-up of a May 1973 performance strikes a similar note, calling *Trumpet* "an open-form, largely aleatoric piece, in which seven trumpeters played set figures according to card cues flashed by the leader. Some marvelously brazen sonorities were produced, but at self-defeating length"; Donal Henahan, "Music in Review: 'Definitive Version' of Foss's *MAP*," *New York Times*, May 6, 1973.

21. "UB Department of Music to Present Concert of Works by Faculty Composers," *Tonawanda News*, May 9, 1972. In the recording at the Music Library at UB, Eastman's vocal fireworks can be made out alongside an amplified violin and the patter of dancers.

22. Putnam, "Eastman Works," 32.

23. The Ligeti received highly publicized performances on the Evenings for New Music series in March 1965. By the time of Eastman's arrival, these had entered into Buffalo lore. See Renée Levine Packer, *This Life of Sounds: Evenings for New Music in Buffalo* (New York: Oxford University Press, 2010), 42. That said, the immediate impetus for *Wood in Time* came courtesy of Karl Singletary, who needed a dance score that could be toured without live instrumentalists.

24. Joel Chadabe, e-mail interview with the author, August 29, 2010. Elsewhere, the piece was listed alternately for four and eight amplified metronomes; "SEM Concert Will Feature Electronics," *Tonawanda News*, April 8, 1975; and Anderson, *American Composers*, 148. Chadabe may be thinking of an early version of the work.

25. Rockwell, "S.E.M. Ensemble."

26. Putnam, "Eastman Traces." Eastman also studied with Warren Benson, but it is more likely that he was referring to Vauclain.

27. Terry Riley, *In C*, Sony Masterworks 45368, 2009, 1 compact disc. For further information about the recording, see Robert Carl, *Terry Riley's In C* (New York: Oxford University Press, 2009), ch. 5.

28. The "encore," not under the official auspices of the CAs, was organized by trumpeter Donald Montalto for May 14, 1971. In the interim, Riley had been invited back to the Center in the spring of 1969, to present his *Kundalini Dervish*; Levine Packer, *This Life*, 93.

29. An April 20, 1974, recording featuring an all-star lineup of violinist Benjamin Hudson, violist Maureen Gallagher, and double bassist James

VanDemark is in the holdings of the Music Library at UB. In Eastman's spoken introduction to the piece, he states that vocalists using frequency counters may also perform the string parts.

30. Kotik interview.

31. Program for S.E.M. Ensemble concert at Paula Cooper Gallery, New York City, March 16, 2010.

32. "U.B. to Present New Music Evening," *South Buffalo-West Seneca News*, December 9, 1971. The S.E.M. performance was given on September 30, 1970, at the UB Student Union. For another S.E.M. performance of the piece on October 15, 1971, see "Penney Art Collection Display at Kenan House Art Gallery," *Lockport Union Sun and Journal*, October 15, 1971. On the December 12, 1971, Evenings for New Music concert, Eastman conducted music by Makoto Shinohara and may very well have played in *Les moutons*. Either way, the CAs subsequently took up the piece, and Eastman performed it with them into 1974; Levine Packer, *This Life*, 134.

33. Tom Johnson, "Frederic Rzewski, Petr Kotik, and Melodies" (originally published April 13, 1972), in *The Voice of New Music: New York City, 1972–1982. A Collection of Articles Originally Published in the* Village Voice (Eindhoven, the Netherlands: Het Apollohuis, 1989), 25. A sure sign that he was drawn to the music, *Coming Together* remained a part of Eastman's repertoire until at least as late as 1979; see John Rockwell, "Music: Philharmonia 'Meets the Moderns,'" *New York Times*, April 9, 1979.

34. Ad, "New Newer Music," *New York Times*, January 20, 1974; and Raymond Ericson, "Two Barns, Horses, and a Church—for Mozart," *New York Times*, January 27, 1974. Eastman's performance was reviewed positively; see Leigh Landy, "New Music around Town: Ensemble: Impressive Mixture," *Columbia Daily Spectator*, January 30, 1974; and Tom Johnson, "A Dark, Unpredictable World," *Village Voice*, February 7, 1974. *Struggle* was the final section of a projected "long cantata" of the same name (sometimes listed as *No Progress without Struggle*); Rzewski subsequently revised the title as *Struggle Song*; Walter Zimmermann, *Desert Plants: Conversations with 23 American Musicians* (Vancouver: Self-published, 1976), 310.

35. David Gibson, telephone interview with author, September 26, 2012. Gibson added, with a touch of whimsy, "I think of Fred Rzewski as being like Hindemith and Julius as Debussy." Gena also pointed to the stylistic affinity connecting Eastman to Rzewski; Gena, interview.

36. As Gena mused, "This kind of stuff was in the air"; Gena, interview. Ned Sublette, who first met Eastman in 1976, insisted that "nobody in Reich and Glass's generation, which Julius was, was influenced by them. They were two of many"; Ned Sublette, e-mail communication with author, June 2, 2014. Whatever the case, Reich did not pass through Buffalo with his ensemble until late 1973, when he presented *Four Organs*, *Phase Patterns*, *Clapping Music*, and part 2 of *Drumming* in Baird Hall on October 10; "Rock Briefs," *Griffin of Canisius College* 44, no. 2

(October 5, 1973): 8. Philip Glass did not make his way to the area with his own ensemble until even later, when they were slated to be in residence at Artpark from August 5–12, 1974; "Artpark's Artists-in-Residence Aim to Involve Large Numbers of Visitors in the Creative Process," *Tonawanda News*, July 19, 1974.

37. Eastman, Glasgow spoken introduction.

38. Jan Williams, e-mail interview with author, August 20, 2010.

39. Kotik interview. Kotik played on the December 16, 1973, performance of *Stay On It* included on *Unjust Malaise*, where he notes that he is mistakenly credited as pianist. Violinist Benjamin Hudson, who participated in the majority of the work's performances, concurred that Kotik only ever performed on flute; Benjamin Hudson, e-mail interview with author, October 12, 2010. Correspondingly, Douglas "Trigger" Gaston, a noted Buffalo-area pianist, is erroneously credited on saxophone.

40. Frank Owen, "Echo Beach," *Melody Maker*, April 11, 1987.

41. Eastman spoke of "a purely improvisational school, and one in which the composer just gives an idea about the piece and the performer carries it out. Of course, this last form some performers have complained about, they say that they're making the piece, they should get credit"; Eastman, Glasgow spoken introduction.

42. Jan Williams, e-mail communication with author, June 3, 2014.

43. Eastman, Glasgow introduction.

44. Ralph Jones, e-mail communication with author, January 14, 2015. Jones accompanied the CAs on the 1974 European tour, and so would have heard at least ten performances of *Stay On It*.

45. Kahle e-mail.

46. Gibson interview; Hudson interview. Appropriating from popular song was nothing new for Eastman, who had already explored the practice in *Creation* and *Macle*; see Dohoney, "Homosexual Ego." In the three known recordings of *Stay On It*, the May 22, 1973, world premiere in the holdings of the Music Library at UB, the December 1973 performance released on *Unjust Malaise*, and the videotaped Glasgow performance, no quotations from "Stop! In the Name of Love" can be identified, though Hudson did not participate in the first of these.

47. Sublette e-mail. Also in vogue at the Hibachi Room during this period were songs like "Midnight Love Affair," "Turn the Beat Around," and "More, More, More"; John Love, "Disco Chat," *Fifth Freedom: Newsletter of the Niagara Frontier Gay Community* 8, no. 6 (December 1978): 4.

48. Renée Levine Packer, e-mail communication with author, August 19, 2012.

49. Julius Eastman, *Stay On It*, May 22, 1973, archival recording. To the audience's audible amusement, Eastman continued: "On sax, we have Jay Beckenstein and Phil DiRe; on flute we have Petr Kotik; on vibes, Jan Williams; and our *beee-autiful* female singer is Georgia Mitoff!" Beckenstein, who went on to cofound Spyro Gyra, was conversant with Eastman's working methods, having received composition lessons from him. They also performed together in *There Is Singularly Nothing*; see Tom Johnson, "Sights of the Second Music," *Village Voice*, June 15,

1972. Beckenstein participated in the premiere and possibly one subsequent performance of *Stay On It* in June 1973. The same holds for Phil DiRe, who by May 1973 had already amassed a wealth of experience as a member of the official White House jazz quartet. Upon arriving at UB, DiRe founded the Buffalo Jazz Ensemble, an influential "jazz fusion" group. Another saxophonist, UB student Art Levinowitz, joined in for *Stay On It*'s penultimate performance, at Islip Arts Theatre at Suffolk County Community College on March 22, 1974.

50. Herman Trotter, "Computer Composition Enlivens UB Concert," *Buffalo Evening News*, May [n.d.], 1973.

51. I am grateful to Ned Sublette for this insightful distinction.

52. In his *Femenine* review, John Rockwell refers directly to Riley's "Pulse," while offering the unhelpful cavil, "some of the textures sounded a bit too reminiscent of Philip Glass"; Rockwell, "S.E.M. Ensemble."

53. Kahle e-mail.

54. "El público se contagia de la euforia que hacen gala los instrumentistas que . . . el público parece haberla captado y se percata que debe participar con los ejecutantes . . . en diferentes puntos de la sala, la onda se va extendiendo a otros espectadores que agitan sus llaveros y los ejecutantes parecen en extremo complacidos porque han transmitido el mensaje de Eastman y un regocijo general invade la sala"; Jaime Rosal, *La(s) falsa(s) ceremonia(s)* (Barcelona: Producciones Editoriales, 1976), 105. Appearing in a collection of short stories and criticism, Rosal's account is stylized and lightly fictionalized, but there is no reason to doubt the veracity of his narrative. As for the audience at the Glasgow performance, the video features a number of heads bobbing contentedly along to the music. For a brief summing-up of the Glasgow show, see Edward McGuire, "Concerts: Scotland," *Music and Musicians* 22, no. 8 (April 1974): 60.

55. Thomas Putnam, "Contrasts Heard at Gallery," *Buffalo Courier-Express*, December 17, 1973.

56. Simon Frith, *Performing Rites: On the Value of Popular Music* (Cambridge, MA: Harvard University Press, 1996), 139.

57. George Lipsitz, *American Studies in a Moment of Danger* (Minneapolis: University of Minnesota Press, 2001), 145.

58. Jones e-mail. Unlike Jones, Williams suspects that amplification may only have been used when appropriate to the venue; Williams e-mail of June 3, 2014. The performance at Carnegie Recital Hall certainly featured amplification; see Donal Henahan, "Concert: Monotony Glorified in New Music Evening," *New York Times*, December 7, 1973.

59. Sims Warren appears only to have performed *Stay On It* once, on a December 7, 1973, Evenings for New Music program at SUNY/Albany in which Mitoff did not participate.

60. Tim Lawrence, *Hold on to Your Dreams: Arthur Russell and the Downtown Music Scene, 1973–1992* (Durham, NC: Duke University Press, 2009), 160.

61. Renée Levine Packer, telephone interview with author, March 9, 2009.

62. Henahan, "Monotony Glorified," 36. Jones recalls that Eastman would chant the phrase as many times as "he could comfortably manage in a single breath"; Jones e-mail. Reich received credit for first using this technique in his *Music for Mallet Instruments, Voices, and Organ* of 1973, but it seems that Eastman got there simultaneously.

63. Walter Hughes, "In the Empire of the Beat: Discipline and Disco," in *Microphone Fiends: Youth Music & Youth Culture*, ed. Andrew Ross and Tricia Rose (New York: Routledge, 1994), 149.

64. "Stay on It" is, however, the title of a 1939 rhythm changes chart by Tadd Dameron. He later offered "Stay on It" to Dizzy Gillespie, who recorded it with his big band in 1947. Eastman does not quote Dameron's tune, and there is no evidence that he knew it.

65. Or, for that matter, the aggressive hypermasculinity of a Charles Ives, whose *Largo* Eastman played on the CAs' European tour. For two influential discussions of the gender politics of musical modernism, see Fred Everett Maus, "Masculine Discourse in Music Theory," *Perspectives of New Music* 31, no. 2 (Summer 1993): 264–93; and Susan McClary, "Terminal Prestige: The Case of Avant-Garde Music Composition," *Cultural Critique* 12 (Spring 1989): 57–81.

66. Tim Lawrence, "Who's Not Who in the Downtown Crowd (or: Don't Forget about Me)," *Yeti* 6 (2008): 96.

67. Sublette e-mail.

68. Gibson interview.

69. Ibid. Eastman remained on close professional terms with Hudson until the end of his life. According to Gena, one of his last projects was a series of violin and piano concerts with Hudson; Gena interview.

70. For example, two years later Tom Johnson covered an improvised piano performance at which Eastman "began singing along in a crazed baritone: 'Why don't you treat me like a real woman?' and later, 'Open, open wider'"; Tom Johnson, "Two Composers Become Performers," *Village Voice*, October 25, 1976, 83. Amusingly, the *Times* reviewer whitewashed Eastman's capers, labeling them "provocatively cryptic" without further explanation; Joseph Horowitz, "Julius Eastman Sings, Plays Piano at Environ," *New York Times*, October 12, 1976.

71. Gibson interview.

72. See Program for S.E.M. Ensemble concert at Albright-Knox Art Gallery, Buffalo, NY, June 7–8, 1975. On the program, as in John Rockwell's review, the title is spelled *Feminine*; Rockwell, "S.E.M. Ensemble."

73. Susan Sontag, *Against Interpretation and Other Essays* (New York: Picador, 1966), 284.

74. "semble avoir pour but de lancer un défi au public en éprouvant sa résistance. Mais le très jeune public barcelonais a fait preuve de la plus extraordinaire patience et ce sont les exécutants qui ont dû finalement—mais combien tardivement—s'avouer vaincus"; Franz Walter, "Barcelone: Semaine de musique

nouvelle," *Schweizerische Musikzeitung (Revue musicale suisse)* 114, no. 2 (March–April 1974): 105.

75. Stephen Walsh, "The Buffalo Sound," *Observer*, February 17, 1974.

76. "In the end, Julius Eastman—also from New York—beat them all with his *Stay On It*, an unvarying, loud, and simpleminded rhythmic ostinato"; "En cuanto a largo, Julius Eastman—otro de Nueva York—, ganó a todos con su "Stay On It," que es un "ostinato" rítmico invaríable, ruidoso y simple"; Xavier Montsalvatge, "Dos jornadas de la 'IV Semana de Nueva Música,'" *La Vanguardia española*, February 24, 1974.

77. "Gay Pride Week Buffalo," *Fifth Freedom: Newsletter of the Niagara Frontier Gay Community* 3, no. 9 (June 10, 1973): 8. The performance apparently took place at the UB Student Union. In addition to *Stay On It*, Peter Maxwell Davies's *Eight Songs for a Mad King*, Kotik's *Aria*, and Ralph Vaughan Williams's *Five Mystical Songs* were programmed.

78. "Gay Pride Week in Buffalo," *Fifth Freedom: Newsletter of the Niagara Frontier Gay Community* 3, no. 10 (July 15, 1973): 3.

79. See "Hibachi Room Triumphs!" *Fifth Freedom: Newsletter of the Niagara Frontier Gay Community* 5, nos. 1–2 (January–February 1975): 4.

80. John M. Yanson, "On Julius Eastman's Second Performance Lasting One Hour," *Fifth Freedom: Newsletter of the Niagara Frontier Gay Community* 5, nos. 1–2 (January–February 1975): 10. The performance took place before mid-January 1975, at the Gay Community Services Center, then located at 1350 Main Street, Buffalo. *Femenine* had been presented previously on a November 6, 1974, SUNY/Albany Composers Forum concert; see "Dorian Woodwind Quintet to Feature Chadabe Work at Composers Forum," *Schenectady Gazette*, September 20, 1974, 14. It was subsequently given by the S.E.M. Ensemble on March 13, 1975, at The Kitchen; see Rockwell, "S.E.M. Ensemble."

81. Julius Eastman, *Femenine* (1974), facsimile, Mary Jane Leach's website, accessed January 5, 2015, http://www.mjleach.com/Eastman%20Scores/Eastman-Femenine.pdf; Julius Eastman, *Femenine*, November 6, 1974, archival recording.

82. Joe Ford, e-mail communication with author, September 27, 2012. Ford went on to have a successful jazz career, working with the likes of Lester Bowie, Sam Jones, Idris Muhammad, and McCoy Tyner.

83. On the extant manuscript the timings actually follow the format 0, 3:00, 3:45, and so on.

84. Hudson interview.

85. Gibson interview.

86. Williams interview.

87. "concede una gran libertad de improvisación a los intérpretes dentro un esquema de sucesiones"; Montsalvatge, "Dos jornadas," 57; "liberar al intérprete de la esclavitud que supone la partitura escrita"; Rosal, *Las falsa(s) ceremonia(s)*, 104.

88. Williams did without his part after a certain point, and he believes the rest of the CAs probably did so as well; Jan Williams, e-mail communication with author, June 8, 2014.

89. Kahle was the lone dissenting voice, questioning the existence of scores in the first place: "I'm not even sure there were notated parts; the riff was really very simple and could be learned by rote in a matter of a few seconds"; Kahle e-mail.

90. Williams interview.

91. Renée Levine Packer, e-mail communication with author, July 12, 2010; Williams interview.

92. Gibson interview.

93. Williams interview.

94. In both the printed and draft versions of the program, Blum is listed as playing in *Stay On It*; program for Evenings for New Music concert at Hopkins Center, Dartmouth College, Hanover, NH, January 28, 1974. My thanks to Barbara Krieger at the Dartmouth College archives for providing me with copies of these documents. As is clear from the video, by Glasgow, Blum was most certainly not performing in the piece.

95. His precise words were, "I have never taken part in any performance of Julius Eastman's *Stay On It*"; Eberhard Blum, e-mail communication with author, September 11, 2010.

96. Gibson interview.

97. Kotik interview.

98. Williams interview; Gibson interview.

99. Williams interview.

100. Tom Johnson, "'I Personally Like Getting Paid,'" *Village Voice*, April 3, 1978, 35.

101. Gibson interview.

102. Williams interview.

103. In the premiere, the start of the piano coda coincides with the tambourine entrance.

104. Williams believes the D-major section was a regular feature of Eastman's performances, at least during the European tour; Jan Williams, e-mail communication with author, June 8, 2014.

105. Williams interview.

106. Kahle e-mail.

107. Gibson interview.

108. Eastman, Glasgow introduction.

109. Williams interview.

110. James A. Snead, "Repetition as a Figure of Black Culture," in *Black Literature and Literary Theory*, ed. Henry Louis Gates Jr. (New York: Methuen, 1984), 67.

111. Putnam, "Contrasts Heard."

112. William Mann, "Park Lane Group," *Times* [UK], February 13, 1974.

113. Henahan, "Monotony Glorified," 36.

114. "simpáticos músicos de Buffalo a lo mejor todavia están tocando"; Montsalvatge, "Dos jornadas," 57. This is in direct contradiction to the accounts

of Rosal and Walter. In general, Kahle and Gibson recalled getting booed, with the former suggesting that the Barcelona crowd may have become restless; Kahle e-mail, Gibson interview. According to Levine Packer, however, the sold out Barcelona concert was "the most enthusiastically received of the whole tour"; Levine Packer, *This Life*, 128. She also offered that "if there were boos (which I don't remember), it may have been the kind of thing that became an arena of traditionalists vs. new music people"; Renée Levine Packer, e-mail communication with author, June 5, 2014.

115. See Levine Packer, *This Life*, 134–35.

116. Kotik interview.

117. Putnum, "Eastman Works."

118. Julius Eastman, "The Composer as Weakling," *EAR Magazine, A New Music Literary Journal* 5, no. 1 (April/May 1979): ninth page (pages unnumbered).

119. Gibson interview.

120. "pues la música se ha convertido en puente entre el autor y el auditorio y la música ya no se ciñe a una partitura eternamente estática, sino que la composición es dinámica y sus posibilidades se tornan infinitas, ya que cada vez que sea nuevamente ejecutada será totalmente distinta, dependiendo del grado de integración entre el público y los instrumentistas"; Rosal, *Las falsa(s) ceremonia(s)*, 105.

121. For a critical discussion of the afterlife of Paik's oeuvre, see the epilogue to Holly Rogers, *Sounding the Gallery: Video and the Rise of Art-Music* (New York: Oxford University Press, 2013).

CHAPTER ELEVEN

CONNECTING THE DOTS

Mary Jane Leach

Julius Eastman was an opportunistic composer, and I mean that in the best way. He had a habit of situational writing, using whatever resources were available. When all else failed, he would create solo works for himself, most of which weren't notated (with the exception of his college compositions, assuming that they had to be notated). Since he was a singer and a pianist, his solo works were for solo voice, solo piano, or both. He also observed and synthesized musical ideas/approaches that he was exposed to into his own compositions.

I will be writing about the arc of Julius Eastman's compositions through his instrumentation, from his earliest known pieces to his last ones, beginning with solo or duo notated pieces; to writing pieces with an expanded instrumentation, using a combination of traditional notation, graphic notation, and improvisation; and ending with solo or duo notated pieces.[1] I will also write about his two *Joan* pieces: *The Holy Presence of Joan d'Arc* (*Joan*), for ten cellos, and *Prelude to The Holy Presence of Joan d'Arc*, for solo voice. They form an interesting pair: a solo piece that was a structured improvisation, paired with a fully notated piece as dense as the solo piece is transparent. In addition, I will explore some of his influences from other composers and performers, and how these were incorporated into his work. Other essays in this book extensively discuss *Stay On It*, *Crazy Nigger*, *Evil Nigger*, and *Gay Guerrilla*, four of Eastman's most substantial pieces that explore some of his other compositional trends.

There are no scores or recordings of the pieces that Eastman wrote while attending Curtis Institute; there are only titles, instrumentation, and remembrances.[2] They were primarily for piano, or piano and voice, and had fairly traditional titles (*Sonata*, *Birds Fly Away*, *I Love the River*), and a few had somewhat provocative titles (*Insect Sonata* and *The Blood*). *The Blood* had the most expansive instrumentation—nine singers and piano—and was written mostly for friends of his at Curtis.[3]

The only works that appear to have been written in the few years after Eastman's graduation from Curtis are short pieces for solo piano (*Piano I–IV*) and a string quartet.[4] Once he arrived on the music scene in Buffalo in 1968, his compositional palette gradually expanded, writing for piano and voice (*Poems with Piano Interlude*), piano and string quartet (*Four Songs with String Quartet*), and viol and piano (*Three Pieces for Viol and Piano*) all written in 1969. Once he joined the Creative Associates in the fall of 1969, though, along with the arrival of Petr Kotik that same year, he had access to a broader range of musical forces, and he began to rapidly expand the instrumentation of his compositions.[5]

Eastman wrote *Thruway* (soprano, chorus, flute, clarinet, violin, cello, jazz combo, and tape) and *The Moon's Silent Modulation* (flute, percussion, two pianos, speaker, chorus, string quartet, and dancers) in 1970. *Thruway* used some improvisation and was the longest of his pieces (that we know of) up to that time, at almost thirty-two minutes. It was also the first time he incorporated prerecorded sound into a piece. He truly had found a great musical situation, with a wide variety of performers to choose from, and was taking the fullest advantage of it.

He still wrote the occasional solo piece, only now it was for other performers: *Bread* for solo violin (1970), and *Comp 1* for solo flute (1971), but he also took advantage of being able to write for larger ensembles, using the performers available to him from both the Creative Associates and the S.E.M. Ensemble (S.E.M.), which Kotik had founded shortly after arriving in Buffalo.[6] He was not only writing for an expanded instrumentation but also had begun to write titles that were more poetic: *The Moon's Silent Modulation* (1970), or more provocative: *Touch Him When* (1970), *Five Gay Songs* (1971), and *Joy Boy* (1973).

He continued to write for the small chamber ensembles of the Creative Associates and S.E.M. until he left Buffalo and moved to New York City in 1976. During the first couple of years that he lived in New York, he performed solo shows. His first big piece there, *If You're So Smart, Why Aren't You Rich?* (two French horns, four trumpets, two trombones, tuba, two chimes, piano, violin, and two basses), was commissioned by Lukas

Foss and premiered in the Meet the Moderns series at the Brooklyn Academy of Music in December 1977. It was also the last piece he wrote for so many instruments, with the exception of *Symphony No. II* (two oboes, two English horns, three flutes, two bass clarinets, three double bass clarinets, three bassoons, three double bass bassoons, three trombones, three tubas, six tympanis, and five strings (three treble clef, two bass clef)), for which there is an unfinished score dated 1983, and which was never performed.[7]

If You're So Smart, Why Aren't You Rich? shares similar timbral explorations with *Trumpet* (1970), which was for seven trumpets (or seven soprano instruments). They both feature the trumpet, and have sections in which the instruments are almost overblowing sustained high notes in close dissonant intervals. *Colors* (1973), for fourteen women singers and tape, also has some sections of sustained dissonant notes, and shares a similarity with *Thruway*, in which the performers (primarily the singers) move throughout the performance space.

In 1978 Eastman began to write a series of pieces with "nigger" in the title,[8] which ranged from small ensemble (*Dirty Nigger* for two flutes, two saxophones, bassoon, three violins, and two double basses; and *Nigger Faggot*, also known as *NF*, for bell, percussion, and strings), to the three pieces for which he is possibly best known: *Crazy Nigger*, *Evil Nigger*, and *Gay Guerrilla*,[9] which were usually performed on four pianos (although *Crazy Nigger* was performed on two pianos by Eastman and Joseph Kubera).[10] All of these pieces were written in 1978 and 1979. Although the titles for the three four-piano works are provocative, the music is not, and they are probably the pieces that sealed Eastman's reputation as an excellent composer.

Starting at least in Buffalo, and continuing into his time in New York, Eastman wrote using a kind of compositional shorthand frequently employed in those days, which necessitated, and relied on, working closely with musicians with whom you had an ongoing relationship, and which involved a lot of discussion.[11] Over the years Eastman had worked with musicians who were familiar with his compositions and what he was trying to accomplish in them. They were willing to work through compositional problems with him, and come up with the best solution, in order to achieve his musical goal. Not all composers are so flexible. A musician who performed with both the Steve Reich Ensemble and the Philip Glass Ensemble in their early incarnations, tells of how, if a performer was unable to correctly play something that Reich had written, he would replace that musician, whereas Glass would adjust the music for that performer.

Starting approximately in the 1970s, the composer-performer began to reemerge—with the exception of composers who were pianists and had continued these dual roles—after too many years of separation. Many composers began to write music that they could perform. This occurred partly because of the music that they wanted to write or perform, as well as for expediency—it is much easier to book and pay for a solo concert than for one requiring rehearsal time, as well as having to pay the musicians. It also eliminates having to rely on other people and waiting for someone else to choose to perform your music. An added benefit is the ability to hear what you have written while it is still fresh in your composing state of mind.[12]

In his article "The Composer as Weakling," Eastman wrote about

> the poor relationship between composer and instrumentalist, and the puny state of the contemporary composer in the classical music world. If we make a survey of classical music programming or look at the curriculum and attitudes in our conservatories, we would be led to believe that today's instrumentalist lacks imagination, scholarship, a modicum of curiosity; or we would be led to believe that music was born in 1700, lived a full life until 1850 at which time music caught an incurable disease and finally died in 1900.[13]

Eastman certainly did not lack scholarship, having graduated from the Curtis Institute with a degree in composition. And he most assuredly did not lack imagination or curiosity. He was both a composer and a gifted vocalist and pianist. In addition to performing his own compositions, he played a wide variety of music. Best known for singing *Eight Songs for a Mad King* by Peter Maxwell Davies, which has one of the most demanding vocal parts in twentieth-century music, he also performed music from all periods, from Bach to Haydn to Richard Strauss to Menotti to Stockhausen, often under the baton of famous conductors such as Lukas Foss, Pierre Boulez, and Zubin Mehta. He was familiar with jazz and improvisation, at times performing with his brother Gerry, a bassist with the Count Basie Band, among other groups. His compositions evince the assimilation of the wide variety of music that he was exposed to, and reveal his creation of music that is indisputably and uniquely his own.

Shortly after moving to New York, Eastman had two solo concerts, one at Environ, *Praise God from Whom All Devils Grow* (October 9, 1976), which was reviewed, and another at Experimental Intermedia Foundation (December 15, 1976),[14] which was recorded. Both concerts were improvisational in nature. In his review of the Environ concert, Tom Johnson wrote:

> There are probably more composers-performers today than ever before. Many composers have had traditional performing skills, but people like Paganini and Rachmaninoff, whose music really depended on their performance abilities, have been rare. . . . But of course, there are also purely artistic reasons why musicians sometimes prefer to write for themselves instead of for other performers. In some cases composers really seem to find themselves once they begin looking inside their own voices and instruments, and come up with strong personal statements that never quite came through as long as they were creating music for others to play.

He went on to note that Eastman played piano in a "high-energy, free-jazz style," and sang in a "crazed baritone."[15] Joseph Horowitz also noted that the singing was "often demonic."[16] It seems that Eastman did not combine voice and piano very often in these concerts, that his piano playing tended more toward free jazz, while his vocal solos were more minimal, and in the style of avant-garde classical music.[17]

Listening to his Experimental Intermedia concert, which was primarily for solo voice, the singing was fairly ornate and melismatic. At times it even seemed medieval, especially similar to Spanish medieval music, with rhythms being tapped out in that style. Although he had used extended vocal techniques in earlier pieces—such as *Macle*, for four voices and electronics (1971)—this singing is fairly straightforward. His use of text, source unknown, is very interesting and is reminiscent of Gertrude Stein. For the first 2:20, only four words are sung: "To know the difference," usually in groups of one or two words. Gradually, words are added, usually one at a time, so that by 3:12 eight words are being sung "To know the difference between the one after zero," and by 4:42, sixteen words are being sung in various combinations: "To know the difference between the one without another, the one after zero. But he is the one behind the zero. To know the difference between the one and the two." By 6:28, twenty-four words are being sung, adding: "Be known to you and to me that the one is after zero, and his place is one. His place is behind the zero. His name is one."

The work of Gertrude Stein was very well known in Eastman's circles. He performed in S.E.M. with Petr Kotik from 1969 to 1975, during which time Kotik was writing *There Is Singularly Nothing* and *Many, Many Women*, which both use text by Stein. He also had met and performed with Virgil Thomson,[18] who had written two operas using texts by Stein,[19] and one of his close collaborators, the choreographer Andy de Groat,[20]—for whom Eastman wrote *Joan*—was a big fan of Stein. She wrote in a repetitive style, using a limited vocabulary, as in the example below.

> Fortunately to be interested in Saint Teresa.
> To be interested fortunately in Saint Teresa.
> Interested fortunately in Saint Teresa
> Saint Ignatius and saints who have been changed from the evening to the morning.[21]

Besides having their use of repetition in common, Stein was searching for the "bottom nature" of her characters,[22] whereas Eastman was searching for "that which is fundamental, that person or thing that attains to a basicness, a fundamentalness."[23]

Eastman's *Praise God from Whom All Devils Grow* concert at Environ, which made a profane interpretation of the hymn "Praise God from Whom All Blessings Flow," is the first instance of an overt reference to a religious text by him, although in a transgressive way. His Experimental Intermedia concert, while it had no overt religious references, juxtaposed Super 8 film showing dog shit and close-ups of a drag queen, displaying an in your face sexuality and depravity.[24]

There was a duality going on in Eastman's work—provocative titles, texts, and multimedia, paired with ecstatic music. Gradually, he began to incorporate and improvise on actual religious texts. At least by spring of 1980 he was improvising using religious texts, with titles such as *Humanity* and the *Four Books of Confucious*. Three of his last four pieces were: *Buddha* for an unspecified instrument (1984), *One God* for piano and voice (1985–86), and *Our Father* for two male voices (1989). *Buddha* is drawn on staff paper, with notes written within a drawing of Buddha, but the other two pieces use regular notation. Eastman was a spiritual person and used texts from many religions.

Eastman wrote *Joan* in 1981. It is scored for ten cellos and was paired with de Groat's dance *Gravy*, which was presented at The Kitchen in New York City (April 1–5, 1981). Only the first two pages of the score for *Joan* exist, with the first system printed in the program.[25] It is a vital, through-written, dense piece, full of rhythm and many melodies. Although it is for ten cellos, it does not explore the timbre of the instrument the way he did in *Trumpet, If You're So Smart, Why Aren't You Rich?* and *Colors*, as well as the three four-piano works—pieces that incorporate sound phenomena, which usually require sustained notes.[26] Instead, he wrote a rhythmically gripping piece. He had heard, and was inspired by, Patti Smith's "Rock N Roll Nigger." He used the rhythm of her singing "Nigger, nigger, nigger, nigger, nigger, nigger, nigger" as the opening rhythm in *Joan*, and continued to use it as a rhythmic motif throughout much of the piece.[27]

In the early 1980s, the Creative Music Foundation received a grant to make three radio programs featuring three composers. Eastman was chosen to be one of these composers, and *Joan* was recorded at the Third Street Music School Settlement with ten freelance cellists, in a barely rehearsed and quickly recorded session. Steve Cellum was the recording engineer, and he remembers that a couple of weeks after the session, while trying to choose which take to use, Eastman casually mentioned that he wanted to record a vocal introduction, something that had not been mentioned before then. So Cellum lugged his equipment to Eastman's tiny East Village apartment (at 314 East Sixth Street), which was not a very good recording environment, but it is how *Prelude* came to be recorded. As far as I know, it was never performed in a live performance. Also recorded was a spoken introduction, which was from the program notes for The Kitchen performance:

> Dear Joan,
>
> Find presented a work of art, in your name, full of honor, integrity, and boundless courage. This work of art, like all works of art in your name, can never and will never match your most inspired passion. These works of art are like so many insignificant pebbles at your precious feet. But I offer it none the less. I offer it as a reminder to those who think that they can destroy liberators by acts of treachery, malice, and murder. They forget that the mind has memory. They forget that Good Character is the foundation of all acts. They think that no one sees the corruption of their deeds, and like all organizations (especially governments and religious organizations), they oppress in order to perpetuate themselves. Their methods of oppression are legion, but when they find that their more subtle methods are failing, they resort to murder. Even now in my own country, my own people, my own time, gross oppression and murder still continue. Therefore I take your name and meditate upon it, but not as much as I should.
>
> Dear Joan when meditating on your name I am given strength and dedication. Dear Joan I have dedicated myself to the liberation of my own person firstly. I shall emancipate myself from the materialistic dreams of my parents; I shall emancipate myself from the bind of the past and the present; I shall emancipate myself from myself.
>
> Dear Joan there is not much more to say except Thank You. And please accept this work of art, *The Holy Presence of Joan d'Arc*, as a sincere act of love and devotion.
>
> Yours with love,
> Julius Eastman
> One Dedicated to Emancipation[28]

As verbose as this spoken introduction is, the *Prelude* is the opposite. It is 11:45 long, but uses only fifteen words, three of which are used just once.

Saint Michael said
Saint Margaret said
Saint Catherine said
They said
He said
She said
Joan
Speak Boldly
When they question you [used only once]

The three saints mentioned are the ones that Joan of Arc claimed to hear, who counseled her to speak boldly at her trial for heresy.

Compare Eastman's words above with these from Thomson's *Four Saints*:

COMMÈRE
Saint Teresa Saint Martyr Saint Settlement Saint
Thomasine Saint Electra Saint Wilhelmina Saint
Evelyn Saint Pilar Saint Hillaire Saint Bernadine.
COMPÈRE
Saint Ignatius Saint Paul Saint William Saint Gilbert
Saint Settle Saint Arthur Saint Selmer Saint Paul
Seize Saint Cardinal Saint Plan Saint Giuseppe.[29]

Even more minimal than the text in *Prelude*, is the musical material: consisting almost exclusively of descending notes in a minor chord, a minor rising third, and alternating minor seconds. The piece is so engrossing, that you do not notice how little is happening musically. There really is no musical development, no compositional sleight of hand, and the words are repetitious. Just plain singing, no extended techniques, no ornamentation. There is the voice, though, and the conviction behind it, the meditation on Joan of Arc, that draws you in. It is probably Eastman's most minimal work, pared of any excess, and it is ironic that it is paired with *Joan*, which is probably the most through-written and dense piece he wrote.

Many composers in the days when Eastman was the most active, the 1970s and 1980s, would agree to do a concert, and sometimes realize a few days before the concert, that they did not have enough material—one of the hazards of doing one-composer concerts of mostly new material—so it was not uncommon to perform a structured improvisation to fill out the concert.[30] Although Eastman did not need to stretch out the length of the recording for the broadcast, I envision him using this same process of preparing for a structured improvisation before recording *Prelude*, selecting the text he wanted to use and having an idea of what he wanted to do musically. Usually the tension of performing in front of an audience tightens one's focus, and brings an energy to a performance that cannot be recreated in a rehearsal. That Eastman was able to do so much with so little, in a small, noisy apartment with no audience, is amazing.

Eastman had many influences and assimilated many of them, including composers from the past. I cannot know for sure if he was familiar with the operas of Giacomo Meyerbeer, but there are at least a couple of synchronicities between their works. Meyerbeer used the Lutheran hymn "A Mighty Fortress Is Our God" in the overture to *Les Huguenots*, and Eastman used the hymn in *Gay Guerrilla*. In *Robert le Diable*, Meyerbeer has Bertram, a disciple of Satan, singing to the ghosts of sinful nuns.[31] His solo is very similar to the beginning of *Prelude*, in which Eastman is channeling Joan of Arc's conversations with her three saints—they have the same first three descending pitches (B–F♯–D), the same rhythm, and they create the same ambience, a cappella, with Bertram repeating the D and continuing down to the next note in the chord (B). Fantasy perhaps, but the musical similarity is very striking, and the contrast in characters—saints and sinners—even more so.

Eastman continues in his article on composer/performers:

> If we look closely before 1750, we will notice that composer/instrumentalist were one and the same whether employed by the church, the aristocracy, or self-employed (Troubadors).
>
> At the beginning of the age of virtuosity, beginning with the life of Paganini, we see the splitting of the ego into two parts, one part instrumentalist, one composer. At this time we also notice the rise of the solo performer, the ever increasing size of the orchestra, the ascendance of the conductor, and the recedence of the composer from active participation in the musical life of his community, into the role of the unattended queen bee, constantly birthing music in his lonely room, awaiting the knock of an instrumentalist, conductor, or lastly, an older composer who has gained some measure of power. These descending angels would not only have to knock, but would also have to open the door, because the composer had become so weak from his isolated and torpid condition. Finally, the composer would be borne aloft on the back of one of the three descendants, into a life of ecstasy, fame, and fortune.
>
> This being the case, it is the composer's task to reassert him/herself as an active part of the musical community, because it was the composer

> who must reestablish himself as a vital part of the musical life of his/her community.
>
> The composer is therefore enjoined to accomplish the following: she must establish himself as a major instrumentalist, he must not wait upon a descending being, and she must become an interpreter, not only of her own music and career, but also the music of her contemporaries, and give a fresh new view of the known and unknown classics.
>
> Today's composer, because of his problematical historical inheritance, has become totally isolated and self-absorbed. Those composers who have gained some measure of success through isolation and self-absorption will find that outside of the loft door the state of the composer in general and their state in particular is still as ineffectual as ever. The composer must become the total musician, not only a composer. To be only a composer is not enough.[32]

Eastman was the embodiment of a composer/performer, one who could construct a dense piece full of counterpoint, such as *Joan*, and then create *Prelude*, using so little material that you wonder how it can hold together and work, but through the strength of his performance and musical vision, he made it work, discovering what was indeed fundamental, by discarding the superficial.[33]

Notes

Portions of this chapter originally appeared in Mary Jane Leach, "Julius Eastman's *Prelude to Joan d'Arc*," *Sound American* 9 (June 2014), http://soundamerican.org/sa9-julius-eastman, and are reproduced with permission.

1. For details of Eastman's compositions, see the appendix.

2. Eastman graduated from the Curtis Institute of Music in 1963 with a degree in composition.

3. Research on these early pieces was conducted by Renée Levine Packer and included in chapter 1.

4. Eastman first showed up at UB trying to arrange a performance of a string quartet. His bio for Creative Associate programs mentions "two ballets, songs, orchestral and piano works." Renée Levine Packer, *This Life of Sounds* (New York: Oxford University Press, 2010), 92. It's not clear when these pieces cited in this bio were written.

5. Eastman was a member of the Creative Associates at the University at Buffalo (UB) from 1969 to 1975. Research on these early pieces was conducted by Renée Levine Packer and included in chapter 1.

6. The S.E.M. Ensemble was founded in 1970 by Petr Kotik. Its first concert was in April 1970 at the Domus Theater in the former showroom of the Pierce-Arrow

car manufacturer. From the Ensemble's Web site, accessed December 4, 2014, http://www.semensemble.org/about.

7. Given the unusual instrumentation, it seems more of a hypothetical piece, than one intended to be performed, considering that Eastman usually had specific situations and performers that he wrote for.

8. Dennis Kahle, who was a Creative Associate from 1972 to 1974, claimed that Eastman told him that *Stay On It* (1973) was the beginning of a "nigger" series of pieces, but no other mention of this or the names of any other subsequent pieces that would be part of this series surfaced until Eastman began writing pieces with "nigger" in the titles in 1978 (see ch. 1).

9. *Gay Guerrilla* was written in the same period as *Evil Nigger* and *Crazy Nigger*, and I am including it as part of the "nigger" series, since its title is equally provocative.

10. Joseph Kubera was a Creative Associate from 1974 to 1976 at UB. He and Eastman continued to perform together once they both lived in New York City. They performed a two-piano version of *Crazy Nigger* at The Kitchen, February 8–9, 1980.

11. This was not unusual—for many years I was a member of the DownTown Ensemble, a new music group based in New York. We performed many pieces similar in style to Eastman's, and many of our rehearsals involved a lot of discussion—sometimes as much as 80 percent of our rehearsal time would be spent talking about the piece—trying to figure out the intent of the composer, the best placement of the performers on the stage, and other performance issues not easily conveyed with conventional notation.

12. The emergence of computers, music notation software, and midi playback has been a great boon for composers, and has given them the capability of immediately being able to hear what they have just written.

13. Julius Eastman, "The Composer as Weakling," *EAR Magazine* 5, no. 1 (April/May 1979): 9th page (pages unnumbered).

14. The two reviews of this concert do not give a title for the performance. However, Ned Sublette remembered the title as such in an interview with Ryan Dohoney, February 2, 2009 (chapter 7).

15. Tom Johnson, "Julius Eastman and Daniel Goode: Composers Become Performers," *Village Voice*, October 25, 1976, reprinted in: Tom Johnson, *The Voice of New Music: New York City 1972–1982* (Paris: Editions 75, 1989), accessed February 25, 2015, http://www.editions75.com/Books/TheVoiceOfNewMusic.PDF.

16. Joseph Horowitz, "Julius Eastman Sings, Plays Piano at Environ," *New York Times*, October 12, 1976.

17. Ryan Dohoney has also written about the Environ and Experimental Intermedia concerts in chapter 7.

18. Eastman performed in Lukas Foss's *Map* with Jesse Levine, Jan Williams, Petr Kotik, and Virgil Thomson, May 2, 1973, in the Whitney Museum's Composer Showcase. Eastman's *Trumpet* was also performed at this concert.

19. *Four Saints in Three Acts* (1927–28) and *The Mother of Us All* (1947). The original production of *Four Saints* was performed in 1934 in Hartford, Connecticut, and then on Broadway in New York with an all-black cast.

20. Andy de Groat also goes by the name Andrew de Groat. He listed Stein as a big influence in an e-mail to the author, dated August 21, 2012.

21. From act 2, *Four Saints in Three Acts*, libretto by Gertrude Stein, music by Virgil Thomson. Thanks to Luciano Chessa for pointing this out to me.

22. I was able to find many references to this, but not the original source of the quote.

23. Julius Eastman, in his introduction to his January 1980 concert at Northwestern University. Julius Eastman, *Unjust Malaise*, New World Records 80638, 2005.

24. Based on the author's conversations with Phill Niblock and Warren Burt (1999–2000).

25. Two pages of *Joan* are in the Performing Arts Research Collections–Music Library at Lincoln Center. They had been in an exibit, "Contemporary American Composers: Photography by Gene Bagnatto," in the New York Public Library's Performing Arts Research Center in spring 1982, were never reclaimed by Eastman, and subsequently deposited in the library's archives.

26. Sound phenomena (combination, difference, and interference tones) are created by playing two or more notes, which then produce at least one more note discernible from the number of notes being played—that is, you hear notes that are not notated or played.

27. Based on the author's correspondence with Ned Sublette, and also referred to in chapter 7.

28. This exact text was printed in The Kitchen program of April 1–5, 1981.

29. From "The Prologue," *Four Saints in Three Acts*, libretto by Gertrude Stein, music by Virgil Thomson.

30. Before this time, concerts of twentieth-century contemporary music generally were not devoted to just one composer. The advent of the composer-performer also heralded concerts devoted to just one composer.

31. Bertram's aria "Nonnes, qui reposez," in act 3 of Giacomo Meyerbeer's *Robert le Diable*.

32. Eastman, "The Composer as Weakling," 9th page.

33. Paraphrased from Julius Eastman's introduction to his January 1980 concert at Northwestern. Julius Eastman, *Unjust Malaise*, New World Records 80638, 2005.

CHAPTER TWELVE

GAY GUERRILLA

A Minimalist Choralphantasie

Luciano Chessa

Composed about a year before AIDS was first clinically observed in the United States, on the tenth anniversary of Stonewall's riots (a coincidence?), *Gay Guerrilla* (1979) is not Julius Eastman's first piece to make reference to homosexuality.[1] Neither is it the first of Eastman's compositions in which the word "gay" is used in the title.[2] Yet if all of Eastman's music but this one were to disappear, *Gay Guerrilla* would still be enough to guarantee him a firm place in the history of twentieth-century music.

Considered thirty-five years later, and thus observed from a more historically advantageous perspective, this piece in fact constitutes at once Eastman's most powerful tribute to the modern fight for gay rights and one of his most compositionally memorable—and moving—works.

Other Eastman "queer-themed" pieces:

Touch Him When (1970)
Five Gay Songs (1971)
That Boy (1973)
Joy Boy (1974)
Femenine (1974)
Nigger Faggot (1978)

Since the moment they hit the scene, titles like the ones above, and a handful of others also including the word "nigger" (Eastman notoriously composed a whole "nigger" series of works), have raised many eyebrows. They still do, which somewhat inconveniences concert producers who may be willing and able to program what survives of this music. But if the titles still makes us uncomfortable in 2015, one should then try to imagine just how outrageous they must have sounded in 1971: prior to Richard Pryor, prior to N.W.A., prior to *Philadelphia*, prior to the Bravo Channel.[3]

Eastman was obviously conscious of the potentially controversial implications of his titles, and he even addressed the controversy in public in the opening remarks to the formidable concert he gave at Northwestern University in January 1980. Here, he proceeded to explain to an uneasy audience what he meant by the word "nigger" and what he meant by "gay guerrilla": all this without necessarily helping to shed much light on the correlations between the titles and the actual pieces.

Had Eastman's music not been as relevant as it is, I probably would not have been able to go beyond the provocation of these titles, which seem to aggressively beg for our attention. The remarkable quality of the musical construction, however, requires a critic to observe the work with special patience and care. It leads to the realization that such titles are more than just simply a way of flipping the bird at the (contemporary) musical establishment of the time.

There is no self-hatred in these title choices but, rather, self-empowerment: the titling was, among other things, a way of exercising power, a way of taking control over words and their meaning. Naturally, such political hijacking of language was common in the history of civil rights movements, and not exclusively in the United States.

There's more. In *Crazy Nigger* and *Evil Nigger*, two of the three pieces Eastman presented in four-piano versions for the above-mentioned concert at Northwestern University, the process unfolding in the music is clear, yet so abstract that no title would really be needed.[4]

Choosing not to name the pieces would leave an empty slot, a slot that one could then fill arbitrarily or purposefully: with an agenda. I believe that, much like Oliviero Toscani's ad campaign for Benetton in the 1980s,[5] Eastman chose to fill what would otherwise have been an empty slot with a sociopolitical commentary: a vindication of sorts. He chose to fill that void with something that could make people think more than they would had these compositions been titled *Symphony*, or *Concerto*, or *Piece* for pianos, and so on. As in Toscani's case, this act surely led Eastman to be misunderstood; for one thing, he could likely be perceived as using cheap tactics and shock value to call attention to his "products." Unfortunate as this may sound, it had to be expected.

Deeper relationships between many of these titles, including *Crazy Nigger* and *Evil Nigger*, and the musical structure of the corresponding pieces may be critically constructed, but I do not think Eastman usually chose them with a specific purpose. However, in the case of the third composition presented at the same Northwestern concert, *Gay Guerrilla*, particularly due to the militant character of the chorale tune he chose to quote in it, I would like to argue otherwise.

Among the Eastman scores we have left, *Gay Guerrilla* is possibly the finest example of what Eastman himself called organic music: a sort of large-scale additive process of accumulation of harmonic materials that proliferates and grows organically across considerable time spans. Unlike Philip Glass's additive minimalism, a process based on lines that rhythmically expand and contract, Eastman's organic music is based on the piling up of pitch over pitch, harmony over harmony, in curves of decreasing and increasing harmonic density and harmonic rhythm. This process really makes these compositions breathe as if they were living organisms.

Eastman's *Gay Guerrilla* is loosely structured like a *Choralphantasie* (chorale fantasia). The chorale fantasia is a musical composition based on a Lutheran chorale, whose characteristic feature is that the presentation of the chorale melody is delayed via an "edging," often constituted by an extended fugue-like section that prepares the stage for the rhetorical climax: the entrance of the chorale as a cantus firmus to accompany and complete the contrapuntal splendor of the fugal devices already deployed, and which typically leads the piece, triumphantly, to its end. Chorale fantasias were the opening movement of many of Johann Sebastian Bach's Chorale Cantatas and are among the most thrilling participatory moments of the entire Lutheran liturgy. Chorale melodies in general can be conducive to militancy: they are constructed so as to be easy to memorize; some look and function as a "call to arms"; they are a powerful tool to unify a group, as everyone in the congregation is familiar with the melody; and as a chorale is first heard, the congregation is typically frenzied with enthusiasm and tends to participate in the singing. In "A Mighty Fortress Is Our God," by Martin Luther, images of warfare are conjured up already in the title, and the text is a call for fortitude and strength (pride!) to overcome oppression:

1. A mighty fortress is our God,
a bulwark never failing;
our helper he amid the flood
of mortal ills prevailing.
For still our ancient foe
doth seek to work us woe;
his craft and power are great,
and armed with cruel hate,
on earth is not his equal.
2. Did we in our own strength confide,
our striving would be losing,
were not the right man on our side,
the man of God's own choosing.
Dost ask who that may be?
Christ Jesus, it is he;
Lord Sabaoth, his name,
from age to age the same,
and he must win the battle.
3. And though this world, with devils filled,
should threaten to undo us,
we will not fear, for God hath willed
his truth to triumph through us.
The Prince of Darkness grim,
we tremble not for him;
his rage we can endure,
for lo, his doom is sure;
one little word shall fell him.
4. That word above all earthly powers,
no thanks to them, abideth;
the Spirit and the gifts are ours,
thru him who with us sideth.
Let goods and kindred go,
this mortal life also;
the body they may kill;
God's truth abideth still;
his kingdom is forever.

After reading the text of this chorale, Eastman's own description of "guerrilla" as "someone who is . . . sacrificing his life for a point of view,"[6] makes even more sense. The rhetoric of a Gay Liberation Front–inspired language is all over the composition.[7]

Though Eastman might have sung the chorale "A Mighty Fortress" from the Episcopalian hymnal in his childhood years as a chorister in

Ithaca, the interest in this chorale and especially in Bach's famous chorale cantata based on it, *Ein feste Burg ist unser Gott*, BWV 80, could also be traced to his association with Lukas Foss, which started in 1968, the year in which Eastman moved to Buffalo, New York, and subsequently became a member of a group formed and headed by Foss, the Creative Associates.

Foss was a well-known champion of Johann Sebastian Bach, as is attested by his *Baroque Variations* (1967), whose last movement, *On a Bach Prelude*, Foss brilliantly reconceived in his later *Phorion* (1994). And Eastman would not have been the first composer Foss directed toward Bach: Foss's fascination for Bach had previously informed what for me is the most striking Italian opera of the twentieth century: Sylvano Bussotti's *La Passion selon Sade* (1965). Bussotti's queer Passion according to the Marquis de Sade, first conceived in Buffalo for Foss, references Bach via Foss in its title, instrumentation (the performance forces include the oboe d'amore), and musical material, much of it derived by musical cells originated from the names BACH and SADE.

Just as in the equally outrageously titled *Passion selon Sade*, Eastman's *Gay Guerrilla* mixes sacred and secular references with an effect that can rightly be perceived as shocking and provocative. Yet here again, Eastman's action (in this case the mixing of sacred and secular) is not merely offered for the sake of creating a controversy. A sincere, if queer religiosity animates this and a number of other Eastman works, from the equally militant *Holy Presence of Joan D'Arc* (1981), to *Our Father* (1989), Eastman's late homage to Petr Kotik's *Many Many Women* (1975). But exactly like Pier Paolo Pasolini's militant and queer *Gospel according to Saint Matthew* (1964), Eastman's attraction to Christianity is cultural and political before being per se religious.[8]

Gay Guerrilla is a penetrating sixteen-page essay with an unequivocally clear dramatic trajectory. The relentless repetition of notes in similar metrical arrangements that make up most of the piece's material and fabric, is at times lamenting, at times alienating, but eventually trumpeting/marching in an evocation of military fanfares.

Elements of a chorale fantasia (a fugal exposition with a subject based on a repeated note, a countersubject, episodes, stretti, and the memorable entrance of the chorale melody as a cantus firmus) are all discernible, if stylized, from the manuscript. The above-mentioned four-piano realization that Eastman presented at Northwestern also unfolds with a kind of baroque, fugal dignity. All of this should not come as a surprise at all. The list of Eastman's compositions includes a piece written in 1963, while he was studying at Curtis, and titled *Chorale and Fugue on a Theme of Constant*

Vauclain; it is sufficient to testify that Eastman handled chorale and fugue writing from an early age.[9]

I would like to close this brief essay by offering some of the formal highlights of *Gay Guerrilla*:[10]

Page 1: A minimal subject based on a repeated note breaks the silence. Parts enter one after the other, fugue-like, though always somewhat unmeasured. Harmony thickens. An equally minimal countersubject is introduced.

Page 6: A counterpoint entirely built over a series of entrances of the countersubject.

Page 10: A more strict rhythmical event based on the A-minor chord melts (an unmeasured crossfade) over and back into a less strict rhythmical event based on a G-sharp-minor-seventh chord, producing a successful contrast in harmonic color. Both events melt into one another. This being the first time in over twelve minutes of music in which the harmonic rhythm significantly changes, the occurrence is new and poignant. This event lasts only forty seconds, after which the harmonic rhythm slows down once again.

Page 12: The harmonic rhythm suddenly and dramatically again increases its pace: this second time, up to six changes of harmony take place in only one minute.

Pages 13 and 14: A large-scale crescendo, which includes as part of the counterpoint a quote of the refrain of Eastman's *Evil Nigger*.

Page 15: The crescendo leads to the presentation, in various octaves, of Martin Luther's chorale *Ein feste Burg ist unser Gott*: it is the emotional climax of the composition.

Once the climax is reached, the piece slowly dissolves in two stages:[11]

> (a) at first through a stunning section (bottom of page 15 to top of 16) also based on an unmeasured crossfading of chords into another, but this time built on repeated notes of the same length (a new rhythmical idea). This section, particularly when performed with cyclically recurring dynamic hairpins, as the one heard in the Northwestern recording, results in an original electronic-sounding effect created analogically by the unmeasured crossfading and phasing of the instruments. This extraordinary effect is not exclusive to *Gay Guerrilla*; only, here becomes more palpable and more electronic-sounding because of the crossfading and the hairpins. (b) finally, with a process of evaporation: a musical line based on the upward scale C♯, D♯, E, F♯, G♯, B, and C♯: all steps of the

scale presented in different octaves and rhythmically repeated as in (a). Once all performers
reach the high C♯ at the end of the scale,
there they finally relax and enjoy the
large-scale pacification of the
opening D-minor key now
gently leaning its head on
a C♯: a suspension?
A place of
wonder?

Notes

This essay is dedicated to Mary Jane Leach, who fiercely fought the oblivion.

1. See his piano four-hands piece *Touch Him When* of 1970.

2. It is preceded by the *Five Gay Songs* of 1971, now lost. Interestingly, the composition *Gay Life* by David del Tredici, one of Eastman's colleagues in Buffalo, created some kind of controversy when it appeared in 1996. Twenty-five years later, the presence of the word "gay" in the title could still generate some kind of negative attention.

3. N.W.A (Niggaz Wit Attitudes), active from 1986 to 1991, was one of the most infamous West Coast hip-hop groups. *Philadelphia*, starring Tom Hanks, was one of the first Hollywood films to deal with homosexuality and AIDS. The Bravo channel, which started out as a culture and arts channel, transformed itself with reality shows, most notably *Queer Eye for the Straight Guy*. Both *Philadelphia* and Bravo brought homosexual topics into the mainstream.

4. If one looks at Eastman's list of compositions, there are many cases in which the works are labeled with titles that either feel a bit like anonymous placeholders (*Piano Piece I–IV*, *Piano 2*, Untitled, etc.), or in which the titles feel just as outrageous as they are arbitrary: all occurrences in which there seems to be no correlation between titles and music. Besides *CN* and *EN*, see also *If You're So Smart, Why Aren't You Rich?* on which title Kyle Gann too has pondered: "The piece's relation to its title, aside from the latter's obvious relevance to Eastman's life, is anyone's guess." In Gann's "'Damned Outrageous': The Music of Julius Eastman," liner notes for the New World Record's 2005 *Unjust Malaise* release). The relevance of this title on Eastman's life is confirmed by a piece of writing Gann must have been unaware of, which was pointed out to me by Renée Levine Packer. In an article by Thomas Putnam, in the February 11, 1979, issue of the *Buffalo Courier Express*, Eastman says about the title: "It's what my mother always asked." Naturally, this still does not allow us to gain any further understanding of a correlation between this personal exchange with his mother and the very musical structure of the piece.

5. Oliviero Toscani, the art director for the Benetton Group, a clothing company, brought controversial subjects to mainstream advertising. One of his most famous campaigns included a photo of a man dying of AIDS.

6. From Eastman's introduction to the 1980 Northwestern performance.

7. And not only that: Eastman's *Gay Guerrilla* is unthinkable without assuming Eastman's direct knowledge of how the politics of race, gender, and queer liberation all intersected and aligned in the baffling, compassionate, and politically wise speech, "The Women's Liberation and Gay Liberation Movements," given at Boston College by Huey P. Newton, on August 15, 1970: a speech in which the founder of the Black Panther Party calls for the Panthers to "unite in revolutionary fashion" with "the various liberation movements among homosexuals and women," both movements understood by Newton as being just as equally "oppressed groups" as the "Blacks." Claiming that "a homosexual could be the most revolutionary," Newton famously took everyone—including members of his own party—by surprise, by requesting the end of misogyny and queer bashing within black power politics.

8. The cocktail of Christianity and queerness brings to mind a ménage that held a considerable place in New York City art culture, and one that would have influenced Julius Eastman profoundly: the collaborative work of the queer-power couple Gertrude Stein and Virgil Thomson, especially their groundbreaking pseudo-Catholic 1927–28 opera conceived for an all-black cast: *Four Saints in Three Acts*. Thomson and Stein's work (repetitive, overtly banal, circular, combinatorial, preminimal, vexational, directionless) was so relevant to this New York milieu—which would inspire theater works by Bob Wilson and Philip Glass, as well as Robert Ashley—that two key collaborators of Eastman, Arthur Russell and Petr Kotik, both had an early Thomson/Stein–inspired composition period (Eastman even participated in Kotik's pieces). Thomson and Stein's popularity in these progressive circles was not merely due to the fact that Thomson was still a powerful pen. It was also due to John Cage, who often spoke (in *Silence*, for example) of Thomson's "athematic continuity of clichés": as if he were some kind of American Erik Satie. Cage's endorsement (blessing?) and critical enlightenment surely allowed Virgil Thomson's work to receive proper attention by a younger generation of composers. Even more so it must have solicited the attention of a black and queer composer like Eastman. Thus, I feel that a composition like the *Holy Presence of Joan d'Arc* would be unthinkable without the knowledge of Thomson and Stein's *Four Saints in Three Acts*. This can be confirmed by comparing the descending arpeggiated incipit of Saint Ignatius's aria "Once in a While," from act 3 of *Four Saints*, with the main descending cell of the *Prelude to The Holy Presence of Joan d'Arc*. And surely, definitive validation comes from Mary Jane Leach, who showed me documentation that proves Eastman and Thomson knew each other.

9. Andre Constant Vauclain was a professor of music composition at the Curtis Institute of Music from 1939 to 1953, before moving to the University of Pennsylvania; he died in 2003 at age ninety-five. The presence of a fugal subject by

Vauclain in Eastman's *Chorale and Fugue* suggests that this piece may have been a classroom assignment produced when Eastman was enrolled in composition classes at Curtis.

10. The scores and other information about *Gay Guerrilla* and *Evil Nigger* are available; accessed January 22, 2015, http://www.mjleach.com/EastmanScores.htm.

11. This last paragraph mirrors the process of "evaporation" described above: the decreasing harmonic density used by Eastman at the last section of *Gay Guerrilla*. Naturally, in other pieces Eastman adopts comparable ending devices, so one can safely argue that this very paragraph is also a visual reverse of the penultimate page of *Crazy Nigger* (see ex. 9.5).

APPENDIX

Julius Eastman Compositions

Mary Jane Leach

Starting in 1998, when I first began to search for the music of Julius Eastman, I kept a running list of pieces found or mentioned. I have prepared this list by culling information from many sources. Primary among them, with helpful assistance from John Bewley, was the Archives in the Music Library at the University at Buffalo (UB), which includes listings for Creative Associate (CA) concerts, Evenings for New Music (ENM) concerts, and Faculty Concerts (FC). Maurice Edwards supplied me with a lot of information centering around Eastman's work and performances at the Brooklyn Philharmonia, including many programs and newspaper articles. I also culled information on pieces by Eastman from the essays in this book, primarily those by Renée Levine Packer, with information on pieces from Eastman's Curtis Institute days, as well as those from his time in Buffalo; Ryan Dohoney, with Eastman's New York City period; and Matthew Mendez, with both the Buffalo and New York periods. Tom Bogdan, Sean Griffin, Elliott Sharp, and Thomas Sokol all found individual scores and shared them. I have tried to limit the list to pieces that were notated. Some of Eastman's improvised pieces were given titles in passing, often for a one-time performance, and in a few cases I did make an exception and included some that were mentioned specifically in essays in this book.

One of the hazards encountered in compiling lists like this is how to deal with typos that have appeared in print (such as with *Femenine*, commonly misspelled as *Feminine*), misquotations, and works discussed in interviews that never actually got written, but were only aspirational. I hope that I have managed to avoid any of these pitfalls, that this list of compositions will continue to grow, and that additional information about each piece will surface.

Insect Sonata (1962 or earlier): piano. No score or recording available.

The Blood (1963): clarinet, piano, and nine singers. Performed February 27, 1963, on Eastman's graduation recital at the Curtis Institute of Music with student performers, including pianist Richard Goode and clarinetist Frank Ell. No score or recording available.

Song Trilogy: O, Go Not; *Birds Fly Away* (with cello); *I Love the River* (1963): voice, piano, and dancer. Performed February 27, 1963, on his graduation recital at Curtis Institute, with student performers. Performed July 1966, at the Alice Statler Auditorium at Cornell University, with Eastman performing as the dancer. No score or recording available.

Piano Compositions: *Chorale and Fugue on a Theme of Constant Vauclain*, *Plié*, *Vergiu's Dance* (1963): solo piano. Performed February 27, 1963, on his graduation recital at Curtis Institute, with student performers. No score or recording available.

Sonata (1963): piano. One movement was titled "Allegro." Performed February 27, 1963, on his graduation recital at Curtis Institute, with Eastman playing the piano. No score or recording available.

Tripod (1960s): unspecified instrumentation. Score in the archives of the University at Buffalo (UB) Music Library; also available online, accessed November 25, 2014, http://www.mjleach.com/EastmanScores.htm. No known recording.

Piano Piece I (1968) 0:50: piano. No score available. Premiered December 15, 1968, in an Evenings for New Music (ENM) concert at the Albright-Knox (A-K) Art Gallery, Buffalo, Julius Eastman—piano; recording in the archives of the UB Music Library.

Piano Piece II (1968) 2:50: piano. No score available. Premiered December 15, 1968, in an ENM concert at the A-K Art Gallery, Buffalo, Julius Eastman—piano, recording in the archives of the UB Music Library.

Piano Piece III (1968) 0:40: piano. No score available. Premiered December 15, 1968, in an ENM concert at the A-K Art Gallery, Buffalo, Julius Eastman—piano, recording in the archives of the UB Music Library.

Piano Piece IV (1968) 2:20: piano. No score available. Premiered December 15, 1968, in an ENM concert at the A-K Art Gallery, Buffalo, Julius Eastman—piano, recording in the archives of the UB Music Library.

Poems with Piano Interludes (1969): spoken voice and piano. No score or recording available.

Four Songs with String Quartet: There Was a Man; Speed Me Life's Fluid; To Those Who Live without the Liquid Love; Baby, Baby, Baby (1969): voice and string quartet. No score or recording available.

Three Pieces for Violin and Piano (1969): violin and piano. No score or recording available.

Symphony for Strings (1969): instrumentation unknown. No score or recording available.

Contrapunctus I–IV (1969): string quartet and/or flute and cello. No score or recording available.

The Moon's Silent Modulation (1970): flute, percussion, 2 pianos, speaker, chorus, string quartet, and dancers. Premiered April 19, 1970, by the Creative Associates in Domus, Buffalo. Score has his first use of graphic notation, uses some improvisation. Score currently in private collection, which will be donated to the UB library. No known recording exists.

Thruway (1970) 31:30: flute, clarinet, soprano, chorus, violin, cello, jazz combo, film projections, and tape. Eastman conducted premiere May 3, 1970, in an ENM concert in the A-K Art Gallery, UB. Score uses some improvisation. Score currently in private collection, which will be donated to the UB library. Recording in the archives of the UB Music Library.

Touch Him When (1970) 9:00: piano four hands. No score available. Recording, with Eastman and Steve Marrow performing, was issued commercially on cassette-only release in 1984, *Tellus IV*, and is available on custom CD from Harvestworks.

Bread (1970): violin. No score or recording available.

Trumpet (1970): seven trumpets (or seven soprano instruments). Premiered March 25, 1971, on an ENM concert in Domus at UB, using oboe, clarinet, tenor saxophone, and four trumpets; recording in the archives of the UB Music Library. No score available. Performed August 18, 1971, by the Los Angeles Philharmonic players at the Hollywood Bowl.

Macle (1971) 33:00: four voices and electronics. Performed February 13, 1972, in an ENM concert in the A-K Art Gallery. Score in the archives of the UB Music Library; recording in the archives of the UB Music Library.

Comp 1 (1971) 14:20: solo flute. Written for and premiered on October 18, 1972, by Petr Kotik in a CA recital. No score available. Recording in the archives of the UB Music Library.

Five Gay Songs (1971): instrumentation unknown. No score or recording available.

Eine Kleine Nachtmusik (1972): performed by S.E.M. Ensemble: flute, clarinet, percussion, piano, and voice. No score or recording available.

Mumbaphilia (1972) 10:00: solo performer and dancers. Premiered May 10, 1972, on a faculty recital in Baird Recital Hall, UB. No score available; recording in the archives of the UB Music Library.

Wood in Time (1972) 15:15: eight metronomes and dancers. Written for Karl Singletary. Premiered March 5, 1973, on a faculty recital in Baird Recital Hall, UB. No score available, recording in the archives of the UB Music Library.

Colors (1973): Fourteen women's voices and tape. Premiered July 22, 1973, in Barnes Hall, Cornell University, Ithaca, NY. Score available online, accessed November 25, 2014, http://www.mjleach.com/EastmanScores.htm. No known recording.

Creation (1973) 20:00: flute, percussion, piano, and recorded sounds. Premiered by S.E.M. Ensemble at A-K Art Gallery, UB. No score or recording available.

Stay On It (1973) 25:00: no fixed instrumentation, although piano, percussion, and voice were always included. Premiered May 22, 1973, on a faculty recital in Baird Hall, UB. No score available, piece uses some improvisation. Several transcriptions have been made, including a version by Paul Pinto available online, accessed November 25, 2014, http://www.mjleach.com/EastmanScores.htm. Recording issued on the three-CD set *Unjust Malaise*, New World Records 80638, 2005, using the UB concert recording. Video recording, courtesy of Francis McKee, Third Eye Centre Video Archive, Centre for Contemporary Arts, Glasgow from a Creative Associates concert on February 16, 1974, in Glasgow, Scotland.

440 (1973) 18:40: voice, violin, viola, and double bass. Performed April 20, 1974, on a Benjamin Hudson (CA) recital, Baird Hall, UB. No score available. Recording in the archives of the UB Music Library.

That Boy (1973): small instrumental ensemble. Performed by the S.E.M. Ensemble March 13, 1975, at The Kitchen, NYC. No score or recording available.

Joy Boy (1974): four treble instruments. Commissioned by the Composers Forum in Albany, NY, and premiered there by S.E.M. on November 6, 1974. Performed by S.E.M. March 13, 1975, at The Kitchen, NYC. Score available online, accessed November 25, 2014, http://www.mjleach.com/EastmanScores.htm. Score uses some improvisation. No recording available.

Femenine (1974) 73:00: winds, marimba/vibraphone, sleigh bells, piano, and bass. Performed by S.E.M. March 13, 1975, at The Kitchen, NYC. Score available online, accessed November 25, 2014, http://www.mjleach.

com/EastmanScores.htm. Score uses some improvisation. Concert recording is in the archives of The Kitchen.

Masculine (1974): small instrumental ensemble. No score or recording available.

Praise God from Whom All Devils Grow (1976): voice and piano improvisation. Performed by Eastman November 12, 1976, at Environ, NYC. No recording available.

Untitled improvisation performed at Experimental Intermedia Foundation (1976) 71:20: voice, piano, and tape. Performed by Eastman December 15, 1976, at Experimental Intermedia Foundation. Improvisation, no score. Private recording exists.

If You're So Smart, Why Aren't You Rich? (1977) 25:00: two French horns, four trumpets, two trombones, tuba, two chimes, piano, violin, and two basses. Eastman conducted premiere December 10, 1977, on the Meet the Moderns series at the Brooklyn Academy of Music; later performed February 11, 1979, on an ENM concert at A-K Art Gallery, UB. No score available. Recording issued on the three-CD set *Unjust Malaise*, New World Records 80638, 2005, using the UB concert recording.

Conceptual Music for Piano (1977): voice and piano. Premiered by Eastman February 27, 1977, in a Brooklyn Community Concert at the Billie Holiday Theater in Bedford-Stuyvesant, Brooklyn. No score or recording available.

Dirty Nigger (1978): two flutes, two saxophones, bassoon, three violins, and two double basses. Premiered December 1, 1978, at the Third Street Music School Settlement, NYC. The first two pages are in the Performing Arts Research Collections Music Library at Lincoln Center. No recording available.

Nigger Faggot, also listed as *NF* (1978): bell, percussion, and strings. Premiered as *NF* November 12, 1978, on a Brooklyn Community Concert, Bethlehem Lutheran Church, Brooklyn. No score or recording available.

Crazy Nigger (1978) 55:00: to be performed by any number of similar instruments, most commonly four pianos. Performed January 16, 1980, in Pick-Staiger Concert Hall at Northwestern University. Performed as a piano duo with Eastman and Joseph Kubera, pianos, on February 8–9, 1980, at The Kitchen, New York City. Score available online, accessed November 25, 2014, http://www.mjleach.com/EastmanScores.htm. The two-piano version of *Crazy Nigger* from the February 8–9, 1980, performances at The Kitchen was recorded (The Kitchen archives). Recording issued on the three-CD set *Unjust Malaise*, New World Records 80638, 2005, using the Northwestern concert recording. DVD of March 13, 2008, performance in the Atrium den Haag, issued as *Crazy Nigger by Julius Eastman* by Dag in de Branding, Swaan Productions, 2008.

Evil Nigger (1979) 22:00: to be performed by any number of similar instruments, most commonly four pianos. Premiered January 16, 1980, in Pick-Staiger Concert Hall at Northwestern University. Also performed June 13, 1980, at New Music America in Minneapolis. Score available online, accessed November 25, 2014, http://www.mjleach.com/EastmanScores.htm. Recording issued on the three-CD set *Unjust Malaise*, New World Records 80638, 2005, using the Northwestern concert recording. Recording issued on: Tomasz Sikorski and Julius Eastman, *Unchained*, Bolt Records DUX 1188, 2014.

Gay Guerrilla (1979) 29:00: to be performed by any number of similar instruments, most commonly four pianos. Premiered January 16, 1980, in Pick-Staiger Concert Hall at Northwestern University. Also performed June 13, 1980, at New Music America in Minneapolis. Score available online, accessed November 25, 2014, http://www.mjleach.com/EastmanScores.htm. A performance of *Gay Guerrilla* was recorded in October 1980 in Berlin, as part of The Kitchen's European tour, in which Eastman participated. Recording issued on the three-CD set *Unjust Malaise*, New World Records 80638, 2005, using the Northwestern concert recording. Recording issued on Tomasz Sikorski and Julius Eastman, *Unchained*, Bolt Records DUX 1188, 2014.

Humanity (1980–81): solo voice. Performed by Eastman January 30, 1981, at The Kitchen, New York City. No score or recording available.

Not Spiritual Beings (1980–81): voice, two pianos, and instrumental ensemble. Performed January 30, 1981, at The Kitchen with flute, bass clarinet, four percussionists, two pianos, two violins, two violas, cello, bass, and voice. No score or recording available.

The Holy Presence of Joan d'Arc (1981) 20:30: for ten cellos. Premiered April 1–5, 1981, at The Kitchen, in a dance (*Gravy*) choreographed by Andy de Groat, Eastman conducting. Also performed June 8, 1981, at New Music America 1981 in the Japan Center Theater, San Francisco. Recording made at the Third Street Music School Settlement, New York City for radio broadcast, as part of a series produced by the Creative Music Foundation, date unknown. Score available online, accessed November 25, 2014, http://www.mjleach.com/EastmanScores.htm. See also example 6.1. The first two pages are in the Performing Arts Research Collections Music Library at Lincoln Center. Recording issued on the three-CD set *Unjust Malaise*, New World Records 80638, 2005, using the recording made for the radio broadcast.

Prelude to The Holy Presence of Joan d'Arc (1981) 15:45: for solo voice. Improvisation, no score. A transcription has been made by Richard Mix. Recording made in Eastman's apartment for radio broadcast, as part of a series produced by the Creative Music Foundation, date unknown. Recording issued on the three-CD set *Unjust Malaise*, New World Records 80638, 2005, using the recording made for the radio broadcast.

His Most Qualityless Majesty (1983) 40:00: piano. Improvisation by Eastman, performed October 20, 1983, at Roulette, New York City No score or recording available.

Symphony No. II (1983): three flutes, two oboes, two English horns, three bassoons, three double bass bassoons, two bass clarinets, three double bass clarinets, three trombones, three tubas, six timpani, and five strings (three treble clef, two bass clef). Score available online, accessed November 25, 2014, http://www.mjleach.com/EastmanScores.htm. Unperformed to date. No recording available.

Buddha (1984): unspecified instrumentation. Score available online, accessed November 25, 2014, http://www.mjleach.com/EastmanScores.htm. No recording available.

One God (1985–86): voice and piano. No score or recording available.

Piano 2 (1986) 15:45: solo piano. Premiered February 21, 1991, by Joseph Kubera at Merkin Concert Hall, New York City. Score available online, accessed November 25, 2014, http://www.mjleach.com/EastmanScores.htm. Recording issued on *Book of Horizons*, Joseph Kubera, New World Records CD 80745, 2014.

Our Father (1989): two male voices. Score available online, accessed November 25, 2014, http://www.mjleach.com/EastmanScores.htm. No recording available.

CHRONOLOGY

Date	Event
October 27, 1940	Julius Dunbar Eastman Jr. born in Harlem Hospital, New York City.
Early 1940s	Family moves to Syracuse, New York.
May 11, 1945	Gerald Eastman born in New York City.
1947	Family moves to Ithaca, New York.
	Julius Eastman Sr. and Frances Famous Eastman separate.
1950	Julius visits New York City with his mother.
	Begins playing piano.
	While in grade school is a paid soprano singer in the Boys Choir of Saint Johns Episcopal Church in Ithaca.
	Attends Boynton Junior High School in Ithaca, sings in glee club.
1954	Attends Ithaca High School, sings in glee club throughout high school.
	Begins piano lessons with Roger Hannah.
1957	Has job accompanying dance classes at Iris Barbura Studio.
	Studies dance with Vergiu Cornea, founding director of the Ithaca Ballet.
Summer 1957	Attends Indian Hill Summer Camp in Massachusetts on scholarship as dance pianist. Meets the dancer Billie Kirpich.

(continued)

Date	Event
1958	Graduates from Ithaca High School, wins Hollis Dann Glee Club Award for outstanding work as glee club member.
Summer 1958	Studies piano with Seymour Lipkin in New York City.
1958–59	Attends Ithaca College, studies piano with George Driscoll.
May 1959	Auditions and is accepted as a piano major by Mieczyslaw Horzowski at Curtis Institute of Music in Philadelphia.
September 1959	Moves to Philadelphia, begins classes at Curtis Institute, lives in YMCA, meets Zeyda Ruga (Suzuki), Marta Garcia Renart, and Beatriz Lima. During this period receives Federation of Music Clubs Award and National Association of Negro Musicians Award.
Summer 1960	Studies composition with Warren Benson at Ithaca College.
Fall 1960	Continues studies at Curtis Institute, begins study with Constant Vauclain.
February 1961	Petitions Curtis for permission to switch to composition major.
1962	Composes *Insect Sonata.*
July 29, 1962	Performs piano recital, Saint Augustine Episcopal Church, Bronx, New York.
February 27, 1963	Graduation recital of his compositions: *The Blood, Song Trilogy, Piano Compositions* ("Chorale and Fugue on a Theme of Constant Vauclain," "Plié," "Vergiu's Dance"), *Sonata for Piano.*
May 11, 1963	Graduates from Curtis Institute of Music with diploma in composition.
Summer 1963	Studies piano and composition at Ithaca College.
Early 1960s	Composes *Tripod.*
Fall 1963	Goes to New York City, stays with his grandmother, Caroline Famous, in the Bronx.
	Possibly studies piano with Frances Dillon at the Mannes College of Music.

(continued)

Date	Event
1963–66	Teaches music therapy at Willard State Hospital.
	Visits family members in Virginia, works on farm.
	Is offered job in chorus at Metropolitan Opera—turns it down.
1964	Performs as vocal soloist in Leoncavallo's *Pagliacci.*
1964–65	Participates in Cornell University Summer Series with Thomas Sokol.
July 1966	Presents vocal and piano recital, including his own compositions, at Alice Statler Auditorium, Cornell University: *Chorale and Fugue on a Theme of Constant Vauclain*, *Vergius's Dance*, *Song Trilogy*, and an improvised work.
	Vocal soloist in work by Vaclav Nelhybel, Cornell Summer Series.
August 1966	Vocal soloist in Strauss's *Der Rosenkavalier*, Saratoga Performing Arts Center.
December 8, 1966	Presents debut Town Hall recital in New York City. Program includes *Chorale*, *Fugue on a Theme of Constant Vauclain*, and *Vergiu's Dance*, plus an improvisation.
Spring 1967	Goes to Buffalo, New York. Reunites with Billie Kirpich, who is teaching dance at the University at Buffalo (UB), where he accompanies dance classes. Meets Karl Singletary.
November 19, 1967	Performs Stravinsky's *Oedipus Rex* at Cornell with Sokol.
December 26, 1967	Vocal soloist in Menotti's *Amahl and the Night Visitors* with the Buffalo Philharmonic Orchestra.
1967–68	Composes dance piece *Star Jazzer* (string quartet and voice).
1968	Composes *Piano Pieces I–IV*.
April 1968	Vocal soloist in Stravinsky's *The Soldier's Tale*, Cornell University.
May 1968	Performs Haydn's *The Creation* with Buffalo Choral Arts Society.
Summer 1968	Tours Europe and the United States with the Gregg Smith Singers.

(continued)

Date	Event
October 1968	Vocal soloist in American premiere of Bohuslav Martinů's *The Prophecy of Isaiah*, Ithaca.
	Meets Peter Yates, Music Department chair at State University College (formerly Buffalo State Teachers College). Hired as teaching assistant on SEEK Program by Yates.
	Meets Lukas Foss, conductor of Buffalo Philharmonic Orchestra.
December 15, 1968	Performs his compositions *Piano Pieces I–IV* on Evenings for New Music concert series (ENM), Albright-Knox (A-K) Art Gallery, Buffalo.
December 27, 1968	Vocal Soloist in *Amahl and the Night Visitors*, Buffalo Philharmonic Orchestra.
	Meets Donald Burkhardt.
1969	Performs in Stravinsky's *Les Noces* with Buffalo Philharmonic, Lukas Foss, conductor.
	Composes *Contrapunctus I–IV* for string quartet and/or flute and cello and *Symphony for Strings*.
Early 1969	Composes *Four Songs with String Quartet*, *Poems with Piano Interludes*, and *Three Pieces for Violin and Piano*.
February 2, 1969	Guest pianist with Yuji Takahashi and Creative Associates in Bernard Rands's *Expressione IV* for two pianos, ENM, A-K Art Gallery.
February 4, 1969	Performs his compositions *Piano Pieces I–IV* and Rands's *Expressione IV* on ENM, Carnegie Recital Hall, New York City.
April 1969	Presents his music, poetry, and dance at A-K Art Gallery under auspices of State University College: *Poems with Piano Interludes*, *Four Songs with String Quartet*, and *Three Pieces for Viol and Piano*.
Summer 1969	Cross-country trip with Donald Burkhardt.
June 28, 1969	Stonewall Inn riots against police harassment sets new dynamic for emerging gay liberation movement.
September 1969	Begins Creative Associate (CA) Fellowship, maintains part-time appointment with State University College.

(continued)

Date	Event
November 1969	Composer /flutist Petr Kotik joins the Center of the Creative and Performing Arts as a CA, forms the S.E.M. Ensemble several months later (March 1970).
November–December 1969	Performs works by James Fulkerson, Barney Childs, Arne Nordheim, Istvan Anhalt on ENM concerts.
1969–70	Composes *The Moon's Silent Modulation*, *Thruway*, *Bread*, *Trumpet*, and *Touch Him When*.
February 1970	Declines State University College full time instructorship appointment.
February–March 1970	University at Buffalo campus student uprisings.
April 19, 1970	Premiere of *The Moon's Silent Modulation* by the CAs in Domus, Buffalo, New York.
Late April- early May 1970	Conducts premiere performances of *Thruway* on ENM at Rutgers University, Carnegie Recital Hall, and A-K Art Gallery.
June 1970	Spends summer in New London, Connecticut, with Donald Burkhardt.
July 1970	Appointed instructor in UB Music Department.
	Performs US premiere of *Eight Songs for a Mad King* (*Eight Songs*) by Peter Maxwell Davies at Aspen Music Festival.
	Requests leave of absence from teaching for fall semester.
July 19, 1970	Cornell Summer Series directed by Thomas Sokol presents performances of *Moon's Silent Modulation* and *Thruway*.
Fall 1970	Moves to his own apartment on Allen Street, invites Karl Singletary to share apartment.
	Joins Kotik's S.E.M. Ensemble.
	Performs Peter Maxwell Davies's *Eight Songs* on ENM in Carnegie Recital Hall, SUNY Albany, and A-K Art Gallery.
	Records *Eight Songs* under Maxwell Davies with Fires of London in UK (Unicorn 9052).

(continued)

Date	Event
1971	Composes *Five Gay Songs*, *Macle*, and *Comp 1*.
February 1971	Performs as vocalist in Peter Schat's *Improvisations uit het Labyrint* on ENM in Buffalo and Carnegie Recital Hall.
	Contributes sound score for *Othello*, directed by Louis Criss.
March 1971	Performs American premiere of Hans Werner Henze's *El Cimarrón* at University of Pittsburgh.
May 1971	Performs Henze's *Essay on Pigs* and Maxwell Davies's *Eight Songs* under Zubin Mehta and the Los Angeles Philharmonic's on the Contempo 71 Series.
Summer 1971	Visits Donald Burkhardt in Charleston, South Carolina.
August 18, 1971	Los Angeles Philharmonic performs *Trumpet* at Hollywood Bowl; Eastman sings songs by Charles Ives on the "All American Dream Concert," directed by Lukas Foss.
September 1971	UB instructorship renewed.
	Attica Prison uprising.
October 1971	Performs Henze's *Essay on Pigs* in Tel Aviv with Israel Philharmonic with Zubin Mehta, conductor.
December 1971	Conducts Makoto Shinohara's *Consonance* for ensemble on ENM at A-K Art Gallery, Carnegie Recital Hall, and short SUNY campus tour.
1972	Composes *Eine Kleine Nachtmusik*, *Mumbaphilia*, and *Wood in Time*.
	Lines and Spaces performed with S.E.M. at A-K Art Gallery (this was in all probability a group improvisation).
February 1972	Performs in *Black Ivory* with UB's Company of Man.
February 17, 1972	*Macle* performed at State University College at Geneseo, followed by performances at Carnegie Recital Hall and at Orange County Community College, Middletown, New York the next week.
March 1972	Performs Karlheinz Stockhausen's *Refrain* on Garry Kvistad's CA recital.
March 13, 1972	*Macle* performed at A-K Art Gallery.

(continued)

Date	Event
April 1972	Performs R. Murray Schafer's *Requiems for the Party Girl*, on ENM at A-K Gallery in Buffalo and SUC Fredonia.
May 10, 1972	*Mumbaphilia* premiered on a faculty recital, Baird Recital Hall, UB.
September 1972	Promoted to assistant professor at UB (three-year appointment)
October 6, 1972	Makes New York Philharmonic debut on Prospective Encounters Series, performing *Eight Songs*.
October 18, 1972	*Comp 1* premiered by Petr Kotik in a CA recital.
October 28, 1972	Performs US premiere of Feldman's *Pianos and Voices* with Feldman, Foss, Del Tredici, and William Appleby, ENM in A-K Art Gallery.
December 1972	Performs *Night Conjure Verse* by Del Tredici on ENM in Carnegie Recital Hall and A-K Art Gallery.
1973	Composes *Colors* (1972–73), *That Boy*, *Creation*, *Stay On It*, and *440*.
	Gerald Eastman moves to Buffalo.
	Creation performed by S.E.M. at A-K Art Gallery.
	Narrator on Barbara Kolb's *Three Place Settings* (Desto 7143).
	Receives Creative Artists Public Service Program Award for Music Composition from the New York State Council on the Arts.
	Eight Songs under Maxwell Davies with Fires of London remastered.
	Nominated for Grammy Award for remastered recording of *Eight Songs* on Nonesuch Records.
February 15, 1973	Performs on WBAI's Free Music Store with John R. Adams, Petr Kotik, and Stuart Dempster.
March 5, 1973	*Wood in Time* premiered on a faculty recital in Baird Recital Hall, UB.
May 2, 1973	*Trumpet* and Foss's *Map* performed at the Composers Showcase, Whitney Museum, New York City.
May 22, 1973	*Stay On It* premiered on a faculty recital in Baird Recital Hall, UB.

(continued)

Date	Event
Summer 1973	Purchases house on Bird Avenue in Buffalo.
July 3–8, 1973	Participates in Petr Kotik's summer music school at Chocorua, New Hampshire.
July 22, 1973	*Colors* premiered in Barnes Hall at Cornell, Ithaca.
October 20, 1973	Performs *Eight Songs* with Brooklyn Philharmonic at Brooklyn Academy of Music (BAM).
November 1973	*Colors* performed in Buffalo, with Gwendolin Sims.
December 1973	*Stay On It* performed at Carnegie Recital Hall, SUNY/ Albany, and UB on ENM.
December 29, 1973	Performs Henze's *El Cimarrón* on ENM concerts in Buffalo and Brooklyn Philharmonic's Meet the Moderns series.
1974	Composes *Joy Boy* (commissioned by the Albany, NY Composers Forum), *Masculine*, and *Femenine*.
	Here He Goes performed by S.E.M. at ORTF (Radio France) (this was in all probability a group improvisation).
January 27, 1974	Performs premiere of Frederic Rzewski's *Struggle* in Here and Now Series at Alice Tully Hall in Lincoln Center with Juilliard Ensemble, under direction of Dennis Russell Davies (Cathy Berberian performs Berio's *Circles*).
February and March 1974	CAs go on five-week tour of Europe. *Stay On It* performed/recorded on tour more than twelve times (pretour concert at Dartmouth College January 28).
April 1974	Performs Rzewski's *Coming Together* on ENM at UB and in New York City.
April 20, 1974	Performs *440* on Benjamin Hudson's CA recital, Baird Hall, UB.
May 25, 1974	Performs *Stay On It* and Rzewski's *Les Moutons de Panurge* at Attica Prison.
October 1974	Performs *Crow* with Pauline Oliveros, ENM, A-K Art Gallery.
November 6, 1974	*Joy Boy* premiered by the S.E.M. Ensemble in a Composers Forum concert in Albany, New York.
	Eastman quits S.E.M. while it is preparing Europe tour.

(continued)

Date	Event
December 1974	Performs Alvin Lucier's *Still* and *Moving Lines of Silence in Families of Hyperbolas*, ENM, WBAI's Free Music Store.
January 29, 1975	Performs *Crow* by Oliveros on WBAI's Free Music Store.
January 30, 1975	Performs Luis de Pablo's *Berceuse* and Oliveros's *Crow*, ENM at Cooper Union, New York City.
March 13, 1975	S.E.M. concert, all Eastman works: *That Boy*, *Joy Boy*, and *Femenine* at The Kitchen, New York City.
March–April 1975	UB Music Department does not renew faculty appointment.
June 4, 1975	Performs John Cage's *Song Books* in June in Buffalo festival.
Summer 1975	Returns to Ithaca.
	Teaches in summer school—students slip away (Sokol thinks he is drinking).
June 29, 1975	Performs *Eight Songs* in New York Philharmonic Rug Concert with Boulez, stays with grandmother in Bronx.
June 30, 1975	Performs Oliveros's *Crow* and *Eight Songs* at Artpark, Lewiston, New York.
Fall 1975	Performs *Crow Two* with Oliveros at opening of Mandeville Art Center, University of California-San Diego, meets Ned Sublette. Increased involvement in jazz. Performs frequently at the Tralfamadore in Buffalo with Gerry Eastman and others.
Summer 1976	Vocal coaching at Cornell.
	Sonora Festival in Haines Falls, New York.
	Moves to New York City (grandmother's house in the Bronx). Gerry Eastman stays in Buffalo house for one more year.
	Nomadic—probably living between New York City, Buffalo, and Ithaca.
July 1976	Renate Strauss interview in *Buffalo Evening News*: "Eastman is clearly groping."
October 9, 1976	Performs *Praise God from Whom All Devils Grow* at Environ, New York City.

(continued)

Date	Event
November 12, 1976	Conducts Brooklyn Philharmonia, and CETA Orchestra in Langston Hughes Remembered concert at Bethlehem Lutheran Church, Brooklyn.
December 1976	Performs Menotti's *Amahl and the Night Visitors* at Cornell, Ithaca.
December 15, 1976	Performs at Experimental Intermedia Foundation, New York City.
1977	Composes *If You're So Smart, Why Aren't You Rich?* for piano and orchestra, a commission from Lukas Foss and the Brooklyn Philharmonia.
January 28, 1977	Performs Bartok's *Mikrokosmos* on Meet the Moderns series at BAM.
February 27, 1977	Brooklyn Community Concert at Billie Holiday Theater in Bedford-Stuyvesant, Brooklyn. Music of Eastman (*Conceptual Music for Piano*), Hale Smith, Omar Clay, Dorothy Rudd Moore, Noel da Costa, Carman Moore, and Oliver Lake.
March 1, 1977	Performs in *EAR Magazine* benefit.
March 27, 1977	Brooklyn Community Concert at I.S. 391, East New York. Music of Eastman (*Conceptual Music for Piano*), Hale Smith, Omar Clay, Noel da Costa, and Oliver Lake.
April 24, 1977	Brooklyn Community Concert at P.S. 307 in Fort Greene, Brooklyn. Music of Eastman (*Conceptual Music for Piano*), Howard Swanson, Arthur Cunningham, Noel da Costa, Talib Hakim, and Tania León.
Summer 1977	Sonora Festival in Haines Falls, New York.
October 23, 1977	Brooklyn Community Concert at Bushwick United Methodist Church. Music of Eastman, Angela Bofil, Chou Wen-chung, Jon Gibson, Joyce Solomon, and Yuji Takahashi.
December 10, 1977	Conducts premiere of *If You're So Smart, Why Aren't You Rich?* on Meet the Moderns series at BAM.
1978	Composes *Nigger Faggot* (also listed as *NF*), *Dirty Nigger*, and *Crazy Nigger*.

(continued)

Date	Event
January 19, 1978	Community Concert organizers (Eastman, León, Hakim) appear on *The Listening Hour* with Robert Sherman on WQXR.
February 5, 1978	Performs on Brooklyn Community Concert at Hanson Place Methodist Church, Brooklyn.
May 10, 1978	Eastman conducts CETA Orchestra in Arthur Russell's *Instrumentals* at The Kitchen.
Fall 1978	Gerry Eastman sells Buffalo house.
	Directs concerts for Brooklyn Philharmonia Outreach program.
November 12, 1978	Premiere of *NF* on Brooklyn Community Concert, Bethlehem Lutheran Church, Brooklyn.
December 1, 1978	Produces concert at Third Street Music School Settlement with proceeds from house sale: *Dirty Nigger*, *Nigger Faggot*, and Rocco Di Pietro's *Donizetti in Buffalo*.
1978–79	Tim Page noninterview at WKCR.
1979	Andy de Groat and Dancers' *Bushes of Conduct*, using *Crazy Nigger*, at Dance Umbrella, New York City.
January 20, 1979	Brooklyn Community Concert at Third Street Music School Settlement. Conducts chamber music ensemble of Brooklyn Philharmonia in music of William Grant Still, Howard Swanson, and Virgil Thomson.
January 24–27, 1979	Performs with Meredith Monk in *Dolmen Music* at The Kitchen. Tours in Europe soon after.
February 11, 1979	*If You're So Smart Why Aren't You Rich?* performed on ENM at A-K Art Gallery.
Spring–summer 1979	Records *24→24 Music* with Arthur Russell under group name Dinosaur L.
April 1979	"The Composer as Weakling" published in *EAR Magazine* (vol. 5, no. 6).
April 6, 1979	Performs Rzewski's *Coming Together* in Meet the Moderns with Brooklyn Philharmonia at BAM.

(continued)

Date	Event
April 27–28, 1979	Eastman, Peter Gordon, Rome Neal, Mustafa Ahmed, Jeff Berman, Larry Saltzman, and Peter Zummo perform two nights of orchestral disco jam at The Kitchen, New York City.
April 30, 1979	Conducts music of Jeffrey Lohn (of the band Theoretical Girls) at the Mudd Club (concert also features Rhys Chatham).
Fall 1979	Composes *Evil Nigger* and *Gay Guerrilla.*
November 1, 1979	Performs Henry Cowell piano pieces on Meet the Modern series at BAM.
November 23, 1979	Conducts Jeffrey Lohn's *Uber Gewissheit* at The Kitchen.
1979–80	Third Street Music School Settlement concerts.
1980	Meets R. Nemo Hill—together for six months.
January 16, 1980	*Crazy Nigger*, *Evil Nigger*, and *Gay Guerrilla* performed at Northwestern University.
February 8–9, 1980	Double bill at The Kitchen with Ned Sublette. Performs in Sublette piece, *Simulated Catholic Music. Crazy Nigger* performed as duo with Joseph Kubera.
April 3, 1980	Performs an evening-length improvisation on his own religious texts, *Sacred Songs* at 33 Grand Street, New York City. Gerry Eastman brings their father to the concert.
June 13, 1980	*Gay Guerrilla* and *Evil Nigger* performed at New Music America in Minneapolis.
October 1980	The Kitchen European tour.
1980–81	Composes *Humanity* and *Not Spiritual Beings.*
1981	Meredith Monk's *Dolmen Music* released (ECM 1197).
	Composes *Prelude to The Holy Presence of Joan d'Arc.*
January 30, 1981	All-Eastman concert at The Kitchen: *Humanity* and *Not Spiritual Beings.*
February 1981	Conducts Arthur Russell's *Tower of Meaning.*
Spring 1981	Plays keyboards on *Turtle Dreams* with Meredith Monk in New York City.
	Composes *The Holy Presence of Joan d'Arc.*

(continued)

Date	Event
April 1–5, 1981	Andy de Groat and Dancers perform *Gravy*, using *The Holy Presence of Joan d'Arc* at The Kitchen.
June 8, 1981	*The Holy Presence of Joan d'Arc* performed at New Music America 1981 in the Japan Center Theater, San Francisco.
Fall 1981	Dinosaur L's *24→24 Music* is released on Sleeping Bag Records.
October 21, 1981	Sonora Ensemble (C. Bryan Rulon, Matt Sullivan, Judith Martin, Cynthia Bell, R. Nemo Hill) at Mostly Magic in New York City.
December 8, 1981	Concert at Synaesthetics, 10 Leonard Street, New York City.
Late 1981–early 1982	Evicted from East Sixth Street apartment; music and belongings confiscated.
March–May 1982	Scores and photo displayed in "Contemporary American Composers: Photographs by Gene Bagnato," in the Astor Gallery in Lincoln Center.
June 1982	Records *In the Light of the Miracle* with Arthur Russell.
December 5, 1982	Performs an improvised set at The Kitchen: *The Four Books of Confucius*.
1983	Meredith Monk's *Turtle Dreams* released (ECM 1240).
	Arthur Russell's *Tower of Meaning* released (Chatham Square 145).
February 1983	Composes *Symphony No. II*.
July 4, 1983	Cornell "Concert of Poetry and Music" with R. Nemo Hill (performs Mompou).
October 20, 1983	*His Most Qualityless Majesty* performed at Roulette, New York City.
December 1983	Cornell job disappointment.
December 4, 1983	Bach's *Christmas Oratorio* performance in Ithaca with Cayuga Chamber Orchestra, Karel Husa, conductor.
1984–86	Tompkins Square Park period.
1984	Andy de Groat and Dancers, *La Petite Mort*, using *Gay Guerrilla* at la Chartreuse de Villeneuve-les-Avignon, France.

(continued)

Date	Event
	Touch Him When for piano four hands released on Tellus #4 (cassette).
	Concert (2 pianos) at Clocktower, New York City.
October 1984	Composes *Buddha.*
1984–85	Grandmother dies.
1985–86	Composes *One God.*
1986	Composes *Piano 2.*
	Records soundtrack for Kathy Acker, Peter Gordon, and Richard Foreman's *The Birth of the Poet*, performed at BAM in 1987.
November 1986	*Geological Moment* choreographed by Molissa Fenley using revised *Thruway* at BAM.
Late 1980s	Works at Tower Records.
	Has psychiatric therapy sessions.
1987	Jazz incorporated as an official department of Lincoln Center.
	Reissue of *Eight Songs.*
1989	Composes *Our Father.*
December 1989	David Borden sees Eastman in Ithaca.
1990	Appears as vocalist on Peter Gordon's *Leningrad Express* (Newtone Records 6702-2).
May 1990	Karl Singletary encounters Eastman on Main Street in Buffalo.
May 28, 1990	Julius Dunbar Eastman Jr. dies at Millard Fillmore Hospital in Buffalo.

SELECTED BIBLIOGRAPHY

Some of the essays in this volume were written by people who knew Julius Eastman or are members of his family. Their sources may include private notes, letters, and scores, as well as recollections. In addition to these firsthand accounts, the list below consists of books relating to Julius Eastman, his music, and his period. References to articles are included among the notes to the essays.

Als, Hilton. "A Pryor Love." *Life Stories*. Edited by David Remnick. New York: Modern Library, 2001.

Anderson, Ruth E. *Contemporary American Composers: A Biographical Dictionary*. 2nd ed. Boston: G. K. Hall, 1982.

Ashe, Arthur. *Days of Grace*. New York: Ballantine, 1993.

Avena, Thomas. "Interview: Diamanda Galás." In *Life Sentences: Writers, Artists, and AIDS*, edited by Avena, 177–96. San Francisco: Mercury House, 1994.

Brown, Richard, and Bob Watson. *Buffalo: Lake City in Niagara Land*. Buffalo, NY: Buffalo and Erie County Historical Society, 1981.

Carl, Robert. *Terry Riley's In C*. New York: Oxford University Press, 2009.

Dohoney, Ryan. "John Cage, Julius Eastman, and the Homosexual Ego." *Tomorrow Is the Question: New Directions in Experimental Music Studies*, edited by Benjamin Piekut, 39–62. Ann Arbor: University of Michigan Press, 2014.

Dwyer, John. "Eastman's 'Mad King' Mighty Work of Theater." *Buffalo Evening News*, November 2, 1970.

Ellison, Ralph. *Invisible Man*. New York: Vintage International, 1995.

Fossner, Alvin K. "Eastman in Debut As Pianist." [unidentified periodical], December 1966.

Frith, Simon. *Performing Rites: On the Value of Popular Music*. Cambridge, MA: Harvard University Press, 1996.

Gann, Kyle. "That Which Is Fundamental: Julius Eastman, 1940–1990." *Village Voice*, January 22, 1991.

———. *Music Downtown: Writings from the Village Voice*. Berkeley: University of California Press, 2006.

Gates, Henry Louis Jr. *The Signifying Monkey: A Theory of African-American Literary Criticism*. New York: Oxford University Press, 1988.

Gendron, Bernard. *Between Montmartre and the Mudd Club*. Chicago: University of Chicago Press, 2002.

Goldman, Mark. *City on the Edge: Buffalo, New York*. Amherst, NY: Prometheus, 2007.

Hisama, Ellie M. "'Diving into the Earth': The Musical Worlds of Julius Eastman," in *Rethinking Difference in Music Scholarship*, edited by Olivia Bloechl, Melanie Lowe, and Jeffrey Kallberg. Cambridge: Cambridge University Press, 2015.

Hughes, Walter. "In the Empire of the Beat: Discipline and Disco." In *Microphone Fiends: Youth Music & Youth Culture*, edited by Andrew Ross and Tricia Rose, 147–57. New York: Routledge, 1994.

Hyde, Lewis. *Trickster Makes This World: Mischief, Myth, and Art*. New York: Farrar, Straus and Giroux, 1998.

Johnson, Timothy A. "Minimalism: Aesthetic, Style, or Technique?" *Musical Quarterly* 78, no. 4 (Winter 1994): 742–73.

Johnson, Tom. *The Voice of New Music: New York City, 1972–1982, A Collection of Articles Originally Published in the Village Voice*. Eindhoven, the Netherlands: Het Apollohuis, 1989.

Katz, Jonathan D., and David C. Ward *Hide/Seek: Difference and Desire in American Portraiture*. Washington, DC: Smithsonian Books, 2010.

Kostelanetz, Richard. *John Cage (Ex)plain(ed)*. New York: Schirmer Books, 1996.

Lawrence, Tim. "Who's Not Who in the Downtown Crowd (or: Don't Forget About Me)," *Yeti* 6 (2008): 90–99.

———. *Hold on to Your Dreams: Arthur Russell and the Downtown Music Scene, 1973–1992*. Durham, NC: Duke University Press, 2009.

Levine Packer, Renée. *This Life of Sounds: Evenings for New Music in Buffalo*. New York: Oxford University Press, 2010.

Lewis, George E. *A Power Stronger than Itself: The AACM and the American Experimental Tradition*. Chicago: University of Chicago Press, 2008.

Maus, Fred Everett. "Masculine Discourse in Music Theory." *Perspectives of New Music* 31, no. 2 (Summer 1993): 264–93.

McClary, Susan. "Terminal Prestige: The Case of Avant-Garde Music Composition." *Cultural Critique* 12 (Spring 1989): 57–81.

Metzger, Suzanne. "Eastman: 'I Always Thought I Was Great, But Why Does Making It Big Take So Long?'" *Reporter*, September 30, 1971.

Ong, Walter J. *Orality and Literacy: The Technologizing of the Word*. New edition. New York: Routledge, 2012.

Piekut, Benjamin. *Experimentalism Otherwise: The New York Avant-Garde and its Limits*. Berkeley: University of California Press, 2011.

———. *Tomorrow Is the Question: New Directions in Experimental Music Studies*. Ann Arbor: University of Michigan Press, 2014.
Schonberg, Harold C. "'Eight Songs for a Mad King' a Delight." *New York Times*, December 11, 1970.
Simon, Jeff. "Cage Stung by Careless Followers." *Buffalo Evening News*, Lively Arts Section, June 21, 1975.
Snead, James A. "Repetition as a Figure of Black Culture." In *Black Literature and Literary Theory*, edited by Henry Louis Gates Jr., 59–80. New York: Methuen, 1984.
Sontag, Susan. *Against Interpretation and Other Essays*. New York: Picador, 1966.
State University of New York at Buffalo, Music Library. *Evenings for New Music, 1964–1980*. Buffalo, 1978, 1981.
Strauss, Renate. "Julius Eastman: Will the Real One Stand Up?" *Buffalo Evening News*, July 16, 1976.
Taylor, Marvin J. "Playing the Field: The Downtown Scene and Cultural Production, an Introduction." In *The Downtown Book: The New York Art Scene 1974–1984*, edited by Taylor, 17–39. Princeton, NJ: Princeton University Press, 2006.
Trochimcyzk, Maja, ed. *The Music of Louis Andriessen*. New York: Routledge, 2002.
Whitesell, Lloyd. "White Noise: Race and Erasure in the Cultural Avant-Garde." *American Music* 19, no. 2 (2001): 168–89.

CONTRIBUTORS

David Borden was born in Boston on December 25, 1938, and was educated at the Eastman School of Music and Harvard University. In 1969, with the support of Robert Moog, he founded the synthesizer ensemble Mother Mallard's Portable Masterpiece Company. Borden has written for various chamber and vocal ensembles and is an accomplished jazz pianist. He is the retired founder and director of the Digital Music Program (now the Cornell Electroacoustic Music Center) at Cornell University.

Luciano Chessa received a PhD in musicology from the University of California, Davis; at the Conservatory of Bologna he earned a DMA in piano and an MA in composition. His research focuses on twentieth-century and experimental music and can be found in *Musica e Storia* (Levi Foundation, Venice). He is the author of *Luigi Russolo, Futurist* (University of California Press), the first English monograph dedicated to the Art of Noises. Chessa is active as a composer, performer, and conductor. Recent compositions include *A Heavenly Act*, an opera with video. His scores are published by RAI TRADE and Carara and performed in Europe, the United States, and Australia.

Ryan Dohoney is assistant professor of musicology in the Bienen School of Music at Northwestern University. He also serves as affiliate faculty in the Gender and Sexuality Studies program. His research explores US experimental music and culture in the twentieth and twenty-first centuries with particular focus on the music of Morton Feldman, Julius Eastman, and Meredith Monk. He is the recipient of a 2015 American Council of Learned Societies Fellowship to continue the research for his book on Morton Feldman and the Rothko Chapel. His work has appeared in the *Journal of the American Musicological Society*, *Women and Music*, and *Dissonance*, and in collections dedicated to experimental music and interdisciplinary collaboration.

Kyle Gann is the Taylor Hawver and Frances Bortle Hawver Professor of Music at Bard College, a composer, and former new-music critic for the *Village Voice*. His most recent books are *No Such Thing as Silence: John Cage's 4'33"* (Yale University Press, 2010) and *Robert Ashley* (University of Illinois Press, 2012).

Andrew Hanson-Dvoracek received bachelor's and master's degrees in guitar performance from Lawrence University and the Boston Conservatory, before pursuing a master's in musicology from the University of Iowa. His thesis concerns Julius Eastman's 1980 residency at Northwestern University.

R. Nemo Hill is the author of a novel in collaboration with painter Jeanne Hedstrom: *Pilgrim's Feather* (Quantuck Lane Press, 2002); a narrative poem based on a story of H. P. Lovecraft, *The Strange Music of Erich Zann* (Hippocampus Press, 2004); and a chapbook *Prolegomena to an Essay on Satire* (Modern Metrics, 2006). His poetry and fiction have appeared in various print and online journals including *Poetry*, *Sulfur*, *Smartish Pace*, *Measure*, *14 by 14*, *Shit Creek Review*, the *Chimaera*, *Literary Bohemian*, *Umbrella*, *Ditch*, and *Big City Lit*. He has lived in New York City for many years (for a time with Julius Eastman), but travels frequently to Southeast Asia.

Mary Jane Leach is a composer-performer whose work reveals a fascination with the physicality of sound, its acoustic properties, and how they interact with space. Leach's music has been performed throughout the world in a variety of settings from concert stage to experimental music forums and in collaboration with dance and theater artists. Recordings are on the Die Schachtel, Starkland, Lovely Music, New World, XI, Wave/Eva, Innova, and Aerial compact disc labels. She also reviews classical music and theater for the Albany (NY) *Times Union*. Following many years of research Leach produced, along with Paul Tai, the New World Records three-CD album of Julius Eastman's music, *Unjust Malaise*.

Renée Levine Packer was a codirector of the Center of the Creative and Performing Arts at SUNY/Buffalo, and a director of the Contemporary Music Festival at the California Institute of the Arts. She has been director of the Inter-Arts program at the National Endowment for the Arts, the producer of Steve Reich and Beryl Korot's multimedia opera *The Cave*, and a dean at the Maryland Institute College of Art. Her book *This Life of Sounds: Evenings for New Music in Buffalo* was published in 2010 by Oxford University Press and was honored by ASCAP with a 2011 Deems Taylor Award for excellence.

George E. Lewis is the Edwin H. Case Professor of American Music at Columbia University. A recipient of MacArthur and Guggenheim Fellowships, his compositions appear on more than 140 recordings. His 2008 book, *A Power Stronger Than Itself: The AACM and American Experimental Music* (University of Chicago Press) received the American Book Award and the American Musicological Society's Music in American Culture Award. He is the coeditor of the forthcoming two-volume *Oxford Handbook of Critical Improvisation Studies*. In 2015, he was elected to the American Academy of Arts and Sciences.

Matthew Mendez (b. 1987) is a music critic with a focus on twentieth- and twenty-first century repertoire. He has written extensively on such contemporary figures as Peter Ablinger, Joseph Beuys, and John Cage. He is a graduate of Harvard University and has master's degrees from the Guild Hall School of Music and Drama (in composition) and the University of Edinburgh.

John Patrick Thomas, born in Denver, Colorado, is a composer-singer living in Hamburg, Germany. His teachers were Darius Milhaud, Andrew Imbrie, and Seymour Shifrin. He taught in the Music Department of SUNY/Buffalo and was a founding member of the Five Centuries Ensemble. Some of the most significant composers of our time—among them William Bolcom, Morton Feldman, Lukas Foss, Mauricio Kagel, Elisabeth Lutyens, Krzysztof Penderecki, and David Del Tredici—have written for his voice. Thomas has himself written an extensive body of music for voice, piano, harpsichord, and various other instruments and ensembles. For a number of years, he was a singing instructor at the Folkwang University in Essen, Germany. Currently, he is completing a series of four related theater pieces called "Borrowed Lives."

INDEX

Eastman Studies in Music

Ralph P. Locke, Senior Editor
Eastman School of Music

Additional Titles of Interest

CageTalk: Dialogues with and about John Cage
Edited by Peter Dickinson

Claude Vivier: A Composer's Life
Bob Gilmore

Composing for Japanese Instruments
Minoru Miki
Translated by Marty Regan
Edited by Philip Flavin

Concert Music, Rock, and Jazz since 1945: Essays and Analytical Studies
Edited by Elizabeth West Marvin and Richard Hermann

Dear Dorothy: Letters from Nicolas Slonimsky to Dorothy Adlow
Nicolas Slonimsky
Edited by Electra Slonimsky Yourke

Harry Partch, Hobo Composer
S. Andrew Granade

The Pleasure of Modernist Music: Listening, Meaning, Intention, Ideology
Edited by Arved Ashby

Samuel Barber Remembered: A Centenary Tribute
Peter Dickinson

The Sea on Fire: Jean Barraqué
Paul Griffiths

The Substance of Things Heard: Writings about Music
Paul Griffiths

A complete list of titles in the Eastman Studies in Music series may be found on our website, www.urpress.com.

Composer-performer Julius Eastman (1940–90) was an enigma, both comfortable and uncomfortable in the many worlds he inhabited: black, white, gay, straight, classical music, disco, academia, and downtown New York. His music, insistent and straightforward, resists labels and seethes with a tension that resonates with musicians, scholars, and audiences today. Eastman's provocative titles, including *Gay Guerrilla*, *Evil Nigger*, *Crazy Nigger*, and others assault us with his obsessions.

Eastman tested limits with his political aggressiveness, as recounted in legendary scandals he unleashed like his June 1975 performance of John Cage's *Song Books*, which featured homoerotic interjections, or the uproar over his titles at Northwestern University. These episodes are examples of Eastman's persistence in pushing the limits of the acceptable in the highly charged arenas of sexual and civil rights.

In addition to analyses of Eastman's music, the essays in *Gay Guerrilla* provide background on his remarkable life history and the era's social landscape. The book presents an authentic portrait of a notable American artist that is compelling reading for the general reader as well as scholars interested in twentieth-century American music, American studies, gay rights, and civil rights.

Contributors: David Borden, Luciano Chessa, Ryan Dohoney, Kyle Gann, Andrew Hanson-Dvoracek, R. Nemo Hill, Mary Jane Leach, Renée Levine Packer, George E. Lewis, Matthew Mendez, John Patrick Thomas

Renée Levine Packer's book *This Life of Sounds: Evenings for New Music in Buffalo* received an ASCAP Deems Taylor Award for excellence. Mary Jane Leach is a composer and freelance writer, currently writing music and theater criticism for the *Albany Times-Union*.

"The publication of this rigorously researched, lovingly produced, multidimensional study of a singular artist will surely be met with joy by those of us who remember Julius Eastman—the inspired creator, the sly provocateur and martyred saint of the avant-garde. For those who are interested in iconoclasts of whatever stripe, this volume will be a revelation and an invitation to rethink what composition, performance, and life at the precipice of madness can be."

—Bill T. Jones, choreographer and dancer

"*Gay Guerrilla: Julius Eastman and His Music* has arrived just in time for Black Lives Matter and gets my deepest praise. This important volume of essays, brought forth by two brilliant women who have long championed Eastman's music, belongs in every music conservatory library and beyond."

—Pauline Oliveros, composer